Recovering the Somali State
The Role of Islam, Islamism and Transitional Justice

Adonis & Abbey Publishers Ltd
St James House
13 Kensington Square,
London, W8 5HD
United Kingdom

Website: http://www.adonis-abbey.com
E-mail Address: editor@adonis-abbey.com

Nigeria:
Suites C4 & C5 J-Plus Plaza
Asokoro, Abuja, Nigeria
Tel: +234 (0) 7058078841/08052035034

Copyright 2017 © Abdurahman Abdullahi "Baadiyow"

British Library Cataloguing-in-Publication Data
A catalogue record for this book is available from the British Library

ISBN: 978-1-909112-62-9

The moral right of the author has been asserted

All rights reserved. No part of this book may be reproduced, stored in a retrieval system or transmitted at any time or by any means without the prior permission of the publisher

Recovering the Somali State
The Role of Islam, Islamism and Transitional Justice

Abdurahman Abdullahi (Baadiyow)

Dedication

In the Name of Allah, the Most Beneficent and the Most Merciful.

This book is dedicated to:

My father, Moallim Abdullahi and my mother Zainab Afrah whom I owe all my achievements;

My wife, Muhubo and her seven children for their endless support, patience and love;

My teachers and mentors who have coached me during my long years of schooling;

Compatriots who have been struggling for decades to recover a collapsed Somali state;

The people of Somalia who have been victimized during the civil war and after;

Those waiting Transitional Justice from mass violations of human rights in Somalia;

Those who want to understand Islam, Islamism and the intricate equation of Somalia.

Preface

After more than 30 years of involvement in Islamic work, civil society activism, and Somali politics, I felt compelled to share my experience and views on the complex subject of Islam, Islamism, and Transitional Justice in the recovering Somali state. During these long years, I realized the prevailing political culture of Somali elites is driven primarily by personal interest promoted through primordial attachment combined with nationalistic and Islamic rhetoric. As such, the previous predatory elite culture that caused the breakdown of the state cyclically reincarnates into the fabric of the polity, dashing the hope for effective state recovery. My interest in this topic began in 1986, when I shifted my study from electronic engineering to social science. In pursuing that objective, I completed MA and PhD programs from the Islamic Institute, McGill University. My primary focus was how to rebuild the Somali state with the available arsenal of ideologies, such as nationalism, clanism, and Islamism. During last three decades of my Somali studies, I concluded that paradigm shifts will be required to recover the viable Somali state. The first paradigm shift is recognizing that Somalia cannot rebuild its state without promoting a concept of citizenship and Islamic values based on consensual culture and collectivity. This paradigm shift calls for ending divisive sectarian discourses and narratives of conflict between Islamists and non-Islamists and instead appeals for promoting a culturally-sensitive Islam understandable to all Somalis. The second paradigm shift is that Somali elites should abandon the predatory culture and embark on good governance practices, whereby effective institutions capable of eliminating corruption and impunity are established. The third paradigm shift is that societal mistrust must be addressed and past injuries of civil war must be healed through suitable mechanisms of Transitional Justice. The fourth paradigm shift is that a culture of tolerance and dialogue must be advanced and all forms of extremism in the name of Islam and clans must be eradicated. The fifth paradigm shift is that Somalia, being weary from horrific internal conflicts and external conflicts with its neighbors, should detach itself from repeating historical mishaps and assertively promote peace, regional integration, and global security. Convinced that these five definitive guidelines are indispensable for rebuilding viable Somali state, I have reviewed and republished these essays to fill some historiographical gaps in Somali studies, hoping to spread these messages and help move Somalia to the deserved position among other nations.

Table of Contents

Preface V

Table of Contents VII

List of Tables and Figures VIII

List of Abreviations IX

Chronology of Islam and Islamism XI

Political Map of Somalia XIV

Introduction 15

Chapter One
Islam and Somali State: Conflict and Compromise 37
I. Islam and Somali Military Regime:
A Showdown on the Secular Family Law 39
II. Recovering Somali State: Islam, Islamism and Nation-Building............61

Chapter Two
Transitional Justice in Islam: Concepts and conceptions 97
I. Islam and Transitional Justices: Principles,
Mechanisms and Historical Role in Somalia 99
II. Conceptions of Transitional Justice in Somalia:
Findings of a Field Research in Mogadishu 139

Chapter Three:
History of the Islamic movements: Phases, Moderation and Militancy.........177
I. Historical Phases of Somali Islamic Movements 179
II. Islamic Moderation in the War-torn Somalia: The Views of Islah on the
Contemporary Issues 207
III. Militancy of the Sufi Orders in the History of Somalia.....................243

References...258

Index 273

List of Tables and Figures

FIGURES

Figure 1

Terminologies of Islamic activism and their logical relations 29

Figure 2

Classification of Human Actions in Islam 107

Figure 3

Development of the Somali elites 196

Figure 4

The logo of Islah Movement ....…...215

TABLES

Table 1

The historical role of Sharia in the Somali Constitutions and Charters ….…..131

Table 2

Islamic persuasions and their jurisprudence schools 136

Table 3

Chronology of mass violations of HRs after the civil war (1991-2009)….…...149

Table 4

The chairmen of Islah Movement and their qualifications 211

Table 5

Somali Sufi Orders and their Headquarters ....…...249

List of Abbreviations

ASWJ	Ahl al-Sunna wa al-Jamaaca (armed Sufi Orders)
AFIS	Amministrazione Fiduciaria Italiana in Somalia
ARS	Alliance for the Re-liberation of Somalia
AMISOM	African Union Mission for Somalia
BMA	British Military Administration
GSL	Great Somali League party
GSP	Great Somali Party
HDMS	Hisbiya Dastur Mutaqil Somali
IGAD	Intergovernmental Authority on Development
ICG	International Crisis Group
MB	Muslim Brotherhood
NBC	Native Betterment Committee
NFD	Northern Frontier District
NUF	National United Front
OAU	Organization of African Union
PRO	Public Relation Office
PBUH	Peace be upon him (this expression follows after naming prophets)
RCC	Roman Catholic Church
SNL	Somali National League
SNM	Somali National Movement
SNU	Somali National Union
SOBA	Somali Old Boys Association
SODAF	Somali Democratic Action Front
SPM	Somali Patriotic Movement
SSDF	Somali Salvation Democratic Front
SRRC	Somali Reconciliation and Restoration Council
SSF	Somali Salvation Front

SYC	Somali Youth Club
SYL	Somali Youth League
TFG	Transitional Federal Government
TFI	Transitional Federal Institutions
TJ	Transitional Justice
TNG	Transitional National Government
UIC	Union of Islamic Courts
UNOSOM	United Nations Operation in Somalia
USC	United Somali Congress
USP	United Somali Party
USC/SNA	United Somali Congress/Somali National Alliance
USC/SSA	United Somali Congress/Somali Salvation Alliance

Chronology of Islam and Islamism in Somalia

613-15	The First Muslim Migration to Abyssinia (the Horn of Africa)
624	Masjid al-Qiblatayn "Mosque of the two Qiblas" in Zaila which has two Mihrabs (niche in the wall of a mosque that indicates the Qiblah): one oriented to the north toward Mecca, and the other oriented to the northwest toward Jerusalem. This indicates that it was built before 624, the time in which direction of Qiblah was changed. This is the first mosque in Somalia
632-33	The exiles of the Riddah (apostasy wars) from Oman settle in Banadir.
695	Migration from Oman led by brothers Suleiman and Sa'id of Juland to settle on the East African Zanj coast.
700	Ummayyad's Caliph Abdul Malik Ibn Marwan sends an expedition to the East African coast to conquer Mogadishu and secure its annual tribute.
755	Abbasid's Caliph Abu Ja'far al-Mansur appoints governor to collect taxes and supervise the teaching of Islam in Mogadishu.
920	A Persian group led by the Seven Brothers of al-Ahsa settle in Mogadishu and Barawa.
1100s	The Construction of Abdulaziz Mosque, the first mosque built in Mogadishu.
1238	The construction of Jama' Mosque in Hamar Weyn quarter in Mogadishu.
1268	The construction of Arba'a Rukun Mosque in Mogadishu.
1269	The construction of Fakhruddin Mosque in Hamar Weyn quarter in Mogadishu.

1330	Abu Bakar bin Fakhruddin establishes the Fakhruddin dynasty in Mogadishu.
1430	Arrival of 44 Islamic scholars under the leadership of SheikhIbrahim Abu-Zarbai.
1488	Abubakar b. 'Abdallah al-'Aidarūsiarrives Harar from Hadramout in Yemen and introduces Qaderiyah Brotherhood.
1527	Imam Ahmad Gurey defeats the Abyssinians decisively at ad-Dir.
1560	The Ajuran Imamate in south-central Somalia emerges.
1600	The Muzaffar dynasty replaces the Fakhruddin in Mogadishu.
1819	Sheikh Ibrahim Hassan Yeberow establishes a Jama'a in Baardeere.
1843	Baardheere Jama'a was burned by Yusuf Mahamud, sultan of Geledi.
1896	Sheikh Ahmed Mahdi incited Lafole incident of killing Italian explorer Antonio Cecchi and most of his troops.
1898	Sheikh Uways ibn Muhammad al-Barawi establishes a jama'a at Balad al-Amin
1907	Sheikh Uways ibn Muhammad al-Barawi was murdered in Biyoley by followers of Sayyid Mahamed Abdulle Hasan.
1924	Sheikh Hassan Barsane leads a revolt against the Fascist attempt to disarm rebels.
1933	The first chapter of Muslim Brotherhood outside of Egypt was established in Djibouti.
1950	The Somali Islamic League was established in Mogadishu by Sharif Mohamud.
1951	Arabic language was adopted as the official language by the First Consiglio Territoriale under Italian trusteeship administration.

1953	Egyptian Islamic scholar Sheikh Moḥamūd Iid, the first known member of Mulsim Brotherhood arrived Mogadishu as part of al-Azhar Mission.
1956	The first Islamic political party called "Hizbu Allāh" (Party of God) was established In the Northern Somalia by Sayyid Ahmed Sheikh Muse.
1963	Adoption of Article 29 of the Somali Constitution prohibiting the propagation of other religions except Islam in Somalia.
1967	Sheikh Nur Ali Olow founded the first Salafia organization known as Jam'iyat Ihyā al-Sunna in Mogadishu.
1967	Munadamat al-Nahda al-Islamiyah, the first Muslim Brotherhood organization was established in Mogadishu.
1969	*Ahl al-Islam* (The Family of Islam), a Muslim student organization was established in Mogadishu, Somalia.
1969	*Wahdat al-Shabab al-Islami* (The Union of Islamic Youth), the first Muslim student organization was established in Hargaysa, Somalia.
1975	Secular Family law was adopted by military regime and 10 Islamic scholars who protested against the secular family law were executed.
1978	Islah Society, a Somali Muslim Brotherhood organization, was established.
1982	Ikhwan (Aala-sheikh) organization was established
1983	Itihad al-Islami was established from unified Jama'a Islaamiyah and Wahdah.
1989	Demonstrations against the military regime were organized from the mosques in protest against the detention of leading Islamic scholars.
2000	Adoption of the Islamic complainant Charter in the Djibouti Peace Conference.
2006	The emergence of the Islamic Courts and Al-shabab.

2009   The Parliament unanimously adopts application of Sharia

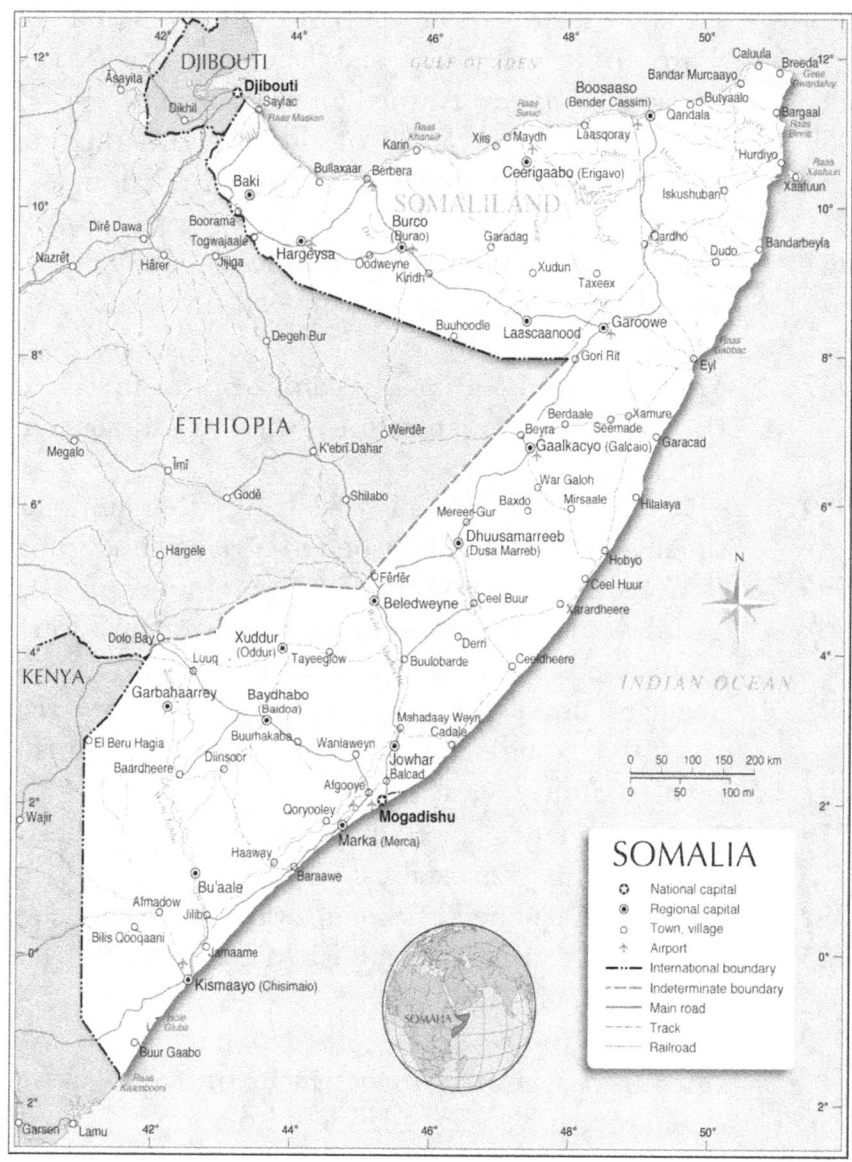

Political Map of Somalia

INTRODUCTION

Islam is a religion that provides general guidelines that aim to develop human beings comprehensively in spiritual, political, social, and economic aspects. The Qur'an and prophetic traditions (the teachings and practices of the prophet Muhammad PBUH) are the two basic sources of Islam. The human interpretation of these sources produces a comprehensive legal framework to regulate the public and private aspects of Muslim life. In addition, Muslim scholars accept two secondary sources: consensus (*Ijma*), the juristic analogy (*Qiyas*), and two complementary sources, general welfare (*Istislah*) and customary practices of particular community (*Urf*). Based on the conceptualization of Islamic legal theories, various interpretations of jurists took into account different spaces, times, and circumstances and produced various schools of jurisprudence called "*Madahib al-fiqh*" and a number of schools of theology.[1] Muslims are required to follow prescribed guidelines as a prerequisite for their harmonious life in this world and rewards in the hereafter. The eminent Islamic scholar Muhammad Qutb succinctly defines Islam as follows:

> Islam is not a mere creed, nor does it represent simply an edification of souls or a refinement and training of human virtues but is rather a harmonious whole that also includes a just economic system, a well-balanced social organization, codes of civil, criminal as well as international law, and philosophical outlook upon life.[2]

---

[1] The Islamic convention in Aman, Jordan, July 2005 that brought together 200 Muslim scholars from over 50 countries recognized eight schools of jurisprudence: four Sunni schools (namely, Hanafi, Maliki, Shafi'I,and Hambali),two Shi'a (namely, Ja'fari and Zaidi),and other schools (namely, Dahiri and Ibadi). Also, recognized four schools of theology: the Asha'ari, Maturidi, real Sufism, true Salafism. This declaration was endorsed by the majority of Islamic scholars and institutions. The Toyal Aal al-Bayt Institute for Islamic Thought, *The Amman Message* (Jordan, 2009), available from http://rissc.jo/books/en/001-Amman-Message.pdf (accessed on June 4, 2016).

[2] Muhammad Qutb, *Islam: the misunderstood religion* (Kazi Pubns Inc,1980), 4. Available from www.Islambasics.com(accessed on May 24, 2016).

Moreover, Islam does not prescribe a specific political system such as monarchies and republics, but it provides a vision of a society founded on justice and benevolence (*adl and ihsan*) that opposes oppression and injustice (*zulm and 'udwan*).³ In addition to offering ethical principles that regulate all forms of human relations, Islam also opposes authoritarianism and calls for consultative form of governance that is, in essence, a democratic governance.⁴ In addition, no specific terminology in the Qur'an and Prophetic traditions qualifies governance in Muslim countries as an Islamic state. The term "Islamic state" was never used in the theory or practice before the 19th century, and its emergence was in reaction to European colonial rule with a secular worldview.⁵ The Arabic term of *"dawlah"* that connotes "state" existed in the Qur'an and its verbal form originally meant "to turn, rotate, or alternate." Also, the term was often used to describe fortunes, vicissitudes, or ups and downs. The first time *dawlah* (Tk., devlet) appears in its modern meaning of state is in a Turkish memorandum circa 1837.⁶ Alternatively, the term used to connote Muslim rule—coined after the death of the Prophet Muhammad (PBUH) in 632 AD—was the term of Caliph "*Khalifah*," which means successor of the prophet as a political leader of the Muslim community, while the territory

---

³ See the Qur'anic verse, usually read at the end of Friday sermons, which says: "Allah enjoins justice, generosity, and kind treatment with kindred."(16:90). In the Qur'an, many terms are used to signify the oppression and injustice, such as *Zulm, Tughyan, Israf, Tabdhir, Ifsad, 'Itida and 'Udwan*. See the Qur'anic verse "And whoever does this aggressively and unjustly, we will soon cast him into fire; and this is easy for Allah (4:30).

⁴ There are two verses in the Qur'an that unequivocally bring forth consultation (Shura) as the basic principle in Islam.The first verse describes the manners of true believers is to consult with each other: "Those who hearken to their Lord, and establish regular prayer; who (conduct) their affairs by mutual consultation among themselves; who spend out of what we bestow on them for sustenance" (42:38). The second verse commands Prophet Muhammad (PBUH)to consult his companions: "Thus it is due to mercy from God that you deal with them gently, and had you been rough, hard hearted, they would certainly have dispersed from around you; pardon them therefore and ask pardon for them, and take counsel with them in the affair; so when you have decided, then place your trust in God; surely God loves those who trust" (3:159).

⁵ Qamaruddin Khan, *Political Concepts in the Quran* (Lahore: Islamic Book Foundation, 1982), 74.

⁶ Turkish Memorandum on 1937 was the beginning of Tanzimat period considered to be the beginning of the rule of the law and Westernization. See Bernard Lewis, *The Political Language of Islam*(Chicago: University of Chicago Press, 1991), 37.

under his rule was called Caliphate. The title of Caliph was conferred to a Muslim ruler similar to a modern political title, such as president. The term was originally derived from the Qur'anic conception that gives authority on earth to the human being. Asserting this notion, the Qur'anic verse says: "And when thy Lord said to the angels: 'I am about to place a successor [*khalifa*] in the earth...'" (2:30). Moreover, other Qur'anic verses (56:55 and 38:26) put forward similar meaning but promise the position of successorship to His true pious believers.[7] Thus, the term caliphate has been in use since the beginning of the rule of the four rightly guided Caliphs until 1924 when the Ottoman Caliphate was abolished. Seemingly, the concept of the Islamic state was developed as a concept in opposition to the secular state and replaced the term caliphate in the era of nation-states. Its modern conceptualization is attributed to the Pakistani scholar Abdul A'la Maududi (1903–1979).[8] A number of states had added the prefix of "Islamic" in their names, such as Iran, Afghanistan, Pakistan, and Mauritania. However, it is not the nature of Islam to give detailed structures or names of any kind because it allows space for human intellect in developing suitable system regarding diverse circumstances, times, and spaces. As of 2015, more than 1.7 billion Muslims are in the world (23.4% of world population), the majority of whom live in the 57 countries that are members of the Organization of Islamic Cooperation (OIC).[9] These countries are the product of colonialism and were shaped to a great extent by the European system of governance and its cultural values. Thus, various

---

[7] See "Allah has promised those who have believed among you and done righteous deeds that He will surely grant them succession [khilafah] upon the earth just as He granted it to those before them and that He will surely establish for them [therein] their religion… (56:55). Moreover, other Qur'anic verse " O David, we have made you successor on earth [Khalifa]. Therefore, you shall judge among the people equitably and do not follow personal desire let it divert you from the path of God"(38:26).

[8] Sayyid abul Ala Maududi, *The Islamic Law and Constitution* (Islamic books, 1980). Also, see Sayyid Vali Reza Nasr, *Mawdudi, and the Making of Islamic Revivalism* (Oxford University Press,1996).

[9] See member states of OIC on their website: www.oicexchanges.org/members/oic-member-state-countries.

organizations working to revive the Islamic message emerged in these countries ranging from peaceful gradualists to revolutionary exclusionists.

Retrospectively, the great Islamic civilization that spanned more than a thousand years was in decline by the dawn of the 13th century while the European Renaissance was at pace.[10] The gradual process of Muslim decadence and European ascendance has stimulated Europeans to conquer Muslim lands since the mid-18th century. Gradually, Islam was portrayed as merely an inherited and outmoded traditional culture rather than a source of a comprehensive way of life for a large part of the educated elite in Muslim societies. This condition was set due to the implication of colonialism and the process of acculturation of Muslim elites. One of the most popular explanations given to the decadence of Islamic civilization was that Muslims had veered away from true Islamic teachings. Indeed, the true Islamic teaching was not limited to performing prescribed rituals and other individual actions, but far beyond that are other aspects of Islam — such as good governance based on justice and benevolence (*adl* and *ihsan*) and advancement of science and technology. Based on that broad view, a number of Islamic scholars began to call for a revival of Islam as a precondition for the rebirth of the Muslim nation and to put an end to their terrible conditions.[11] Therefore, socio-political movements emerged in the early years of the 20th century and, since then, the revival of Islam has been shaping every Muslim country from North Africa to Southeast Asia. The impact of these movements was so overwhelming that it extended even to Muslim minorities and communities in their respected countries around the globe.

---

[10] The Renaissance is the period in European civilization immediately following the Middle Agesin the 14th century; it'scharacterized by a surge of interest in classical learning and values, discovery and exploration of new continents, the decline of the feudal system, and the growth of commerce and the inventions. See William Gilbert and Edwyna Condon Gilbert,*The Renaissance and the Reformation* (electronic edition, 1998), ed. by Judith C. Galas.

[11] The forerunners of contemporary Sunni Islamic revivalinclude Jamal-al-Din Afghani, Muhammad Abduh, Hassan al-Banna, Rashid Rida, Muhammad Iqbal, and Abul-Ala Mawdudi.

The surge of Islamic revival had discredited the secular paradigm of the scholars of modernity — such as Voltaire, Jefferson, Marx, Comte, Muller, Spencer, Durkheim, Weber, and Freud — who predicted the decline of religious belief and institutions with the advent of industrial society and modernity.[12] The puzzling resurgence of Islam provoked Western academia to differentiate between traditional Islam and modern Islamic movements with strong political agenda. Thus, various terminologies signifying this phenomenon were coined by various scholars.

Key Buzzwords of the Islamic Movements

To study the phenomenon of the resurgence of Islam, scholars of different academic fields have used various aspectual taxonomies signifying the nature of the Islamic movements. For instance, proponents of the Islamic movements use friendly terminologies, such as Islamic movement, Islamic revival, and Islamic awakening. The term of Islamic movement has a broad definition and encompasses all activities related to spreading Islam. Its comprehensive definition, as given by the International Crisis Group, is "the active assertion and promotion of beliefs, prescriptions, laws, or policies that are held to be Islamic in character."[13] The movements are not monolithic; they're not wholly integrated and include many different trends, policies, structures, and spheres of influences. According to Bjørn Olav Utvik, the Islamist movement can be delimited by three traits: First, they refer to themselves as the Islamic movement; second, they call for an Islamic state ruled in accordance with Sharia, and third, they organize themselves for the purpose of achieving these goals.[14]

---

[12] R. Wallis &S. Bruce,"Secularization: the orthodox model,"in S. Bruce, ed., *Religion and Modernization* (Oxford University Press, Oxford, UK, 2001), 8-30.
[13] The International Crisis Group Report, "Understanding Islamism," Middle East/North Africa Report no. 37-2 (March,2005), 1.
[14] Are Kndusen, "Political Islam in the Middle East," Chr. Michelsen Institute for Development Studies and Human Rights, Bergen, January 2003. Available at www.cmi.no/publications/file/15 48-political-islam-in-the-middle-east.pdf (accessed on June 7, 2016), 3.

They share many attributes with other social movements primarily studied in social movement theories, which were developed to study secular movements and activities. The scope of these theories was widened and many scholars in the field argue that the dynamics, processes, and organization of Islamic movements can be explained as elements of contention and mobilizations that address Muslim grievances.[15] Adding the epithet of "Islamic" simply specifies the system of meaning and identity and the source of motivations. This specificity was succinctly offered by the preeminent Islamic scholar Yusuf Al-Qaradawi, who defined Islamic movement as follows: "organized, collective work, undertaken by the people, to restore Islam to the leadership of society, and to the helm of life all walks of life...[it] is work: persistent, industrious work, not just words to be said, speeches and lectures to be delivered, or books and articles are indeed required, they are merely parts of a movement, not the movement itself."[16] Hence, being organized and collective work offer common features shared with other movements, and its specificity is driven from the source of its motivation, conviction, and performance —faith in Islam. Other terms used by the proponents of the Islamic movement are Islamic rival or renewal (Tajidid al-Islam), which refer to a periodic trend that transpires at the beginning of every century throughout the Muslim world, led by a reformist scholar or the collective work of a movement. This term is derived from a well-known prophetic tradition that states, "God will send to His community at the head of each century those who will renew its faith for it."[17] Many scholars and movements were qualified as revivers "Mujadiddin" in the history of Islam, such as Egyptian Muslim Brotherhood, Pakistani Jama-Islamiya and

---

[15] Quintan Wiktorowicz (ed.), *Islamic Activism: A Social Movement Theory Approach* (Indiana University Press, 2003).
[16] Yusuf al-Qaradawi, *Priorities of the Islamic Movement in the Coming Phase* (al-Dar; 1st edition, 1992), 5.
[17] Narrated by Abu-Dawud & Al-Hakim.

others.[18] Another related term is Islamic awakening which is the English translation of the Arabic term "*al-Sahwa Al-Islamiyah.*" It denotes alertness, consciousness, and wakefulness from slumber or drunkenness. It connotes a general condition of growing consciousness among the Muslims about their religion, which encompasses individuals and groups, whether organized or diverse. This means that the Islamic awakening paves the way for the Islamic movement, and as such, every Islamic movement is a product of Islamic awakening, but not every individual influenced by the awakening necessarily becomes part of a movement. According to al-Qaradawi's perspective, "an awakening is a tributary that supplies and reinforces a movement; a movement is a guide that steers an awakening in the right direction. They are, however, related through interaction."[19] These three terms — Islamic movements, Islamic revival, and Islamic awakening —are favoured by Islamists who use them in describing themselves.

The other cluster of terminologies used by mainstream Western scholars and media are pejorative, such as radical Islam, militant Islam, revolutionary Islam, extremist Islam, Islamic terrorism, and fundamentalist Islam. Attaching these terms to Islam creates a distorted system of meaning for the Islamic movements, depicting them as a threat to Western civilization. These terminologies are relational and aspectual labelling or designating concepts that indicate a degree of something. Also, they are not value-neutral and always exonymic, which means they are applied by others to a group rather than a group labelling itself. Moreover, these terminologies are derived from the lexicon and historical context of the West. For example, early scholars designated the modern Islamic movement as Islamic fundamentalism. Nonetheless, the use of the term of Islamic fundamentalism to

---

[18] The revivers of Islam are numerous. Examples are Ibn Taymiyyah, Ahmed Sirhindi, Shah Waliiullah, Hassan al-Banna, Sayyid Qutb, Al-Maududi and Ruhullah Khumeini.
[19] Al-Qaradawi, *Priorities of the Islamic Movement*, 4.

denote a wide range of Islamic movements is inaccurate and misleading. This terminology was borrowed from the history of the conservative protestant movement that emerged in the U.S. in the early 20th century. This movement was labelled as fundamentalists asserted against the growing influence of liberal theology and critical bible studies believing the statements in the bible are literally true. This movement is not comparable to Islamic movements because Muslims do not disagree on the authenticity and the literal divine origin of the Qur'an. Another term early scholars used to label Islamic revival was radical Islam, derived from the Latin radix (root) that means going to the origin. Sometimes radicalism becomes interchangeable with extremism. Its meaning had been evolving since the late-19th century when radicalism was considered a progressive liberal ideology in Europe. Thus, the meaning of radical does not always stand for bad things even though its meaning may change with context. Occasionally, it may signify those who want to see significant positive changes to society, like the liberation movements of colonized people and women's liberation movements. In other cases, radicalism may imply the initiation of ruthless behaviour that incline toward extremism and terrorism. Thus, the use of the term radical Islam connotes radical change that Islamic movements are aiming for in their drive to apply Islamic law (Sharia) and advance Islamic values. It also may allude to the activities of some groups among Islamic movements that propagate and exercise extremism and terrorism. As such, without differentiation, branding Islamic movements as "radical" can paint a false picture and bad representation of the religion of Islam and its believers. In addition, another extensively used term is Islamic extremism. This term was widely used after 9/11 and literally means driving (something) to the limit and to the extreme. In the Arabic language, the same phenomenon is called "Tadaruf." There is no consensus in defining this term, but it is closely related to other negative terms, such as terrorism, racism, xenophobia, and interethnic and inter-religious hatred. The term is used to qualify individuals or groups that hold unfamiliar ideas that fall outside the mainstream society. Those who profess to the ideology of extremism can be violent toward mainstream society and isolate themselves from ordinary life. Islam is very critical of extremism and calls for moderation in everything —in belief, worship, conduct, and legislation. Islam warns against all forms of extremism, using a term synonymous with extremism, such as *Ghuluw* (excessiveness), *Tanattu'* (meticulous religiosity), and *Tashdid* (strictness). The narrated prophetic tradition said: "Those who succumb to pedantry and nit-picking religiosity (Al-tanattu) will perish."[20] In the history of Islam, extremism in the name of Islam that led to political extremism and terrorism has been known since the *Kharijites* rebelled against Imam Ali bin Abidalib.[21] That is why the term *neo-Kharijites* (*Khawarij al-asr*) is sometimes employed to signify an armed rebellion claiming Islamic righteousness directed against governments in Muslim countries. As such, labelling current groups, such as Al-Qaida and the Islamic State (ISIS), and their affiliates around the globe as extremists is justified from the Islamic perspective. However, identifying all Islamic movements as extremists, including those moderates who participate in elections and profess democracy, is misleading and erroneous. Conversely, moderation, or balance, is not only a general characteristic of Islam, but it is a fundamental principle. In the Qur'anic verse (2:143), Allah says:

> Thus, have we made of you an Ummah (Nation) justly balanced, that you might be witnesses over the nations and the Messenger a witness over yourselves.

---

[20] Narrated by Al-Bukhari and Muslim in their collection of the prophetic traditions.
[21] Joas Wagemakers, *'Seceders', and 'Postponers'? An Analysis of the "Khawarij" and "Murji'a" Labels in Polemical Debates Between Quietist and Jihadi-Salafi*. Available from www.jihadica.com/wp-content/uploads/2012/04/Seceders-and-Postponers-An-Analysis-of-the-Khawarij-and-Murjia-Labels-in-Polemical-Debates-between-Quietist-and-Jihadi-Salafis.pdf (accessed on June 5, 2016).

Yusuf Al-Qaradawi describes the first manifestation of extremism as

> bigotry and intolerance, which causes a person to be obstinately devoted to his own opinion and prejudices as well as rigidity which deprives him of clarity of vision regarding the interests of other human being.[22]

Summarizing, the use of the terms fundamentalism, radicalism, and extremism demonstrates the ideology and belief system of the group of people who are in the periphery of mainstream society. These groups may resort to militancy, revolutions, and terrorism, as such other set of terminologies were developed focussing on their plausible actions.

The terminologies that derive their meaning from factual or fictional behaviour of those designated as fundamentalists, radicals, and extremists include militant Islam, revolutionary Islam, and Islamic terrorism. The inference is that ideologies of extremism, radicalism, and fundamentalism beget the behaviour of militancy, revolutions, and terrorism, and as such, they are linked in a manner that makes their boundaries porous. To spot their nexus, their definitions must be briefly outlined. To start, militancy simply means having a combative character, i.e., aggressive, especially in the service of a cause. Adding an Islamic adjective signifies that Islamic slogans and banners are used as the guiding ideology of that militancy. Militancy can have both negative and positive meaning depending on the motives and context. For example, most liberation movements and freedom fighters have used some form of militancy to gain their freedom and independence. This type of militancy is considered positive and legitimate. Thus, the use of militancy using an Islamic slogan as mobilizing ideology could be justified if the cause is just. In the Islamic doctrine, a just war is called "Jihad," which carries broader meaning than that which is used currently in mass

---

[22] Yusuf al-Qaradawi, *Islamic Awakening between Rejection and Extremism* (International Institute of Islamic Thought2006), 20.

media and as claimed by terrorist organizations. On the other hand, revolutionary Islam was primarily used in the literature after the Iranian Islamic Revolution of 1979, which overthrew the Pahlavi dynasty under Mohammad Reza Shah, which was supported by the United States. The Iranian Revolution expressed itself in the language of Islam with a charismatic scholar in its leadership: Grand Ayatollah Rohollah Khomeini. This movement had been using Islamic conception and criteria to criticize and oppose the Pahlavi regime and expressed its plans in the language of Islam. The initial success of the Iranian Revolution had instilled hope of the possibility of change among the oppressive regimes in Muslim World. However, the use of the term revolutionary Islam waned afterward. Wrapping up, the most popular terminology used in the current media is Islamic terrorism. The definition of terrorism is highly controversial, as countries define it differently for the purpose of their legal requirements. However, it is commonly understood as violence from groups with political, religious, or ideological objectives. Historically, terrorism referred to state terrorism, which was linked to the reign of terror during the French Revolution (1793-94).[23] The most objective analysis of terrorism may be the one given by Bruce Hoffman who wrote:

> On one point, at least, everyone agrees: terrorism is a pejorative term. It is a word with intrinsically negative connotations that is generally applied to one's enemies and opponents or to those with whom one disagrees and would otherwise prefer to ignore.
> 'What is called terrorism,' Brian Jenkins has written, 'thus seems to depend on one's point of view. Use of the term implies a moral judgment; and if one party can successfully attach the label terrorist to its opponent, then it has indirectly persuaded others to adopt its moral viewpoint.' Hence the decision to call someone or label some organization terrorist becomes almost unavoidably subjective, depending largely on whether one sympathizes with or opposes the person/group/cause concerned.

---

[23] Jan Voerman, *The Reign of Terror* (Andrews University Seminary Studies, 2009, Vol. 47, No. 1), 117-134.

If one identifies with the victim of the violence, for example, then the act is terrorism. If, however, one identifies with the perpetrator, the violent act is regarded in a more sympathetic, if not positive (or, at the worst, an ambivalent) light; and it is not terrorism.[24]

Based on the above stated subjective conception of the term, many scholars and politicians identify terrorists who are of Muslim faith as Islamic terrorism, creating a perverted image that Islam is the religion that condones violence and terrorism. Placing the epithet of "Islamic" to the terrorist organizations disregards the sensitivities of mainstream Muslim believers who are victims of terrorism and at war with them, and it ineptly awards religious legitimacy to the terrorist groups.

Some soft definitions frequently used include political Islam and Islamism. The term political Islam alludes to the phenomenon in the Muslim majority countries where Islamic movements began to propagate comprehensiveness of Islam after centuries of decadence that relegated Islam in the periphery of the political sphere. It was used by many Western scholars perplexed by the strange and unwarranted intrusion of Islam into the secular domain of politics, assumed earlier to be apolitical, and to distinguish Islamic inspired political activities from everyday Islamic practices, such as actions of personal piety, the belief system, and conventional rituals. The new slogan that Islam is a religion and state "*Din wa Dawla*" that has been attracting Muslim masses was a challenge for the established notion of secularity among the states. The term political Islam singles out the political aspect of the Islamic movements, which becomes problematic for the secular conception of politics in the western world and could be defined shortly as "Islam used to a political end." The historic triumph of the secular forces upon church and clergies in Europe, and dominance of secular views were imported to the

---

[24] Bruce Hoffman, "Inside Terrorism".Columbia University Press, 1998, 32.

Muslim lands and Muslim political elites mimicked colonial ways during their reign in the postcolonial states. Moreover, Western thought correlated modernization with secularism while local traditions were associated with backwardness. Furthermore, among the two domains of public and private spheres in the Western worldview, religion is relegated to the private sphere. Conversely, Islam offers comprehensive guidelines to both the public spheres and the privates spheres and requires complete abidance from its believers. The use of the term political Islam has three deficiencies according to Are Kndusen.[25] First, it implies that political Islam is "an illegitimate extension of the Islamic tradition outside of the properly religious domain it has historically occupied."[26] Second, it focuses only on the political aspect of Islam and does not capture that Islam fuses religion and politics (*din wa dawla*). Third, there is a tendency to conflate peaceful protest and militancy. Because of these weakness there is an increasing trend to resort to the term "Islamism."[27]

Islamism is sometimes used as synonymous with political Islam even though their diverse definitions makes it difficult to come up with a concurred one. Its simplified definition used in this book is a popular movement advocating the reordering of Muslim societies and states in accordance with the principles of Islam. Historically, Islamism was first used by the French writers in the 17th century as an interchangeable term with Islam parallel to Christianity and Judaism. However, the meaning of Islamism evolved with the time and was used excessively after the 9/11 attack of vital American targets. The word "Islamism" is compounded in adding the suffix of "ism" to Islam, which connotes an ideology rooted in the principles and values of Islam.[28] The difference between human-created

---

[25] Kndusen, "Political Islam in the Middle East," 2.
[26] C. Hirschkind, What is political Islam? Middle East Report Oct/Dec (1997):12-14,12.
[27] K. Karamé, Social and economic reasons for the recruiting to political Islam (in Norwegian). Internasjonal Politikk, 1996, 54:199-213.
[28] Ideology is a collection of beliefs held by an individual, group, or society and is a normative concept that deals with how society should work and offers guidelines for a social order.

ideologies, such as socialism, nationalism, capitalism, feminism, and Islamism, is that Islamism makes ultimate reference to the supremacy of the teaching of Islam. However, groups belonging to Islamism are not monolithic, even though conceptually they agree to consider Islam their ultimate reference. They differ in their approaches, interpretations, and views on the contemporary issues. The term gained popularity, and many Muslim scholars began to use it and was translated into Arabic language as "*Islamiyyun.*"However, this book, while using the tern Islamism, defied classification of Muslims into Islamists and secularists and adopted the term "non-Islamists" instead. Islamists are those engaged in some form of Islamic activism and may belong to one of the organized groups. Non-Islamists include the majority of Muslims who are neither secular nor Islamic activists.[29] This means that a Muslim cannot be signified as secularist if he is not asserting deliberately to be free from Islamic rule and teachings. Secularism as an ideology in that sense totally opposes basic tenets of Islamic faith. An individual's mere claim to be secular, while deeply believing in Islam and practicing its rituals, does not make him secular; rather, he may be ignorant, fearful, and knowingly indulge in anti-Islamic activities while still believing what he is doing is wrong. As such, many Muslims who pretend to be secular are like "rice Christians" or " scholarship Christians" who claim false conversion to Christianity for worldly benefits rather than religious conviction.[30]

Following Diagram demonstrate development of the various terminologies to quality modern socio-political

---

[29] The Qur'an classifies Muslims into three categoties and classifying them into Islamist and secularist defies proper Islamic conception. See the qur'anic verse "Then we caused to inherit the Book those We have chosen of Our servants; and among them is he who wrongs himself, and among them is he who is moderate, and among them is he who is foremost in good deeds by permission of Allah" (35:32).

[30] "Rice Christians" are people who formally declared themselves Christian for material benefits. Nuruddin Faarax, a prominent Somali novelist, called Somali students who claimed Christianity in the early-1960s "scholarship Christians" who reclaimed their Islamic faith after they graduated from a U.S. university. This story was relayed by Mohamud Siyaad Togane in an interview by the author on November 3, 2009, in Montreal, Canada.

activism in the name of Islam. It shows how Muslims designate themselves and how others brand Muslim activism. The logic of the terminologies used by the Western scholars emanate from the concepts of sociology of religion which does not mind the validity of religious beliefs, but study its effects on society. In view of that, these scholars examine the core ideology and correlated actions of Islamic activists and associate them to Islam. On the other hand, Muslim scholars look Islam from the perspective of being transcendental religion which has its specific principles and normative values. Hence, its reawakening and revival is considered a desirable development. Moreover, Islamic scholars do not relate faulty actions of individuals or groups to Islam such as terrorism or violations of Human Rights, but consider these actions as a deviation from the true nature of Islam.

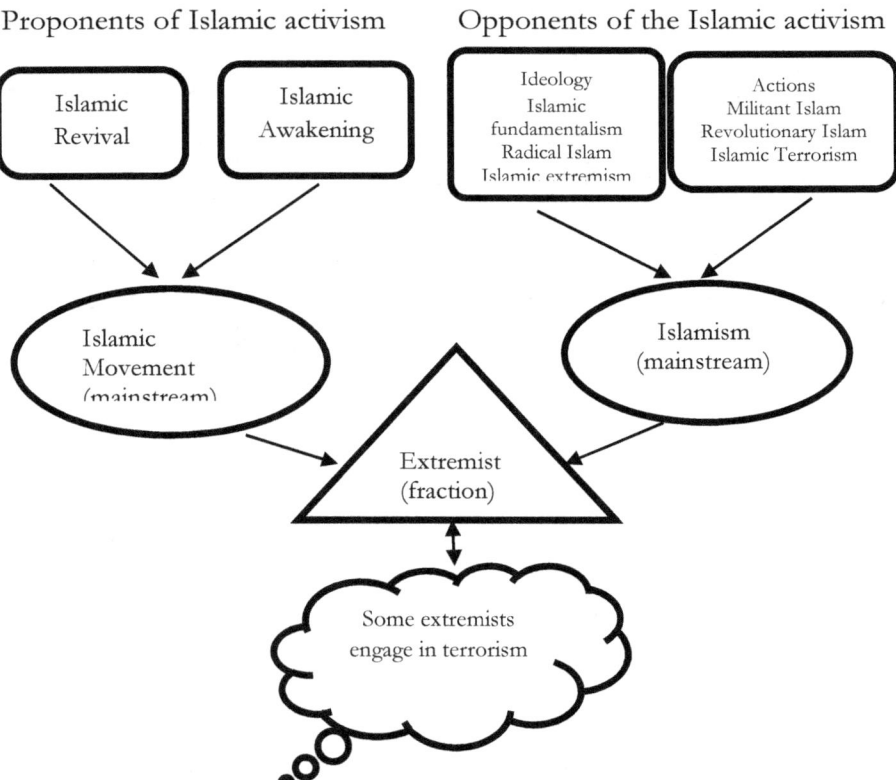

Fig 1: Terminologies of Islamic activism and their logical relations

Having given some remarks on Islam and Islamism, let us now turn to Transitional Justice, the third theme of this book. The collapse of the Somali state in 1991 and the breakdown of the order and state institutions instigated a total breakout of civil war where clan-based, armed militias fought each other throughout the country, wreaking havoc and committing gross violations of human rights against civilian populations. Those violations were not limited to the actions of Somali non-state actors but also implicated other external actors who intervened Somalia militarily. Strangely enough, despite the mass violations of human rights taking place in Somalia, Transitional Justice was not incorporated as part of the international plan for assisting the Somali peace-building process.[31] Indeed, Transitional Justice is considered a precondition for rebuilding a harmonious society after civil wars and mass violations of human rights. In Somalia, a country torn apart for a quarter of century, introducing Transitional Justice was paramount, but its mechanism needed to be in harmony with Islam and local traditions. This topic is less addressed in the literature of Somali studies.[32] The objective of this book is to link these three themes — Islam, Islamism, and Transitional Justice—with the Somali state recovery project. It offers a unique analysis of these three themes as the components necessary to rebuilding a viable Somali state.

---

[31] For instance, the mandate of the African Union Mission in Somalia includes a Transitional Justice component. See Margherita Zuin, "A Model for Transitional Justice for Somalia" *(PRAXIS, The Fletcher Journal of Human Security* (Vol. XXIII), 2008), 89-108.

[32] Academic studies on transitional justice in Somalia are in its infancy. Following are emerging literature since 2008.Rahma Abdulkadir, "*Gender, transitional justice, and failed statehood: can Somali traditional customary law be the basis for viable and inclusive mechanism(s) of transitional justice in Somalia?*(PhD d*iss.*, The University of Texas at Dallas, 2011). Fowsia Abdulkadir & Rahma Abdulkadir, "Transitional Justice & Limited or Failed Statehood: A Case Study of Somalia," available from www.wiscnetwork.org/porto2011/papers/WISC_2011-769.pdf (accessed on June 6, 2016). M. Zuin, A Model of Transitional Justice. Abou Jeng, "*Transitional Justice and Post Conflict Reconstruction in Somalia: The Role of the African Union and Pointers Provided by It*" (North Eastern African Studies, Vol.14, No.2, 2014),45-76. Abdirizak Haji,Somali v.Rwanda-Transitional Justice, available at www.linkedin.com/pulse/somali-vs-rwanda-transitional-justice-abdirizak-hagi (accessed on June 6, 2016).

Organization of the book

This book consists of seven papers previously published as book chapters or in academic journals. I have revised these papers and incorporated them into three focused, cohesive chapters. They cover Islam and the Somali state during conflict and compromise, the Transitional Justice in Islam and its conception in the Somali public, and historical development of the Islamic movements, phases, moderation, and militancy. Collectively, these papers exhibit the dynamics of Islam, Islamism, and Somali state during a military regime and after its collapse. Some of the sections of the book may look repetitive, but for the sake of covering each topic independently, some of these duplications may be indispensable and justified. The author convincingly argued that any success of Somali nation-building depends on the skilful reconciliation of nationalism and Islam on one hand and accommodating clan attachments on the other. Moreover, the author warns that if moderate Islamism is not promoted within the state apparatus in Somalia, the alternative will be the emergence of more extreme groups that may bring social conflict and regional security problems.

The first paper in Chapter one, "Islam and Somali military regime: A showdown on the secular family law,"[33] traces an important historical event that was one of the defining moments of Somali history but that received less historical attention. It fills that historical gap in pulling back the veil of history and examining the dynamics of women, Islamists, and the military regime within the socio-political context of Somalia. It narrates the events that occurred in 1975 when the military regime clashed with the Islamic scholars who criticized secular family law and executed 10 Islamic scholars and imprisoned hundreds others. The military regime's discourse

---

[33] The original paper was published as book chapter under the title: Abdurahman Abdullahi, "Women, Islamists, and the Military Regime in Somalia: The new family Law and Its Implications," in Markus Hoehne and Virginia Luling (ed.) *Milk and Peace, Drought and War: Somali Culture, Society and Politics* (London: Hurst&Company, 2010),137-160.

was that socialist reform would be deficient unless women were liberated from the bonds of culture and religion. On the other hand, the Islamic scholars considered the laws as violating the most sacred domain of the Islamic Sharia, the family. This chapter makes the argument that although the family law placed women in the national agenda, it did not empower them and caused irreparable damage in setting off extreme ideology in the name of Islam.

The second paper, "Recovering the Somali state: Islam and Islamism in nation-building," addresses the dynamics of Islam and Islamism in recovering the collapsed Somali state.[34] The author believes that the complexity of the Somali debacle does not permit emotional solutions, repeating failed approaches, importing external solutions, and creating structures tailored to suit group interest or political advantage of incumbent leaders. This paper focuses on how Islamic moral values – values that supersede and dilute clannish culture of disunity and disintegration – could be revived and reinvigorated in order to recover the Somali state. It brings to the forefront aspects of Islam that bring people closer to each other, uniting their mission and purpose in life. It also explores the nature of the moderate Islamic movement and its role in nation-building and social transformation.

The second chapter deals with the important aspect of nation-building and peace-building less addressed in the Somali scholarly studies: Islam and Transitional Justice and its Somali conceptions. The first paper "Islam and Transitional Justices: principles, mechanisms and historical role in Somalia" aims to investigate Transitional Justices concepts and mechanisms based on the Islamic Sharia and its applicability in Somalia.[35] It offers a theoretical framework on the basic

---

[34] The original paper before current revision was published in 2007 under the following title. Abdurahman Abdullahi, "Recovering the Somali State: The Islamic Factor." In *Somalia: Diaspora and State Reconstitution in the Horn of Africa,* edited by A. Osman Farah, Mamo Mushie, and Joakim Gundel (London: Adonis & Abby Publishers Ltd., 2007), 196-221.

[35] The original paper was published in the website under the title: Abdurahman, Abdullahi. "Islam and Transitional Justice: Principles, Mechanisms, and Historic Role in Somalia" (A paper

concepts and classifications of Islamic Sharia and explores retributive and restorative systems of justice in Islam. Finally, it explains the historical role of Sharia and the development of the schools of jurisprudence "*madaahib*" in Somalia. The second paper, "Somali conceptions of Transitional Justice: findings of a field research in Mogadishu," covers field work in southern Somalia to discover prevailing public opinion of Transitional Justices through sample interviews.[36] It sought to identify the most 'acceptable' mechanisms from the menu of available Transitional Justices approaches, ranging from local customary law to Sharia to national and international law. The findings are based on field research undertaken from June to October 2012 in Mogadishu. This survey showed that modern understandings of Transitional Justices are limited among the general population and mostly confined to small groups of educated elites in Somalia. Most elements of modern Transitional Justices approaches can be found internally accepted norms of Somali customary law and Islamic Sharia, and a place-based approach has the potential to reconcile multiple forms of law as they deal with issues of Transitional Justice.

Chapter three consists of three papers and deals with the historical phases of the Islamic movements, moderate components represented by the Islah movement, and historical roots of the current militancy. The first paper, "Historical phases of Somali Islamic movements," examines the historical development of the Islamic movement in four phases: the Islamic revival (1800-1950), the rise of the Islamic consciousness (1950-1967), the beginning of the Islamic awakening (1967-1978), and the emergence of the Islamic

---

produced as part of research project on Transitional Justice in Somalia commissioned by Max Planck Institute for Social Anthropology, Halle/Saale, Germany,2013), available at www.scribd.com/doc/132832431/Islam-and-Transitional-Justice-Edited1-Doc. (accessed on June 14, 2013).

[36] The original paper was published as: Abdurahman Abdullahi, "Conceptions of Transitional Justice in Somalia: Findings of Field Research in Mogadishu"(*Northeast African Studies* Vol. 14, No. 2, Fall 2014), 7-44.

movements (1978-).³⁷ These historical phases are not mutually exclusive and demonstrate continuity and change. They are dynamic, crosscurrent, and overlap each other. The second paper, "Islamic moderation in war-torn Somalia: the views of Islah movement on the major contemporary issues" delves into Islamic moderation in war-torn Somalia using the Islah movement as a case study.³⁸ It looks at the nature of the organization, its ideological affiliation and historical development in the formative period (1978-1992) and during the civil war (1992-2008). The Islah movement's long period of uninterrupted work has gained experience, sharpened its vision and mission, and improved its views, strategies, and operations. This paper provides views of Islah on major contemporary issues, such as cooperating with traditional Islamic scholars; downplaying disputed issues of religion; rejection of violence and extremism; promoting civil society organizations, democracy, women's rights; and protection of human rights. The third paper, "Militancy of Sufi brotherhoods in the history of Somalia," traces incidents of militancy in the name of Islam that took place among Sufi Orders as evidenced in the history of Somalia.³⁹ It constructs four historical events in the history of Somalia when Islamic scholars led internal fighting to gain politico-religious hegemony. Such events offer historical importance and constitute precedents for current widespread militancy in Somalia. It provides lessons that doctrinal differences and political ambitions can develop into conflict and violent wars among Islamic scholars under the leadership of charismatic and ambitious scholars. These four incidents of militancy that

---

³⁷ The originalpaper was published as: Abdurahman Abdullahi, "Somalia: Phases of Modern Islamic Development," available from www.academia.edu/13227041/Phases_of_the_Islamic_Movement_in_Somalia (accessed on June 6, 2016).

³⁸ The original paper was published under the title, Abdullahi, Abdurahman, "Islah Movement in Somalia: Islamic Moderation in the War-torn Somalia" (A paper presented at the Second Nordic Horn of Africa Conference, Oslo University, 2008), available from www.hiiraan.com/oct2008/ISLAH.pdf (accessed on June 5, 2016).

³⁹ The original paper was published under the title, Abdurahman Abdullahi, "The Roots of the Islamic Conflict in Somalia" In *Somalia: Exploring A Way Out* (National Civic Forum-Somalia, 2011).

occurred among different Sufi orders were, to a certain extent, influenced by the Salafia doctrine and led by scholars with traceable connections and affiliation to the Arabian peninsula.

Collectively, these papers present a narrative on the role of Islam, Islamism, and transitional justice in recovering the Somali state employing a postcolonial perspective. Postcolonial theory offers an oppositional worldview in discovering the other side of previously neglected, concealed, or marginalized narratives of hegemonic powers and their knowledge. This other side draws its analysis from viewpoints of local actors and allows them to tell their stories and come up with their approaches. Accordingly, the major theme of this book is to underline the total failure of western modernity on the traditional Somali society and impossibility of its resuscitation without reconciling with the basics of Somaliness —Islam and clan. Here, I make the case that recovering the collapsed Somali state is contingent upon reconciling Islam, clanism, and nationalism in a well developed system of governance and ethical principles. In doing so, three possible options available. The first option was experimented during postcolonial state building and was based on moving society towards state model inherited from the colonial powers. This model had demonstrated its total failure as it had collapsed in 1991.The second option was moving the state towards society which means building modern state institutions on primordial clan affiliation and traditional structures. This indigenization approach was experimented since Djibouti Peace Conference in 2000 which adopted 4.5 clan power sharing. It has demonstrated imcompatibility of the clan system and modern state concepts based on citizenship. The last available option is moving both the state and the society towards each other, and integrating tradition and modernity in a way that is acceptable to both the state and society.

CHAPTER ONE

Islam and Somali State: Conflict and Compromise

I
Islam and Somali Military Regime : A Showdown on the Secular Family Law

II
Recovering the Somali State: Islam, Islamism and Nation-Building

Islam and the Military Regime:
A Showdown on the Secular Family Law

> Allah enjoins you about [the share of inheritance of] your children: A male's share shall equal that of two females -- in case there are only daughters, more than two shall have two-thirds of what has been left behind.

> The Qur'anic verse on inheritance (4:11)

> As of today, Somali men and women are equal. They have the same equality, the same rights, and the same share of whatever is inherited from their parents.... the era of one half, one third, one quarter is gone forever.

> President Mohamed Siyad Barre, January 11, 1975.

Introduction

The military regime that came to power in Somalia in 1969 introduced a new Family Law on January 11, 1975. Through this law, the President declared that the Qur'anic verses on inheritance were outdated and would not have any legal power in the new socialist Somalia. This pronouncement caught the Somali public by surprise, since it overtly contradicts the historically practiced Sharia law. Though, public reaction was calm and cautious due to the ruthless and repressive nature of the regime, a small number of Islamic scholars had the courage to criticize the new Family Law from the pulpit of one of the mosques in Mogadishu. In panic, the regime used its security agents and detained these scholars and their sympathizers. On January 23, 1975, the military regime executed 10 of the Islamic scholars while incarcerating hundreds more. The military regime's intention in enacting the new Family Law sought to modernize the society through socialist transformations and making the genders 'equal comrades'. The regime argued that socialist reform would be deficient unless women were librated from the bonds of culture and religion through a revolutionary legal reform. In view of this the Islamic scholars focused their arguments on the protection of the last and most sacred domain of the Islamic Shari'a – the family – from the pervasive secularism of the military regime.

The disagreement between the Islamic scholars and the "secular" nationalists took place over the issue of the role and status of women where each party sought to either modernize the role of women or preserve religious society. Yet in all this, it seems that Somali women were not much engaged at the initiation stage of the Family Law, and most likely had much more important priorities and demands. Indeed, women were suffering primarily because of the anachronistic patriarchal system, which both the regime and the Islamic scholars equally represented.[1] Historians and scholars said little on this important historical event, and indeed the situation matches Fleishmann's notion of a "history in search for historians".[2] Considering that this event is one of the defining moments of Somali history, this paper attempts to pull back the veil of history and examine the dynamics of women, Islamists and the military regime within the socio-political context of Somalia. It makes the argument that though the Family Law placed women in the national agenda, indeed, it was a blow against the gradual empowerment of women, and caused enormous hardships to them. Moreover, the secular family law galvanized Islamic revivalism and motivated extremism in the name of Islam.

---

[1] Gender relations in Somalia are derived mostly from the dominant pastoral culture based on the division of labour in the harsh environment and volatile security predicaments. Most of the new elites and Islamic scholars are recent immigrants from the pastoral areas. Reforming that culture in the urban setting is challenging and requires generational change.

[2] Ellen L. Fleichmann, *The Nation and Its "New" Women: The Palestinian Women's Movement, 1920-1948* (University of California Press, 2003).

Defining Key Concepts

In the context of this paper, Women, Islamists and the Military regime are not separate categories of analysis, but are instead interdependent groups interacting within the Somali society. For example, beyond the philosophy that underpins its cosmological outlook, Islam in its social aspects very much accounts for social realities, influencing economic, political, cultural and gender relations within a given time and space. In this context, it has maintained flexibility and reformability within its broader paradigm, while delineations have always existed in interpreting social issues in accordance with a set of methodologies employed by researchers in a particular issue. These methodologies have led to different interpretations of Islam, as reflected in the existing major schools of Jurisprudence.[3] The term Islamist is used here to denote the various Islamic scholars in both traditional and modern Islamic movements who are considered bearers of Islamic knowledge and protectors of Islam against secularizing forces. They are the experts of jurisprudence and those engaged in teaching Islamic doctrines, and those guiding the religious aspects of the Somali communities. Islamist movement represents a popular movement advocating for the re-ordering of Muslim states and societies in accordance with the Islamic laws. Thus, an Islamist is an activist in achieving the objectives of Islamic movement. Conversely, non-Islamists include majority of Muslims who are neither secular nor Islamic activists. On the other hand, the term 'woman' is used to signify the 'Muslim woman' who is part of the larger Somali society, nevertheless marginalised within the cultural system and within class, clan and race dynamics.[4] The Family Law denotes the codified statutory personal law pronounced by the

---

[3] These schools are the four Sunni schools, namely Hanaffi, Malikki, Shafi'i and Hambali, and other Shi'a schools such as Ja'fari and Zaidi.
[4] Somalis belong to the Sunni Muslim of Shafi'i Jurisprudence.

military regime on 11th January, 1975. This law, though supported by a small coterie of elite urban women, affected all women regardless of their location within power configurations. The Military regime ruled Somalia from 1969 to 1990, taking a socialist orientation as its guiding philosophy for social transformation and development, and assigned more roles that are prominent to women.[5]

Women in the Societal Framework

Traditional power configurations in Somalia bind together two groups who perform complementary functions in the society. The first is the worldly function of the primordial or territorial clan groups, bounded by their diverse versions of clan laws in their multi-level structures and hierarchies.[6] These worldly functions are vested on the clan elders of the primary social unit (Diya-paying unit), who have diverse titles and roles in the different localities and sub-cultures, and coordinate the affairs of the clans through the institution of the general assembly or 'Shir'.[7] This assembly is participatory and includes all male members of the clan and mostly exclude women from discussions and decision-making. The second are the religious functions undertaken by the Islamic scholars, such as Islamic education, dispensing and directing religious functions and events.[8] Beyond this, the Islamic scholars have religious

---

[5] Osseina Alidou and Meredith Turshen, "Africa: Women in the Aftermath of Civil War", Race &Class, 2000:41(4): 81-92.

[6] In the pastoral areas, the system is based on primordiality while in the agricultural areas, it is founded on territorial attachments; and accordingly, various legal systems have been developed to respond to the needs of the communities. Moreover, hierarchies of the clan system begin from Diya-paying sub-clan.

[7] Different clans use different titles for their elders. There are Sultan, Ugas, Islan, Boqor, Wabar, Malaaq, imam, Grad and so on. A Diya-paying group is a primary unit that has a common territory, clan wells, Xeer and a leader, and recognized as such by other clans. The function of the clan elder is the provision of security, conflict resolution; administration of Diya system and intra-clan relations. So, it is a sort of mini-state. See Abdurahman Abdullahi, "Tribalism, Nationalism and Islam: Crisis of the Political Loyalties in Somalia", (MA Thesis, McGill University, 1992), 37-39.

[8] These functions include teaching Qur'an and Islamic disciplines; conducting marriage contracts and inheritance; leading prayers, fasting and celebrations of religious festivities and so on.

authority that community members hold in the highest respect and adoration. Nonetheless, women are not part of the religious enterprise, and their involvement in Islamic education and Islamic activities have long been peripheral. Therefore, in the traditional patriarchal power praxis, women have been excluded from decision making. In this, the dominant anthropological school has posited that Somali society in a monolithic representation of pastoralism, secularism and masculinity.[9] This perspective assumes vertical relations between clan elders, Islamic scholars and women, situating clan elders at the top and women at the bottom. These hierarchical relations defy the notion of egalitarian and democratic practices in the society as romanticized by I.M. Lewis's "pastoral democracy", as women have not been part of the pastoral 'democratic' system.[10]

The colonial authorities absorbed traditional leaders within its administrative apparatus and downplayed its traditional authorities. Gradually, the Somalis developed nationalist political parties that led Somalia to independence in 1960. Following this, the post-colonial state adopted policies that curbed the role of the traditional institutions, adopting a framework founded on a vertical state hegemony. In particular, during the era of the military regime, "the hands of the state extended towards family and personal law, standardizing, codifying, reforming and modernizing them."[11] During this period women gained a number of important rights, including equality in citizenship, voting rights, equal opportunities in the social services and jobs and paid maternity

---

[9] Virginia Lulling posited three models of clan formation: pastoral-nomadic model, the agro-pastoral model, and the urban model. See Virginia Luling, *Somali Sultanate: The Geledi City-State over 150 Years* (London: Haan Publications, 2002), 77-80.

[10] Surprisingly, I.M. Lewis qualified a society which half of its population are not represented in the decision-making process to be "democratic". See Lewis, I. M., *Pastoral Democracy*, (Oxford: Oxford University Press, 1961).

[11] Codification of the family law and the process of selection of judges made, in many cases, judicial decisions less flexible. See Amira El-Azhary Sobol (ed.) *Women, the Family and Divorce laws in Islamic History* (New York: Syracuse University Press, 1996), 7.

leave.¹² Beyond this, the main 'feminist' issues of the Muslim World – such as the veil, seclusion, work and education – were not discussed in Somalia until the era of military rule in 1969. In all, Somali women enjoyed enormous freedoms in the traditional and religious society, but did adhere to the pastoral and semi-pastoral culture – until the military regime introduced policies forcefully secularizing the traditional society.

Literature Review

Studies on Somali women and their role in social, political, economic and religious activities is not common. What does exist in English published literature are three main historical perspectives which can be traced to the anthropological, transformational and revisionist perspectives.[13] From the anthropological perspective, I. M. Lewis' *A Modern History of the Somali*, treats Somali Family Law in few lines:

> The public execution of ten local religious Sheikhs in January 1975 had wider and more serious repercussions, touching a deeper nerve. ... By this action, taken in International Women's year, the government demonstrated its secular, reformist intensions – but at the cost of rising in an acute form the whole question of Islamic identity of the Somali people.[14]

Lewis characterized the new Family Law as merely "tokenism."[15] Meanwhile, in her book "Society, Security and Sovereignty and the State in Somalia", Maria Barons hailed the reformist policies of the regime regarding "women's rights", while criticizing the regime for its violation of civil rights. Here, the author wrote,

---

[12] Abdurahman Abdullahi, "Penetrating Cultural Frontiers in Somalia: History of women's Political Participation during four Decades (1959-2000)." *African Renaissance*. 4:1 (2007): 34-54, 41.
[13] Ibid., 42
[14] Lewis, I. M., *A Modern History of Somalia: Nation and State in the Horn of Africa* (London: Longmans, 1980), 213.
[15] *Refugee Survey Quarterly, Vol. 13, Nos. 2 and 3, 1994*, 94

All civil rights were increasingly curtailed. Women's option for voice remained also very restricted, and progressive opinions were suppressed and conservative critique was brutally silenced.[16]

Beyond this, Professor Said Samatar and David Laitin in their well-titled book "Somalia: A Nation in Search of a State" completely ignored the inception of the secular Family Law.

In the transformationist perspective adopted in the book "Socialist Somalia: Rhetoric and Reality", Ahmed Samatar focused on the socialist transformations of the military regime. He related the promulgation of the secular Family Law under the topic of women's rights, flattering the regime's policies and actions towards women. Professor Samatar argued that the Family Law of 1975 was "another important progressive step."[17] Samatar shied away from even mentioning the execution of the Islamic scholars and the possible repercussions of this event. Conversely, Professor Lidwien Kapteijns questioned "Siyaad Barre's state feminism", suggesting that it was "clan-based – and class-based – clientage extended to a set group of women." Though Kapteijns did not emphasise the Family Law and its implications, she did articulate the superficiality of the regime's policies regarding women, refuting the regime's claim that it was improving equality between men and women. She affirmed that women climbed to higher positions within the government simply because of their being a "relative of loyal male client of the regime" or "relatives of men needed to be kept out of power" or a "compromise [for] their sexuality."[18] Finally, Professor Hussein Adam's paper on "Historical Notes on Somali

---

[16] Maria Barons, *Society, Security Sovereignty and the State in Somalia: From Statelessness to Statelessness* (Netherlands: Utrecht: International Books, 2001), 198.
[17] Ahmed Samatar, *Socialist Somalia: Rhetoric and Reality* (London: Zed Press, 1988), 107.
[18] Lidwien Kapteijins, "Women and Crisis of Communal Identity: The Cultural Construction of Gender in Somali History" in *The Somali Challenge: From Catastrophe to Renewal?*, edited by Ahmed Samatar (Boulder: Lynne Reinner Publishers, 1994), 229.

Islamism" totally ignored the event of the Family Law and its impact on instigating extremism in the name of Islam.[19]

Revisionist historians have added a new perspective on this issue. The revisionists view was introduced through Professor Jumale's book "The Invention of Somalia". Yet in this work, the discussion on the "Invention of Somali Women" which was undertaken by Christine Ahmed who criticizes anthropological perspective and Orientalist invention of Somali women, does not include reference to the Family Law reform. Catherine Besteman however, in her book "Unravelling Somalia: Race, Violence and the Legacy of Slavery", did provide a chapter on "Violence and the State." Nonetheless, she did not mention the violence committed by the State in the name of gender equality in 1975. Beyond this, Hamdi's PhD thesis "Multiple Challenges, Multiple Struggles: A History of Women's Activism in Canada", provides a good historical background to the position of Somali women, analysing the implications of the Family Law.[20] Finally, Islamist historians have focused on the execution of the Islamic scholars in 1975, considering it as one of the defining moments in Somali history and the impetus for the modern Islamic revival in Somalia. For them, the event sits as a key moment in the history of the struggle between Islamism and secularism.[21] These notions are well articulated in Professor Ali Sheikh Ahmed's historical work "Judur al-Ma'sat al-Rahina", which provides the most substantial historical reporting on the topic of the Family Law and the local and Muslim world implications.[22] In such scarcity of written references, this

---

[19] Hussein Adam, "Historical Notes on Somali Islamism" (A paper presented at the Conference of the Somali Studies Association, Djibouti: December 12-15, 2007).
[20] Hamdi Mohamed, "*Multiple Challenges, Multiple Struggles: A History of Women's Activism in Canada*" (PhD Thesis submitted to the University of Ottawa, 2003).
[21] Abdurahman Abdullahi, "Perspectives on the State Collapse in Somalia" in *Somalia at the Crossroads: Challenges and Perspectives in Reconstituting a Failed State*, edited by Abdullahi A. Osman and Issaka K. Soure (London: Adonis & Abby Publishers Ltd, 2007), 44.
[22] Ali Sheikh Abubakar, *Al-Somal: Judur al-Ma'sat al_Rahina* (Beirut: Dar-Ibn Hazm, 1992).

paper makes substantial use of oral narrations to fill gaps in the existent literature.

Setting the Stage

After the failure of the nine-years democratic regime that followed the removal of colonial rule, the Military regime took over Somalia through bloodless Coup on 21st October, 1969, and Mohamed Siyad Barre became the new absolute ruler.[23] Few tears were shed for the corrupt civilian government, and the people of Somalia supported the new regime with the hope that the new government will change their socio-economic and political wellbeing. On the first anniversary of the military coup in 1970, scientific socialism was espoused as the guiding ideology of the regime. From this moment, the regime undertook policies designed to curb both the 'elements of traditional Somaliness' – specifically, the clan and Islam – and embarked on the road towards dictatorship. The repressive course of the regime began most clearly with the enactment of the notorious 'Law of 26 Articles', adopted on September 10, 1970. This law listed a number of serious crimes against the State which constitutes death penalties and life imprisonment. Such crimes include "exploiting religion to create national disunity or to undermine and weaken the powers of the state."[24] The policy of the regime with respect to Islam was to emphasize its complementary relationship with socialism in notions of social justice.[25] Occasionally, Islam was even used as an instrument for furthering socialist goals, as evidenced by the declaration that "Anyone opposing socialism

---

[23] Italian government immediately recognized the military regime and provided massive assistance. Moreover, the Communist party of Italy supported the new regime not only because of its socialist path, but also because of its historical connection with the Soviet Union. See Paolo Tripodi, *The Colonial Legacy in Somalia: Rome and Mogadishu: From Colonial Administration to Operation Restore Hope* (London: McMillan Press, 1999), 115.
[24] Luigi Pastaloza, *The Somali Révolution (*Bari: Édition Afrique Asie Amérique Latine, 1973), 318
[25] Lewis, 219.

should at the same time be considered acting against the principles of Islam and against its very system of life."[26]

Opposition to the regime was often considered as having some Islamic inclinations in opposing socialist regime. The first major form of opposition came during an internal rift within the ruling junta, when two prominent Generals of the Revolutionary Council: General Salad Gabeyre Kediye and General Mohamed Ainanshe Guled, and the former Colonel Abdulkadir Dheel, were accused of organizing a counter-coup with the aim of introducing 'Islamic Socialism.' The three officers were publicly executed on July 1972.[27] The second opposition was initiated by Islamic scholars who mutinied against the adoption of the secular Family Law. Ten of these scholars were executed by the military regime. Beyond such explicit acts, the President's speeches also consistently referred to "bad Sheikhs" (*wadaad xume*), casting them as reactionary forces opposed to the progressive state ideology.

After consolidating power in the first five years, by 1974 the military regime had realized a number of important achievements which made them triumphant. For instance, Somalia joined the Arab League in 1974, securing important political and economic support from the Arab world. Moreover, the annual summit of the Organization of the African Union (OAU) was held in Mogadishu in 1974, boosting the image of the regime and the President was elected to the position of chairmanship of OAU.[28] The Cultural Revolution initiated in 1973 succeeded in adopting the historically disputed "Latin Script' as the alphabet of the Somali language. The literacy campaign that began in July 1974 allowed more than 30,000 high school students and teachers, both male and female, to travel to the rural areas to teach

---

[26] Pastoloza, 138.
[27] Ibid.,150.
[28] Lewis, 227.

people writing and reading in their own language.²⁹ In the domestic challenges, Somalis increased their contact with the Arab world through Somali migrant labour which flocked to the Gulf States, facilitating their participation in the Islamic awakening following the Arab-Israeli war of 1973. Moreover, the growing strength of the military regime and its prestige also added to the dissatisfaction of the formerly privileged classes and the clans marginalized in the aftermath of the coup d'état and the execution of counter-coup plotters.

Furthermore, Marxist revolution had triumphed in 1974 in Ethiopia, encouraging the Somali State in its irredentist goals of securing a 'Greater Somalia' from the weakened Ethiopia which was under domestic conflict. In the international arena, the UN adopted a resolution in 1972 proclaiming 1975 the International Women's year and called on all member states to promote equality of men and women.³⁰ In this local, regional and global context, the Family Law was precipitately introduced by the military regime.

The Secular Family Law of 1975

Throughout the colonial period, the Italian and British (the two colonial masters of Somali Republic), had imposed their own legal systems on Somalia – except in the crucial area of Family law. For them, this was simply too religiously sensitive. Traditional Family law in Somalia is a combination of Shafi'i Jurisprudence and elements of a variety of local customs in the various localities and communities. The first attempt at codification of this traditional family law occurred in the British Somaliland which promulgated the Native's Betrothal and Marriage Ordinance in 1928 and the Qadis' Courts Ordinance in 1937. The latter was repealed in 1944 by the

---

[29] Ibid., 216.
[30] The official policy of introducing the secular Family Law was perhaps encouraged by the UN Resolution of 3010 of 18 December, 1972 which proclaimed the year 1975 as International Women's year and called all member states to promote equality of men and women.

subordinate Courts Ordinance, which retained the jurisdiction of the Qadis only in the matter of personal law."[31] After the independence and the unification of the former British and Italian Somali territories in 1960, Family law remained unchanged: consistent with the constitutional decree that bars any law that contradicts Islamic principles. Here, Article 50 of the Somali Constitution clearly states, "The doctrine of Islam shall be the main source of the laws of the State." Moreover, article 98, prescribes that "Laws and provisions having the force of law shall conform to the Constitution and to the general principles of Islam."[32] Family and Property laws remained in the realm of the Sharia and strict interpretation of selective Shafi'i jurists.[33] Nevertheless, the military regime of 1969 adopted a socialist ideology that narrowed the spheres of Islam and tradition, and promoted a secular ethos in line with socialist ideology.

The idea of codifying Family law was initiated in 1972 by the Ministry of Justice and Religious Affairs, which was followed closely by the United Nations' proclamation of promoting gender equality. Nurta Haji Hassan, a member of the drafting commission narrated the history of the codification of the Family Law as follows:

> Sheikh Abdul Gani who was the Minister of Justice and Religious Affairs in 1972-74 attempted to introduce codified Islamic family law in the light of the Egyptian Family Code. Perhaps, that was the reaction of the Minister to the increased awareness of women's issue in the United Nations General Assembly. The Minister provided me copies of the Egyptian Family Law that comply with the Islamic law to share with the most educated Somali women employed in the different Ministries and

---

[31] Mahmood Tahir, *Personal Law in Islamic Countries* (New Delhi: Academy of Law and Religion, 1987), 253.
[32] See Paolo Contini, *The Somali Republic: an Experiment in Legal Integration* (London: Frank Cass & Company LTD., 1969), 58.
[33] Ibid., 35. The main reference book for the Islamic jurists in Somalia is "Kitab Al-Minhaj Li-Al-Imam Al-Nawawi".

requested to comment on it. During this time, most of the women were in the Halane Training Camp.[34] The women selected a committee of five women and I was one of them.[35] We have been closely connected with the Italian Communist Party.[36]

These women received strong support and encouragement from Dr. Mohamed Aden Sheikh, Dr. Mohamed Weyrah and Dr. Abdisalam Sheikh Hussein – known leftists and members of the kitchen Cabinet of President Barre. Moreover, the President nominated a seven-member commission in 1974 to draft the Family Law, stressing that it should be "progressive". The commission submitted the draft to the President in December 1974.[37] In January 11, 1975, Somali Women's Unit under the Public Relation Office (PRO) decided to commemorate the Somali Women's day.[38] This date is known as the historic "Hanoolato". This is a day the SYL freedom fighters clashed with the colonial police force in 1948 and Hawo Taako was among those murdered in that day.[39] Thus, Hawo Tako was recognized as heroine that symbolizes a remarkable role played by woman in Somalia's struggle for independence. Somali Women's Unit, under the Chairlady Marian Haji Ilmi, organized the first commemoration of that

---

[34] Halane is a military training school located in Mogadishu used to train and indoctrinate civil servants on socialist ideology.
[35] Nurta Haji Hassan, interviewed on October 15, 2007. Nurta was a member of the commission assigned to draft the secular Family Law and was a legal adviser to the President Mohamed Siyad Barre.
[36] Italy recovered its influence in Somalia after the establishment of the National University funded by Italian cooperation program by adopting Italian language as the language of instruction and Italian lecturers as the main faculty members. Most of the educated generations of Somalia were educated there and the members of the committee were Italian-speaking women who had graduated from the National University. See Poalo, 116-119
[37] The designated commission included Mohamed Sheikh Osman (High Court), Abdisalam Sheikh Hussein (Minister of Justice), Mohamed Aden Sheikh (Minister of Information) and four women, namely; Nurta Haji Hassan, Marian Haji Ilmi, Faduma Omar Hashi, Raqiya Haji Duale.
[38] Public Relations Office was initially aimed to process communications from the public to the Revolutionary Council but rapidly had grew into multifaceted organization under President's office. It was considered the embryonic socialist political party which was announced lately in 1976.
[39] Barnamijka Xusuus Reeb: Dilkii Culimada Somaliyeed ee 1975. Interview with Maryan Cilmi By Wariye Ducaale on January 23, 2015. Available from https://www.youtube.com/watch?v=JuGv78k6ndg (accessed on May 23, 2016).

day at the Stadio Conis in Mogadishu and invited Supreme Revolutionary Council members to open the celebration.[40] As a gesture of good will for Somali women, President Mohamed Siyad Barre precipitately decided to announce the secular Family Law. In front of thousands of Somali men and women, the President publicly stated that "As of today, Somali men and women are equal. They have the same equality, the same rights and the same share of whatever is inherited from their parents."[41] The president added – in a provocative manner – that the era of "one half, one third, one quarter" is gone forever.[42] The President stressed that the new law would change the "unjust law of inheritance" ordained by the Qur'an that assigns different shares of the inherited wealth to the rightful heirs of men and women. This produced outrageous reactions, though, it was to a large extent subdued through the repressive and merciless measures of the regime.

The Family Law, according to Tahir Mahmood, "has the character of the dominant Shafi'i Jurisprudence and adherence to the general principles of the Islamic law, however, on marriage, divorce and filiations, had many commonalities with the amended Syrian Personal Code of 1975. On the issue of inheritance, Somali Family Law had no similarities in the Muslim world except Turkey."[43] Although the Law contained a number of articles that went against accepted Islamic Sharia law, the most provocative articles were the articles of inheritance. It offered "equal rights of men and women under the rules of inheritance; and drastic curtailment of the list of

---

[40] Ibid.
[41] Mohamed Siyaad Barre, *My Country and my people: Selected Speeches of Jaalle Siyaad* (Ministry of Information and National Guidance, 1979), 3.
[42] You can listen the speech of the president from https://www.youtube.com/watch?v=gVmAqa0OPdE (accessed on June 12, 2016). Also, Interview with Dr. Ali Sheikh on November 30, 2007. Dr. Ali Sheikh has made extensive unpublished research on this topic and currently is the President of Mogadishu University.
[43] Tahir, *Personal Law*, 225.

heirs and application of new rules for the division of estate of a deceased person."[44]

The government organized a huge rally to show public support for the Family Law, where state employees and students were forced to listen to the vice-president Hussein Kulmiye Afrah who made a brief speech in the support of the secular Family Law. Yet within days, the true public reaction was heard in the Abdulqadir Mosque. According to eye witness Sheikh Mohamed Geryare,

> after the Friday prayer in the famous Mosque of Abdulqadir[45] about 1:00 pm, Sheikh Ahmed Mohamed stood and began to deliver his critical speech against the Family Law criticising it as 'arrogance and transgression of the borders of the Law of Allah. He stated that" this is unacceptable to the Somali Muslims" Successive speeches by the other Islamic scholars continued until the afternoon prayer about 3:30 pm where as many as nine other Islamic scholars criticized the Law. Most of the people who prayed in the Mosque also remained listening enthusiastically. After the afternoon prayer, security forces encircled the Mosque and arrested many people in the mosque including the 10 leading scholars.[46]

The campaign of arresting students and Islamic scholars was widespread before and after the execution of the Islamic scholars.[47]

The President was touring the Lower Shabelle region when the news of the Islamic scholars' protestation in the Mosque was reported to him. The situation was seen as an emergency security threat and the President urgently returned to

---

[44] Ibid., articles (158 - 169), 256.
[45] Sheikh Mohamed Moallim used to offer Tafsir al-Qur'an in this Mosque (exegesisof the Qur'an) using the famous "Dhilal al-Qur'an" (in the Shade of the Qur'an) of the renown Muslim Brotherhood scholar Sayyid Qutb,
[46] Sheikh Mohamed Garyare, interviewed in Toronto on November 5, 2007. Sheikh Garyare was the director of the Religious Affairs of the Ministry of Justice (1969- 1975) and a prominent scholar.
[47] Marian Arrif Qassim, a prolific writer and a politician, interviewed in Djibouti on November 12, 2007.

Mogadishu. After the arrest of the Islamic scholars and imprisonment of many young Islamists, the President organized a meeting at the National Theatre which was attended by the most prominent Islamic scholars. Among those who attended the meeting, according to the narration of Marian Haji Ilmi, were Sheikh Ali Sufi, Sheikh Ibrahim Suley, Sheikh Adan Sheikh Abdullahi and Sheikh Mohamed Iman. In his speech, the President defended the arrest of the Islamic scholars and bluntly said: "they spread lies about me and they said I persecuted Islamic scholars of the nation. These are the leading Somali Islamic scholars who are setting in front of me", and then started to name them one by one and each of them stood up. The President then proceeded and said: "Indeed, we have arrested and given death penalty to a few drunken youth propped by the international imperialism aiming to create instability in our national security."The situation was so frightening that all Islamic scholars were stricken with horror and frozen into silence. After two weeks of the proclamation of the secular Family Law, on 26 January, 1975, 10 leading Islamic scholars were executed at the Police Academy. Coincidentally, two Soviet built MIG 17 Military jets collided while demonstrating a show of force on the capital city of Mogadishu. The public perception of that incident was that Allah's wrath had befallen on Somalia and His revenge to the execution of the pious Islamic scholars was immediate. Public support for the regime drastically dwindled and popular prediction were the commencement of calamity for Somalia and the military regime.

Many individuals including women's leaders, Islamic scholars, members of the Revolutionary Council and Cabinet Ministers had appealed the President to pardon the Islamic scholars. Also, international organizations and head of states including the Kingdom of Saudi Arabia had pleaded to spare the lives of these scholars. However, the President was decisive in eliminating what he perceived as imperialistic conspiracy against the "blessed Revolution."[48] There is no much written historical evidence on this point, yet new witness reveals president's ambivalence and hasty execution of these scholars.[49] Most interviewees consented that the execution of the Islamic scholars was a pre-emptive strike to suppress growing Islamic movement and to show the regime's commitment to the secular socialist ideology in competition with the Marxist Ethiopia.[50] Commenting on the outcome of the Family Law, Hamdi has lucidly written,

> The law was contested by many groups from various perspectives. Feminists who drafted it and pushed for its announcement were shocked about the final contents of [the] law because they did not want to challenge Islam in such away. Because it touched the most sacred and protected realm of the society – family – local religious leaders condemned it and advised women against using it. [Also], average women [contested the law,] afraid of the implications of such [an] 'anti-Islamic' approach in resolving domestic matters.[51]

Repercussions of the Family Law

The codification of the Family Law could, in principle, be seen as a legal development that permitted the inclusion in Family law of other schools of Islamic jurisprudence. Moreover, it could be developed as new 'Ijtihad' that does not contradict

---

[48] Some new testimonies indicate conspiratory role of some individuals in the inner circle of President Barre who were using execution of the Islamic scholars to damage the image of regime and boost emerging oppositions. However, this evidence requires more research in order to discover hidden actors who were behind the President's decision. For those claiming to be true socialists some whom interviewed by the author affirmed that they were against persecution of the Islamic scholars and considered as a diversion from the true path of socialist transformation.

[49] The new testimony revealed by Ambassador Dr. Hassan Welli Sheikh Sheikh Hussein Osman indicates that the President was finally convinced to pardon the Islamic scholars and even wrote pardoning letter, but the execution was implemented haphazardly before the letter reaches the officers at the Police Academy. See the testimony of the Ambassador on http://rajonews.net/2015/08/xeerka-qoyska-1975-by-danjire-dr-xasanwali-sheekh-xuseen-cismaan/ (accessed on June 13, 2016).

[50] Marian Arrif Qassim, interviewed in Djibouti on November 12, 2007.

[51] Hamdi, the Multiple, 132-133, 132-133.

with the generally accepted principles of Islam. Conversely, the adopted Family Law of the military regime was one of the most westernized legal reforms in the Muslim world (comparable only to reforms seen in Turkey) applied in one of the most traditional societies. This undertaking created a crack in the fabric of the society, culminating in the brutal execution of the Islamic scholars and violating human rights in the name of defending 'women's rights.' The Family Law placed women in the national agenda at a point where all political and religious positions were represented in the debate. The Family Law had three central repercussions, namely, increased polygamy, divorce and domestic violence; intensified opposition to the regime; and the development of the embryonic Islamic movements.

Increased polygamy, divorce and domestic violence: Most interviewees agreed that debates on the status and role of women were opened in every household; many women who thought that the state was on their side began to challenge their husbands. Distrust also developed amongst family members and many women were suspected of belonging to the notorious intelligence service. The traditionally polygamous Somali society – accustomed to investing men with absolute power within the family – could not swallow easily the secular Family Law. In particular, the issue became more complicated when challenging common practices of Islam. According to Dr. Ali and Nurta Haji, major repercussions of the law for the women included an increase in polygamy, while religious individuals aimed to derail the Family Law. Moreover, due to the distrust created by the promulgation of the law in many households, family violence and divorce rates drastically increased. Finally, traditional relations based on the complementary role of women and men were shaken, the harassment of women increased, and even some women were murdered as a result of quarrel caused by the Family Law.[52]

Increased activities of the oppositions and suffering of the women: Opposition to the regime politically benefited from the promulgation of the Family Law and the subsequent execution of the Islamic scholars. As a result opposition movements gained an extra slogan to include in their anti-state propaganda. Now they could stress, in addition to the dictatorial behaviour and 'Godless' socialist ideology, the regime do not respect even the most sacred segments of the society and poised to destroy family values. The voices of the opposition movements gained sympathetic listeners in conservative Arab countries and in the Western circles working to halt the Soviet Union's growing influence in the Third World. Moreover, the opposition movements found a way to combine clan grievances with religious duty to liberate the country from the 'atheist dictatorial' regime. After the enactment of the Family Law, some women began to offer more support to the regime while their husbands moved towards the opposition movements. Yet, even with this, the regime abused women in order to attack opposition movements, using relatives and wives of the suspected supporters of the opposition movements in unethical manner.[53] These women were subjugated and imprisoned or recruited as collaborators of the regime. In both cases, women suffered greatly; and as a result, families broke up and some women became breadwinners for their family because their husbands, fathers, brothers and sons had been imprisoned or had fled the country.

Boosting Islamic Movements: The previously embryonic Islamic movement gained more members and support thanks

---

[52] Hamdi, the Multiple, 136.
[53] Marian Arrif Qassim, interviewed in Djibouti on November 12, 2007.

to the secular Family Law and the subsequent execution of the scholars. Due to these developments this, a number of high school students and Islamic scholars fled the country to Sudan, Egypt, Saudi Arabia and other Gulf countries. Some of them got employment and many attended universities, in particular, Islamic universities in Saudi Arabia. Importantly, this occurred during the time of booming economies and Islamic revivalism throughout the Arab Muslim World. The economic wellbeing and education offered the emerging Islamic movement an impetus to reorganize and spread their message back in Somalia. Meanwhile, many of the students encountered different brands of revivalist movements, and brought these ideologies and approaches – including their stance on women back to Somalia. As a result, varieties of Islamism, ranging from the evolutionist Muslim Brotherhood to the extreme *Takfir* ideologies began to spread throughout Somalia. This onset of new cultural influences crippled Somali women, and instead of focusing on modest and flexible Islamic forms of dressing, more stringent rules were set in place. In particular, women's conservative dresses were introduced besides face covering (*Niqaab*) projected as representing women's piety and faithfulness. As a result, many women were forced into seclusion, silenced, denied jobs and education. In addition, it was observed that polygamy and divorce increased dramatically among followers of some Islamic movements.

On the other hand, moderate Islamists offered more space for women and advocated the empowerment of women through education and freeing them from un-Islamic societal pressures and literal rigid interpretation of Islamic texts regarding women. As a result, some women became more active, better educated and participated more in public affairs.

Conclusion

This paper has attempted to reconstruct the history of the Family Law in Somalia and its repercussions on women, Islamists and the Military regime. It has posited that Somalia is a hierarchical traditional society in which women are placed at the bottom, a view contrasting with that of the romantic egalitarian representation of Somali society of the anthropological perspective. In the literature review, the paper illustrated that the available literature on this topic remains poor, even though new studies of Islamism and feminism are emerging. This situation necessitated the use of oral recollections to fill gaps in the literature.

The Family Law placed women squarely at the centre of the national agenda – yet this created tremendous socio-political problems. Importantly, both proponents and opponents of the Family Law represented the patriarchal traditional society that shares the same mind-set and attitudes towards women. This suggests that the issue of the role and status of women was used as a stage for socio-political conflict and ideological clash between the Islamists and the "secular" nationalists. Those opposing the regime expressed themselves using Islamic rhetoric to appeal to all Somalis. Meanwhile, the repercussions of the Family law was tremendous, creating irreparable family conflicts, radicalizing Islamic movements and contributing to the emergence of the armed opposition factions. All the interviewed agreed that women suffered more after the adoption of the Family Law in a variety of ways. Nonetheless, the Law did not take off since the public did not sanction it and the law enforcement agencies undermined it in various ways. Moreover, because of the cumulative internal and external oppositions, ideological and economic weakness of the regime in the 1980s, the Family Law was later revised to comply with the general principles of Islam. In conclusion, it is clear that the Military regime not only failed to adopt strategies to empower women without creating disastrous social conflict, but also lost the entire institutions of the state that completely collapsed in 1991. As a result, women suffered even more.

II

Recovering the Somali State: Islam, Islamism and Nation-Building

> Regardless of the subtleties of Islam in Somalia, it is one of the few elements that virtually all Somalis support to some degree. It provides a code of moral and ethical behaviour, it bolsters Somali cultural tradition by offering a system in which rulings of elders are accepted, and it brings a tradition of continuity greatly needed in Somalia's struggle to bring order out of the last decade of chaos. The presence of traditional Islamic ethics, codes, and laws of conduct offer one piece of a foundation upon which the new Somalia can be built.
>
> Hussein Adam, Richard Ford et al,
> Removing Barricades in Somalia: Options for Peace and Rehabilitation

Introduction

When the Somali state completely collapsed in the early 1991, the created vacuum was filled by a patchwork of warlord-dominated regions, clan-based fiefdoms, shaky local administrations and traditionally administered areas. Scholars assumed opposing views in the evaluation of what really collapsed the Somalia State. The debate was focussed on whether the collapse was total or partial. In the process, scholars examined the three components that any given state must possess. Firstly, the idea of the state: the political, economic, religious and social ideologies that lay the foundation for the state in the minds of its people. Secondly, the physical land mass of the nation-state, including territorial borders, natural resources, and the man-made wealth within these boundaries. Thirdly, the institutional entities of the nation-state: the executive, legislative, administrative and judicial branches of the state. Two perspectives on the issue of restoring Somali state came out. The first perspective assumes that everything related to the Somali nation-state had collapsed and proposes to reconstruct the state from scratch through a bottom-up process of state formation based on the concept of "Building Blocks".[1] Opponents of this approach expressed their fear from disintegration of the state. The second perspective held that Somali state is recoverable and only national state institutions collapsed whereas other two components of the state – namely, its population and the physical landmass – remain intact. This view supports a top-down process of state recovery instead of the re-invention of a new state[2]. This perspective triumphed during Djibouti Peace Process in 2000 where the recovery of the national Somali state took the first push and interpreted "building block" in creating federal states as part of the state-building project.

The complexity of the Somali debacle does not permit emotional solutions, repeating failed approaches, importing external solutions and creating structures tailored to suit group interest or political advantage of incumbent leaders. Recovering and reconstructing Somali state requires innovative approach that breaks the vicious circle of chronic failures. This paper focuses on how Islamic moral values – values that supersede and dilute clannish values of disunity and disintegration – could be revived and reinvigorated in order to recover the Somali state. It brings to the forefront aspects of Islam that bring people closer to each other uniting their mission and purposes in life. The paper also, explores the nature of the moderate Islamic movement and its role in nation-building. It is noteworthy to differentiate Islam as a universal religion founded on the authentic sources of the

---

[1] Under Ethiopian pressure, the Inter-Governmental Authority for Development (IGAD) and the international community adopted the "Building Block" approach for Somalia in 1998. This approach was further encouraged with a peace dividend aid package by European Union. Proponents of this approach hoped that these blocks would eventually unite to form a new Somali state.

[2] The concept of national state recovery took the centre stage in Arta peace process in Djibouti and subsequent Mbagathi Peace Conference in Kenya. Both the Arta TNG (Transitional National Government) and Mbagathi TFG (Transitional Federal Government) recognized the imperativeness of decentralized system for Somalia.

Qur'an and the prophetic tradition, and modern development of Islamic movements representing organized groups carrying human deficiencies and limitations. This paper, Firstly, explores the concepts of clan-based society, nation-building and Islam and their manifestations in the Somali state formation. Secondly, it offers notes on the role of Islam in creating social cohesion indispensable in nation-building and the recovery of the state. Thirdly, it traces the nature the modern Islamic movements and their role in social transformation and political participation.

Historical background

Islam reached Somalia in its earlier years, and it is believed that some parts of it fell into the hands of Umayyad Dynasty (685-705).[3] Nevertheless, Somalia remained on the periphery of the Muslim world for quite some time. The Somali race is well known for its ardent belief in Islam to the degree that Somali identity becomes synonymous with being a Muslim, since all Somalis are Muslims by birth. Traditionally, Somalis mainly belong to one of the two Sufi brotherhoods – the Qadiriyah (which has two branches, the Uwesiyah and Zayli'yah) and the Ahmadiyah (also with three branches, the Salihiyah, Rahmaniyah and Dadrawiyah) – and adhere to the Shafi'i school of Islamic Jurisprudence. Prior to colonial rule, clan elders and Islamic scholars ran communities and played important roles in their affairs. Elders with a variety of hierarchical levels and roles managed the affairs of their particular communities during peace time and in conflicts, playing the role of conflict resolution managers in the affairs of the community. Islamic scholars played the role of religious teachers and administered Islam-related affairs like conducting

---

[3] Mohamed Mukhtar, "Islam in Somali History: Fact and Fiction", in *The Invention of* Somalia, edited by Ali Jimale Ahmed (The Red Sea Press, 1995), 3. Mukhtar narrates that during the rule of Abdilmalik Ibn Marwan (685-705), a Syrian general Musa Ibn-Umar Al-khatha'mi was sent to conquer both Mogadishu and the neighbouring East African city-state Kilwa.

marriage contracts, inheritance, resolving conflict by means of the Islamic legal code, and so on.

These Islamic scholars were responsible for all community education matters, as such most of their activities were directed to the fields of education and propagating Islam. The basics of the education system were founded on memorization of the Qur'an, and its higher levels were geared towards teaching Arabic language, Islamic jurisprudence, Sufism and interpretation of the Qur'an and Hadith. Memorization of the Qur'an in the early childhood years and admitting children in the Qur'anic schools known as "*Dugsi*"or "*Malcamat*" was part of Somali culture and widespread in almost every populated area of Somalia. Moreover, circles of Islamic education in the mosques and ancient Islamic propagation centres like Zayla, Harar, Warsheikh, Banadir and Marka were well established as a sustainable system for higher education and as reservoirs of Arabic language-based education. Many leaders of the anti-colonial movements graduated from these schools, which had also produced Islamic activists who were opposed to the conversion undertaken by the Christian Missionaries. Moreover, modern anti-colonial movements were directly connected to these schools. Islamic scholars and clan elders exercised legitimate authority over their communities and were working in a networked system, united and harmonious in every locality in accordance with a set of rules and regulations called Xeer that was blended with Islamic Sharia. The roles of the elders and religious scholars were complementary, and job divisions were clear for both types of leadership. They always cooperated with each other and was observed that clan elders took the leading role in the nomadic areas, where the frequency of outbreaks of warfare was high, whereas, Islamic scholars took prominence in the agricultural and settled communities.[4]

---

[4] It was observed that in the real pastoral areas, clan elders were more powerful than the religious leaders. However, this phenomenon changed in the settled agricultural regions along the banks of the rivers, where religious leaders become top leaders of the communities.

During colonial rule, the authority of these traditional community leaders were greatly weakened. Often, the state authorities intervened in the selection of clan elders; and since they became salaried employees of the state, their autonomous authority in their constituencies were weakened. This did not change in the post-colonial Somalia, even though Islam was officially recognized as the religion of the state and Islamic Sharia was made the main source of the legal system. However, modern understanding of Islam in 1960 was not well developed and thus, all legal matters based on the inherited colonial legal system remained largely intact. The only aspect of law respected all along was the Family Law, which was based totally on Sharia until the military regime tried to change it 1975. Generally, the Somali state was, on the one hand, trying to show its firm commitment to Islamic symbolism, exploiting it to fit into the state objectives while, on the other hand, taking a quasi-secular approach in its practical actions.

Nevertheless, it was only in the early 1970s that the basic Islamic canon, the Family Law, was questioned openly by the military regime under the guise of implementing socialist ideals of equality of men and women in inheritance. Islamic scholars reacted to that attempt by protesting peacefully, and in 1975, the uncompromising revolutionary regime responded with an unprecedented display of arrogance and savagery by publicly executing 10 leading Islamic scholars. This execution shook the Somali people profoundly and gave impetus for the revival of Islam. Moreover, indiscriminate state repression had caused mayhem and the emigration of Islamic activists in search of peaceful havens and opportunities for work and education. The new emigration destinations were Saudi Arabia, Egypt and Sudan, the centres of modern Islamic movements. At the same time, the cruelty of the revolutionary regime led to a great number of the population to gradually express its peaceful resentment by disengaging from involvement in the programs of the regime and took refuge in the mosques.⁵ Thus, in the mosques, underground Islamic groups gained new recruits in the 1970s and established various networks to counter socialist ideology with more organized grassroots Islamic work. As a result of the military regime's alienation of Islamic and clan-based oppositions, clan-based oppositions developed into armed factions and established bases in Ethiopia, while the Islamic oppositions opted for the grassroots strategy based on intensifying the call to Islam and strengthening their underground organizational base. It is believed that the voice of an organized Islamic challenge was first heard loudly in Somalia in the 1989 Black Friday massacre and its aftermath. This incident occurred on July 14 in which about 200-450 persons were massacred while demonstrating against the arrest of Islamic scholars and more than 2,000 were injured.

After the collapse of the state and the outbreak of the civil war, Islamic movements took the center stage in reconciling the warring groups, but in vain. In such tense situation, different Islamic persuasions took different approaches. For instance, Al-Itihad became more radical and took up arms as a way of political participation, while Islah opted peaceful means of propagating Islam, reconciling communities and providing social services. On the other hand, traditional Sufi Orders were either neutral in the conflict or aligned along clan lines. During the civil war, Islam became a solace for many Somalis inside the country and in the Diaspora communities, and many people assembled in the mosques and frequented Islamic study centers. In these mosques, modern Islamic scholars offered explanations of the calamities be fallen on the Somalis from the Islamic perspective and were raising awareness of the Islamic commitment. Besides, hundreds of schools with strong Islamic inclinations were opened throughout the country, reviving traditional Islamic education infused with modernity

---

⁵ The military regime established orientation centres in every district to indoctrinate the population in Marxism and to build popular support for the regime. Participation in the programs of these centres was considered as evaluation criteria for the loyalty to the regime.

in a sustainable system of education. Moreover, Somalis aspiring for unity after the disruptive civil war found Islam to be the only available ideology capable of uniting them. As such, during the civil war, the Somali society was transformed, and the popular understanding of Islam and devotion of the population to it deepened greatly. It is worth mentioning here the popular perception that "Somalis, for the most part, don't by and large apply Islamic values, but they always protect Islam and guard it from abuses by others". Moreover, the Somali wisdom that is "two are inviolable in Somalia: clan culture and Islam" convey the same message which means most Somalis are ready to sacrifice their lives in defending these two inviolable ideals.

In the absence of a strong central authority, traditional elders and Islamic scholars play a pivotal role in managing the affairs of their communities. They have recovered their original role in resolving conflicts and mediating disputes. That is why all the successful conferences for reestablishing local and national state institutions in Somalia have been based on the decisions of the traditional leaders.[6] Moreover, modernity has influenced both traditional elders and Islamic scholars and many of them are highly educated, integrating the best of tradition and modernity. At last, modern Islamic movements have modernized traditional ways of propagating Islam in the mosques and teaching Islamic sciences in public arenas. As a result, traditional methods of education have improved educational opportunities for the Somalis in the absence of national institutions.

Theoretical Framework: Clanism, Nationalism and Islam

The shared values among most Somalis are clanism, nationalism and Islam. In varying degrees, these are present in

---

[6] All successful reconciliation conferences in Somalia, such as the Borama, Growe and Arta conferences, were based on the empowerment of the traditional leaders as truly legitimate leaders of the communities.

the consciousness of almost every Somali. Among these values, only clanism carry the natural virus of divisiveness in the society, while core values of nationalism and Islam can be agents for societal cohesion and if not radicalised can constitute core ideologies for nation-building. Indeed, a single divisive factor cannot overcome two unifying factors unless they are weak and divided. In any case, it is clear today that none of these three components of Somaliness is marginable and thus, recovering Somali state requires reconciling nationalism and Islam on one side and offering space for clan attachments on the other.[7]

Nationalism Versus Clanism: Mistaken Approaches

After a long period of denial, the fact that the Somali social setting is based on clans have finally been accepted by those involved in the reconciliation processes. In the post-civil war Somalia, it seems that all the local administrations and national reconciliation conferences could not find a better formula during the initial institution building stage than clan representation in accordance with an agreed power sharing formula.[8] Any attempt to create other options for power sharing, at this stage, did not receive enough popular and international support.[9] Today, the Somali social setting has become so used to this formula of sharing power based on clans that the first chapter of most academic studies of Somalia begins with clan classification and mapping. In weak states and strong societies like Somalia where clan attachments

---

[7] Reconciling clanism, nationalism and Islam is not an easy undertaking and departs from the conventional perception of their irreconcilability, which has dominated both political and intellectual discourses. This author has also held the theory of irreconcilability (Abdullahi 1992: 6). This project requires immense intellectual input and public awareness besides mutual understanding of the Islamist and non-Islamist scholars.

[8] Regional administrations: the Borama and Growe conferences; and National Reconciliations conferences: the Arta peace process in Djibouti and Mbigathi in Kenya (4.5 formula dividing Somalis into 4 equal clans and a congregation of other clans represented as 1/2 clan share).

[9] Abdulqadir Adan Abdulle, "Djibouti Peace Process: a non-clan approach of distributing MPs"(A paper presented to the Somali Intellectual Symposium held in Djibouti in preparation for the 2000 Somali Peace Conference).

are strong, primordial loyalties generate identity politics.[10] In that situation, tribalism/clanism being a state of mind, an act of consciousness, generates tribal solidarity and a strong loyalty to one's own clan, and triggers high propensity among political leaders to invest in the goal of controlling the government. In rural areas, clan solidarity is vital and necessary as the only viable way of survival where no central authority exists to arbitrate disputes and to provide security.

According to Ibn-Khaldun, "only tribes held together by group feeling can live in the desert".[11] Clan solidarity, however, may be destructive in urban centres if it transgresses the social domain and is widely used as a political instrument. Even so, in the social domain, social relations are usually expected to take another form such as neighbourhoods and professional group interests. But in Somalia, rural migrants to the urban centres brought their tribal allegiances with them. This urban tribalism developed in the 1950s into overt political tribalism. Rural tribalism is based on the fame an individual derives from the glory of his ancestors, loyalty to and self–sacrifice for the sake of the clan, and the fulfilment of the law of revenge. It was this type of tribalism that was institutionalized in the urban centres, creating negative political implications. Strangely enough, this clan culture, instead of weakening with improved education, increased accumulation of wealth and vigorous nationalistic programs, re-emerged and strengthened. In fact, the phenomenon of reverse process, termed as the nomidazation of the urban elite, had been taking place.[12]

The founding fathers of the modern Somali state were very much aware of the obstacles that political clan loyalties pose

---

[10] On the concepts of weak state and strong societies refer to Joel S. Migdal, *Strong Societies and Weak States: State-Society Relations and State Capabilities in the Third World* (Princeton, NJ: Princeton University Press, 1988).

[11] Ibn-Khaldun. *Muqaddimah: An Introduction to History*. Transl. by Franz Rosenthal, (2nd ed.) (London: Routledge & Kegan Paul, 1967), 261.

[12] The reason simply is that pastoral segments of the society, privileged under the military rule, dominated the government; and thus, in accordance with the law that the weak imitates the strong, urban elites conditioned themselves to this new situation.

for the nation-building process. In the 1950s, in the early days of the struggle for independence, smaller clan-based political parties emerged beside the national political parties and political clanism systematically were ingrained in the psyche of the people. The political system coined similar to Italian-style multi-party system and district based electoral constituencies (first-past-the post) promoted political tribalism and laid early seed of political conflict. Thus, the founding fathers were confronted with imperatives for nation-building centred on promoting nationalism in a society that lacked appropriate organizational skills in modern political participation. This dilemma became manifest in the clan alignments of the first-ever elections and the formation of a local administration in Southern Somalia in 1956. Since then, political clanism actively emerged and every politician was compelled to pass through the knotty test of clanism. Clan politics was the only means to mobilize supporters and get elected to the parliament. In this process, Somali political culture, based on imperativeness of clan affiliation, commercialization of politics and nepotism, was developed.

To deal with the issue of political clanism, successive Somali governments developed the following three strategies: Proportional representation of unwritten policy of allocating higher state positions to the various clans;[13] Extreme idealization and glorification of Somali ethnic nationalism, and Stigmatizing and condemning social reality of clan divide; and enacting legislative measures and adopting policies to implement strategies to wipe out clanism.[14] However, all these

---

[13] Aweys Osman Haji & Abdiwahid Osman Haji, *Clan, sub-clan and regional representation 1960-1990: Statistical Data and findings* (Washington Dc., 1998).The dominance of specific clans over the political arena, where others were under-represented, systematically ruined this strategy.

[14] Abdurahman Abdullahi, "Tribalism, Nationalism and Islam: The Crisis of the Political Loyalties in Somalia." (MA thesis, Islamic Institute, McGill University, 1992), 78-82). Three important laws were passed prior to 1969 to curb clanism. The first was intended to reduce authorities of tribal chiefs, the second was to lessen tribal solidarity and the third resulted in banning political parties that utilized tribal names. Moreover, the military regime enacted laws to liquidate "*dabar-goynta*" tribalism, abolishing the Diya(blood money) system, renaming clan chiefs in the rural areas; and introducing compulsory auto insurance and local government responsibility for funeral expenses.

efforts failed to prevent the development of clan-based politics in the government and the emergence of clan-based armed opposition factions. Armed confrontation between these factions and the government forces finally sealed the fate of the Somali state in total collapse in 1991.

Clan solidarity in Somalia is more robust in the pastoral areas and among the extended families in the urban centres. Since these pastoralists traditionally dominated Somali clan politics, they have coloured nomadic culture across the whole political spectrum of Somalia. The problem of nomadic culture vis-a-vis state formation is well studied by the Arab philosopher Ibn-Khaldun, who wrote that:

> Savagery has become the character and nature [of the Bedouins]. They enjoy it, because it means freedom from authority and no subservience to leadership. Such a natural disposition is the negation and antithesis of civilization...the very nature of their existence is the negation of building [urbanization], which is the basis of civilization. Furthermore, since they do not see any value in labour and craftsman and do not appreciate it, the hope for profit vanishes, and no productive work is done. The sedentary population disperses and civilization decays... The Bedouins are not concerned with laws, or with deterring people from misdeeds... they care only for property that they might take away from people through looting... Under the rule of Bedouins, their subjects live as in a state of anarchy. Anarchy destroys mankind and ruins civilizations.[15]

Summarizing the above stated points, nomads have three characteristics which cause destruction of urban life and ultimately the state: (1) Anarchy and Lawlessness, (2) Despising labour and crafts, and (3) Transgressing private and public property. Since nomads and their cultural extension in the urban areas can't produce functional state institutions, due to the behaviours stated above, the question becomes: how

---

Above all, massive propaganda against tribalism was conducted in the name of the 'socialist transformation' of Somali society.
[15] Abdullahi, "Tribalism, Nationalism and Islam", 1992, 17.

can these nomads be transformed or absorbed into a system of modern state institutions? The founding fathers of Somali nationalism answered this question in two ways:

(1) Intensification of modern education and attempting to implement gained experience of running state institutions from the colonial administration.

(2) Raising national consciousness and excessive condemnation of everything related to the clan culture through all forms of state propaganda. However, neither approach came to fruition owing to time constraints and malpractices. In reality, there were no more than 10 years of nation-building time during trusteeship period (1950-1960) which precipitated handing over of the administrative task to the low trained Somali bureaucrats.[16]

Clan divides are neither evil nor good; rather, are a neutral and natural social setting, prevalent in many societies and particularly among Muslims where family values are very strong. A true genealogy through one's paternity is an indication of family sanctity and compliance with desired Islamic values. This neutral entity could be utilized in a positive or destructive way. Unfortunately, in Somalia, clan settings in many instances, were employed wrongly, even in the highest echelon of the state institutions. In fact, contrary to the make-up of clans in many countries where clans don't share much in their ethnicity, clans in Somalia share all the necessary elements of homogeneity. However, criminalization of clan sentiment by Somali Youth League (SYL) and the successive Somali governments stamped all national troubles to be related to political clanism. In this way, public perceptions have been diverted from grasping the complex root causes of the immense challenges of the Somali state. Going even further, many Somalis consider clanism as the

---

[16] Actual programs for state formation began after UN Trusteeship of 1950 after which limited modern schools were opened. Also, Somalis were gradually employed in the higher echelons of the state institutions without having appropriate administrative expertise.

"Cancer of Somali State", which implies its incurability.[17] The implications of such notion are very severe: essentially it leads either to forging a policy of "eliminating tribalism" (*dabar-goynta*"), or to giving up on nation-building measures. Moreover, fixating all Somali problems on clan divide is one of the great farces, deceptive and scapegoats that political elites constantly used to justify their failed leadership. This perspective was promoted by anthropologists I. M. Lewis[18] and Enrico Cerulli.[19] It has been passed on to their disciples like Berhard Helander[20] and Virginia Lulling.[21] Nevertheless, Maria Barons expressed lucidly that

> the clan divide as such is not the core factor of the Somali crisis of state formation: it is rather competition over resources and power, which is seen as safeguarding access to these resources, that is expressed in competitive clan labels.[22]

Nationalism and Nation-Building

Nation-building is linked to other concepts such as Nation, Nationalism and State. Attempts to develop consensus on the definition of nation had failed. This paper uses a brief working definition, the nation is

> ...an extensive aggregate of persons, so closely associated with each other by common decent, language or history, as to form a distinct race or people, usually organized as a separate political state and occupying a defined territory.[23]

---

[17] Abdalla Omar Mansur, "Contrary to a Nation: the Cancer of the Somali State." In *The Invention of Somalia*, edited by Ahmed Jumale (Lawrenceville: The Red Sea Press,1995),112.
[18] Professor of Anthropology, London School of Economics. He wrote his PhD thesis on Somalia in the 1950s and since then he has written extensively on Somalia. His numerous works are considered indispensable references on Somalia.
[19] Italian ethnologist, employed by the Italian Administration in Somalia. He wrote extensively on Somali ethnology
[20] Swedish anthropologist who wrote his PhD thesis on Somalia. Currently works for Uppsala University, Sweden.
[21] An Anthropologist who wrote her PhD on the Somali Sultanate of Geledi.
[22] Maria Barons, *Society, Security, Sovereignty and the State in Somalia: From Statelessness to Statelessness?* (International Books, 2001), 90.
[23] J.A. Simpson and E.S.C Weiner, *The Compact Oxford English Dictionary*, 2nd ed. (Oxford, GB: Clarendon Press, 1991): 231

The conception of Somali nation falls in this definition which produces a sense of ethnic or cultural nationalism, an exclusive conception which bases membership of the nation primarily on the primordial attachments rather than on inclusive civic nationalism of political membership.[24] Cultural nationalism stands for a movement and ideology which garner loyalty to the nation-state and maintain its attributes (language, religion, history, values, etc.). Moreover, nationalism, nation and nation-building are somehow linked to the existence of a State which is briefly defined as "organized political community living under a single system of government".[25] In the international law, the state have four components: a permanent population, a defined territory, a functioning government and recognized by other states. Furthermore, when geographic boundaries of an ethnic population and a political state correspond, which means political and cultural nation coincides in one geographical entity, such state is called Nation-state. Somalia has all the characteristics of ideal Nation-state.

Nation-building is a normative concept that implies different meaning to different people in different contexts. It is often seen as having the same meaning with state-building and peace-building, but each concept is different, though they have many cross-cutting and overlapping commonalities. Social science scholars engaged in studying nation-building projects after the Second World War when the newly emerged independent states employed new definition. This definition was developed to deal with the challenges of constructing national identity of the newly independent states using the state power to integrate its different ethnic groups into one nation. It included the creation of national paraphernalia such as flags, anthems, national days, national stadium, national

---

[24] Benedict Anderson, *Imagined Communities: Reflections on the Origin and Spread of Nationalism* (Verso; Revised edition, November 17, 2006).
[25] Thompson and Della ed.,*"State"*, *Concise Oxford English Dictionary, 9th ed.)* (Oxford University Press, 1995).

sport clubs, national airlines, national languages, national armies and national myths.[26] However, with the change of the time and circumstances, the concept of nation-building took different meaning when some post-colonial state failed or collapsed due to futile nation-building approaches. One of the succinct definition is "the use of armed force in the aftermath of a conflict to underpin an enduring transition to democracy."[27] The rationality of new definition is founded on "that a strong state is necessary in order to provide security [global security], that the building of an integrated national community is important in the building of a state".[28]

In the Somali context, early programs of nation-building after the independence in 1960 included creating a certain degree of national consciousness, which tames nomadic culture and cements segments "clan blocks" into a solid nation. To do this, early Somali nationalists thought that Somalis were already "a nation in search of a state" which means they assumed that Somali nation preceded the state contrary to the most African states where states preceded the nation. And that by strengthening the ideology of nationalism assumed to be ingrained in the fabric of Somaliness "*Somalinimo*" and scorning clanism, nation building could be easily achieved.[29] Therefore, nationalism was focused on and over expressed in the rich Somali heritage of poems and modern songs, and as a result the national flag and anthem were looked at with great respect and adoration.

According to Saadia Touval, in addition to the common factors underlying the rise of nationalism in the colonized countries, three factors in particular contributed to the rise of

---

[26] Anthony Smith, "State-Making and Nation-Building" in John Hall (ed.), *States in History* (Oxford: Basil Blackwell, 1986), 228–263.
[27] James Dobbins, Seth G. Jones, Keith Crane, and Beth Cole De Grasse,*The Beginner's Guide to Nation-Building* (Santa Monica, Calif., : RAND Corporation, 2007).
[28] Carolyn Stephenson, "Nation-building" (January, 2005) available from http://www.beyondintractability.org/essay/nation-building (accessed on June 10,2016).
[29] David D. Laitin and Said Samatar, *Somalia: Nation in Search of a State* (Boulder: Westview Press, 1987).

nationalism in Somalia.[30] First, resentment against colonial governments, which had superficially ruled but had never subjected the Somalis. In the colonial era, Somalis who had never been subjected to an institutionalized government had to bear the burden of heavy taxation, forced labour, and racial policy especially in the era of the Italian fascism. The colonial authorities appropriated rich agricultural lands in the southern part of Somalia and interfered with the traditional authorities of elders and Islamic scholars. Saadia Touval states that "the confrontation of the nomadic, individualistic and independent Somalis with organized government inevitably led to resentments and conflict".[31]

The second factor relates to religious antagonism towards both European powers and Ethiopia. To the Somalis, the colonial powers represented Christianity, whereas they were Muslims; "it was exceedingly difficult and humiliating for them as Muslims to accept a non-Muslim rule".[32] The third factor was a "deliberate encouragement by various governments" to achieve certain goals. Italy with its "la Grande Somalia" program during its invasion of Ethiopia in 1935, the British ambition of a "Greater Somalia" in 1946, and Egypt's revolutionary influence in the 1950s, all contributed to the rise of Somali nationalism in one way or another. In summation, Somali nationalism and its core ideology revolved around the establishment of a united Somali nation-state including all regions inhabited by Somalis in the greater Horn of Africa region. However, it appears that this Somali vision of nationalism did not take into consideration how to preserve the nation-state once it had been founded.[33]

---

[30] Saadia Touval, *Somali Nationalism: International Politics and the Drive for Unity in the Horn of Africa* (Cambridge:Cambridge University Press, 1963), 76-78.
[31] Saadia Touval, Somali Nationalism, 1963: 62).
[32] Ibid.
[33] AbdallaMansur, *Contrary to a Nation*,1995:112. The state was described as a favourite she-camel called "*maandeeq*" which gives abundant milk to the people and was looted by the thieves (colonial powers) but later was retrieved by the owners (Somalis). However, the owners did not know how to care for their new camel (the state).

Somali nationalism was a very emotional feeling of the majority of the people, but did not supersede tribal solidarity, even though all possible efforts were made to do so . The reunification of the former British Somaliland and Italian Somalia, and promulgation of the independence of the Somali Republic on July 1st 1960, was the greatest achievement of the Somali nationalists. Yet clan alignments and clan politics were gradually mounting and Somalia reached the verge of collapse only nine years after the independence. In October 1969, the military took over the power and recreated new symbols for nationalistic zeal, including the adoption of the Latin alphabet for writing the Somali language. Moreover, at the pinnacle of nationalist fervour, the military regime waged war in 1977/78 to liberate Somali territories captured by Ethiopia in 19th century. With the defeat of Somalia in the war and proclamation of the independent Republic of Djibouti, Somali nationalism began to wither. The overstretched goals of Somali nationalism and the low capacity of the state institutions caused the self-destruction of the Somali nation-state. The abysmal level of Somali nationalism and its fragility is evident from the absence of national political institutions and total demise of the former ruling national political parties.[34] In the vacuum left by the declining Somali nationalism and the collapse of the state, radical clan factions and Islamic movements with both moderate and extreme components emerged. Radical clan factions are the continuation of political clanism, while the modern Islamic movements are also continuation of the traditional Islamic scholars with new social and political organizations focusing on the Islamic component of Somali indigenous ideologies.

---

[34] The SYL and the Revolutionary Socialist Party ruled Somalia from 1960-1969 and 1976-1990 respectively, and both have disappeared organizationally. Moreover, Somalis lack national political institutions advocating for the ideals of Somali nationalism. However, recently, in the post-civil war period, emerging and active nationalistic tendencies have been observed both inside Somalia and in the Diaspora communities.

Nation-Building from the Islamic Perspective

The early history of Islam demonstrates how the clans of the Arabian Peninsula changed their political culture after their conversion to Islam. Those converted to Islam in the early years of Makkah period (610-622) were persecuted by the aristocracy of Quraish tribe and lived as a community of believers cross-cutting their clan affiliations. After the migration to Medina in 622, the first state was founded on what was historically termed the Constitution of Medina *"Wathiqat al-Medina"*.[35] This document laid the foundation of trans-clan brotherhood bonds between Muslims and extended common citizenship to all communities of Medina. It combined territorial attachment with a common faith in a form of social cohesion among all community members.[36] This history suggests that present-day Somali clans, having great similarities with these ancient clans, might also be influenced by the revival of Islamic values. Islam abhors anarchy and lawlessness, despising of labour and crafts, looting private and public properties, and internecine wars which are the main features of the Somali pastoral nomads. Islam teaches its faithfuls that they are brothers and sisters, and must be united and shun all forms of divisiveness as the following Qur'anic verse proclaims:

> And hold fast, all together, by the rope of Allah and be not divided; and remember the favour of Allah which He bestowed upon you when you were enemies and He united your hearts in love, so that by His grace you became as brothers; and you were on the brink of a pit off re and He saved you from it. Thus does Allah explain to you His commandments that you may be guided. (3:104).

---

[35] Muhammad Hamidullah, *The First Written Constitution in the World: An Important Document of the Time of the Holy Prophet (3rd ed.)* (Lahore, Pakistan: Ashraf Press, 1975),1–5.
[36] The concept of citizenship in Islam could be traced in the text of the Covenant of Medina laid down by Prophet Mohamed (PBUH) after his migration from Makka to Madina in order to create a unified community from the Muslims, Jews and non-Muslims who were residing in the city of Madina and its environs.

The Qur'anic scholars interpreted (rope of Allah) - the Qur'an and Prophetic tradition, however, in the context of the modern state, "the rope" that every Muslim should hold fast imply the Constitution of the country that is compliant with Islam and ratified through consultative processes and referendum. Generally, in the democratic states where freedom of choice is respected, Muslims do not consent to anything that contravenes their core belief system.

Islam emphasises a sense of belonging and unity beyond primordial attachment which is based on the concept of a community bonded by common belief, vision and mission that constitute a single group (a supra-national community), a commonwealth of the believers "*Ummah wahidah*". Following Qur'anic verse affirms the conception stating "Verily this Ummah [nation] of yours is one Ummah" (21:92). This commonwealth of the believers should adhere to the commands of the Almighty God, seek unity under single law-abiding leader, a leader committed to the values of good governance. This argument is valid for worldwide sentiment for Muslim brotherhood and in the narrower conception, among citizens of modern states. Islam is both an individual and a communal religion that calls for the individual to live in harmony with him or herself, with the community and with the entire creation of God; and for the individual to take direct responsibility for all his actions. Human responsibility on his actions is well articulated in the Qur'an. For instance, the following verses affirms that "And every soul earns not [blame] except against itself, and no bearer of burdens will bear the burden of another" (6:164). Islam teaches an individual to be honest, truthful, patient, content, charitable, cheerful and tolerant. It commands its faithful to control their anger and to forgive when others wrong them.

Besides the early community of believers in Medina, the entire Arabian Peninsula changed drastically because of the new faith that was instilled in the mind set of the segmented clans. Universal values, such as the supremacy of the law, equality, justice, freedom and fraternity, were established. Upon these values, Islamic civilization was built. In later years, the Arab sociologist and philosopher Ibn-Khaldun recorded that

> Bedouins can acquire royal authority only by making use of religious colouring, such as prophet hood or sainthood or some great religious event in general. The reason is because of their savagery: the Bedouins are the least willing of all nations to subordinate themselves to each other, as they are rude, proud, ambitious and eager to be leaders. Their individual aspirations rarely coincide. But when there is religion [among them]…then they have some restraining influence upon themselves. The quality of haughtiness and jealousy leave them. It is, then, easy to unite them [in a societal organization].[37]

Islam also emphasizes social cohesion and harmony. Its basic philosophy is enjoining the right and prohibiting the wrong and the teaching that one should not harm others. As a narrated prophetic tradition that relates: "There should be neither harming nor reciprocating harm."[38] Social cohesion begins in the family and community and extends to human beings at large. This concept is well documented in the Qur'anic verse

> O people, be conscious of your Lord, who created you from one soul and from it created its mate and from them twain scattered many men and women. Be conscious of God and remember the rights of the wombs, surely God is always watching you (4:1).

The law of Islam emphasizes justice and fairness and prohibits cheating, exploitation, fraud, and deception, as well as coercive policies. It also emphasizes good governance under broad moral principles and laws ordained by God. Furthermore, Islamic moral teachings emphasize benevolence, charity, and kindness.

---

[37] Quoted by Mukhtar, *Islam in Somali* History, 1995, 16.
[38] The prophetic tradition in the Sunna Ibnu Majah (Book 13, Hadith 2340).

In view of the above brief conceptualization of some Islamic values, this work now discusses the minimum necessary values for restoring the Somali state. The arguments shall be limited to five major values that Islam emphasises in other to create an orderly community. These are supremacy of the law, protection of public and private properties, supreme loyalty to the state, equality of the people and consultative form of governance (democratic state).

(a) Supremacy of the Law

Supremacy of the law is a fundamental principle in the modern democratic states. It demands both rulers and the ruled to be similarly subjected to known and standing laws. Constitutions are the basic law of modern states and all other laws are developed on the basis of the constitutional principles. Ironically, in the mindset of the Somali people, man-made laws (secular laws) are derived from the inherited colonial laws imposed on the Somali society without considering their Islamic beliefs, cultural heritage and moral values. It is an indisputable fact that

> all laws, whether prescriptive or prohibitive, legislate morality. All laws, regardless of their content or their intent, arise from a system of values, from a belief that some things are right and others wrong, that some things are good and others bad, that some things are better and others worse.[39]

Therefore, breaking secular laws are not seen to be immoral in view of the fact that they are not accepted socially and are considered alien. Accordingly, breaking secular state laws are not considered obnoxious. For instance, imagine when the whole population including those holding public offices do not believe in the supremacy of laws of their state. Conversely, if these laws are considered to be Islamic, in a

---

[39] Michael Bauman, "Law and Morality", available from http://www.equip.org/article/law-and-morality/ (accessed on June 9, 2016).

broader sense, breaking it will arouse feeling of personal guilt and subsequent remorse is likely to occur to avoid grave consequences in this world and hereafter. Moreover, infringing on Islamic laws are not socially acceptable and perpetrators are publicly reprimanded. In case Islamic laws are adopted, the effect of the following three compounded layers reduces criminality and violations of the laws. These are self-regulation of the individuals in fear from Allah's wrath, social pressure that requires conformity to the community values and law enforcement institutions of the state. In the current condition, only component of law enforcement institutions are functional and they also don't give ultimate and supreme loyalties to the secular state laws.

Practically, all laws of the state could be made Islamic if these laws are codified and examined comparatively in relation to the Islamic Sharia by the Islamic legal experts. Moreover, state laws that do not contravene with the Islamic laws will be considered Islamic and is safeguarded as such by the community at large. Certainly, prevailing perception in Somalia sees those who break the laws of Allah as evildoers. Hence, they are looked down upon while those who break state laws are often considered "bona fide" or even "heroes" among their fellow clan members. In the contrary, individuals who do shy away to accumulate public wealth for personal benefits or strictly comply with laws are despised in the most corrupt environment of the state institutions and society. Therefore, legal awareness and legal conformity is in high demand in Somalia . It is the gateway for good governance in which laws are accepted, respected and abided by most citizens of the state. Therefore, Islamic laws are the only means capable of restoring respectability for the state laws that invigorate self-restraining moral codes in the individuals and communities.

(b) Protection of public and private properties

The concept of public property is not well entrenched in the culture of many Somalis. In the pastoral society as well as in agricultural communities, private property is well understood, but public property is merely no-man's property. Nothing is shared in the Somali culture except blood wealth (Diya–paying), clan wells and common defence during conflicts. Zakat and charities, which are Islamic concepts, are also not well developed in the culture. What Somalis know mostly is not pure charity, but returning favours *"abaal ergasho"*. Modern states are built with public property collected in the form of taxation and redistributed to the society through allocations in the budgetary system, social services and developmental programmes. This requires huge administrative apparatus that is transparent and accountable. In Somalia, on the other hand, the culture of nomads, which regards raiding and looting other's properties as normal practices, was transferred to the cities in a new urban cultural practices. The ripple effect of this nomadic culture is evident in the public financial and human resource management. In particular, the process of looting of public property occurs in a setting where the higher and lower echelons of the government are inter connected in a complex web of kinship. Therefore, reviving the Islamic values of what is 'lawful' and 'prohibited' (*Halal and Haram*) in a community that is very much attached to Islam may create additional added value for the protection of public property. This concept inculcates all citizens that taking a way something that belongs to the whole community - public property is prohibited *"Haram"* in Islam and even more damaging and sinful than pillaging personal properties. The family, friends and the relatives pressure individuals who dare to take *"Haram"* even before the state apparatus and law enforcement began to prosecute. This means that community self regulation and restraints will take place and public plundering will be greatly minimized.

(c) Supreme loyalty to the state

The modern state demands supreme loyalty and has the responsibility of protecting its citizens from internal as well external threats. This loyalty is divided in clan-based societies, where the individual's loyalty is pulled in opposing directions between clans and the state. The pastoral culture of leadership is based on the fact that the clan elder is first among equals, while the hierarchical system of the modern state is not well entrenched in that culture. Most Somalis are of pastoral/nomadic culture which creates insubordination towards state institutions. This creates extra-institutional connections between clan members in the different levels of the state bureaucracy. In this way, for instance, a member related to the minister working in the ministry may easily meet with the minister and give him unofficial reports and then ruin the hierarchy required for the modern state management. Most often wrong administrative decisions are made based on these informal reporting systems of the clans. Islam enjoins its believers to give loyalty to their state and its leadership as long as the leadership abides by the policies and procedures of the state laws, supposedly non-contradictory to the Islamic principles. This notion is well stated in the Qur'anic verse:

> O you, who believe, obey Allah and obey the Messenger and those charged with authority among you. If ye differ in anything among yourselves, refer it to Allah and His Messenger, if ye do believe in Allah and the last day. (4:59).

Therefore, loyalty to the state and elected leaders are ingrained in the Islamic faith that teaches the Muslim community to abide by these guidelines. Reviving this concept belittles clan attachments for the benefit of loyalty to the state.

(d) Equality of the people

Equality is a relatively self-centred concept in the pastoral communities. Paradoxically, equality among one family clan is well respected in the egalitarian society but the universal equality of all people, races and clans in Somalia is not deeply-rooted in the culture. Strong and big clans despise smaller and weaker clans. Warrior clans in the pastoral regions look down on peaceful agricultural communities. Sometimes, individuals with no clan attachments or belonging to smaller clans are considered to be of the lower caste while members of the large and strong clans may consider themselves as nobility. The impact of this culture is extremely disastrous in a way that members belonging to specific clans claim the right to be the natural leaders of the nation, while on the contrary, the concept of the modern state is founded on equality of all citizens irrespective of their traditional cultural heritage. Somali nationalists failed to create a society where every citizen feels equal among others. However, Islamic practices in Somalia has shown a totally different picture. For instance, Sufi brotherhoods in Somalia had proven the supremacy of the Islamic brotherhood over clan attachments in their *Jama'a* communities. Members of larger clans have become disciples of Sheikhs from smaller clans or even despised clan groups[40]. Thus, in the Sufi orders, clan supremacy was diminished drastically and Islamic equality superseded over artificial clan pride. This shows that when Islamic values are revived and disseminated in the community, equal citizen's concept is better accepted in the society.

(e) Consultative Governance

In theory, Islam calls for consultative form of governance using the Arabic term of "*Shura*" which was narrated in the

---

[40] Clear examples are legendary Sufi brotherhood Sheikhs such as Sheikh Aweys Al-Barawi, Sheikh Suffi of Banadir, Sheikh Ali Maye of Marka and many others.

Qur'an in the form of direct command for the prophet to consult his companions and in the form of being a general characteristics of true believers.[41] Muslim nations like other nations are imploring for political participation and freedom of choice. However, in the postcolonial era, there are a number of obstacles to the democratization of the Muslim countries. The first one is colonial legacy which had created family based monarchies in the wealthiest Muslim countries who are adamant to keep the status quo and oppose any form of democratic movements. Unfortunately, these monarchies use Islam as a tool to legitimize their power and sponsor distorted interpretation of Islam emphasizing its incompatibility with democracy. Moreover, Western countries have also been supporting authoritarian rule in the Muslim countries believing that security is more important than democratic transformation and as such they constitute an obstacle for democratic transformation. Finally, traditional culture ingrained in the educational curriculum and popularized in the mass media enjoins citizens to be submissive to the authoritarian system of governance. Nonetheless, there is nothing wrong in Islam that is an obstacle to democracy provided that it is sensitive to its core belief. Offering succinct explanation, Sudanese politician and scholar Sadiq al-Mahdi have articulated that democracy is like *Shura* (consultation) that have developed modern institutions such as political parties and *Shura* is like democracy that is bounded by the Islamic ceiling and conforms to the general Islamic principles.[42] Giving a simple example, democracy in its ideal form is like

---

[41] Following the two verse in the Qur'an about consultation. the first Qur'anic verse is "*Those who hearken to their Lord, and establish regular Prayer; who (conduct) their affairs by mutual consultation (Shura); who spend out of what We bestow on them for Sustenance*" [are praised] (42:38). The second verse is "*Thus it is due to mercy from God that you deal with them gently, and had you been rough, hard hearted, they would certainly have dispersed from around you; pardon them therefore and ask pardon for them, and take counsel with them in the affair; so when you have decided, then place your trust in God; surely God loves those who trust*"(42:39).

[42] Sadiq al-Mahdi. "*Al-Shura ka Asaas li-Nidum Al-Hukm Fi Al-Alam Al Islami.*" (Unpublished paper submitted to the 15th Conference of the Muslim Affairs held in Cairo, May, 2003): 9-12.

pure water that does not have a shape and colour; however, it takes the shape and colour of its container. Likewise, democracy takes the colour and the shape of the society in which it is applied. Therefore, democracy exists in different forms corresponding to the will and the choices of the different cultures. Since nations are different in their culture, religions and system of governance, their application of democracy eventually takes different forms. Combining pastoral culture that IM. Lewis romanticized as "pastoral democracy" and Islamic conception of consultation, democratic transformation has a great opportunity in Somalia in the post-civil war period. In addition to that, the legacy of the democratic precedents in the first nine years of Somalia's independence (1960-1969) provides additional inspirations and lessons to be learned.

Moderate Islamism and Nation-building

Islamic movements in Somalia in general should be understood in the context of a modernist comprehension of Islam as a complete way of life, an understanding that does not sit well with the secular tendencies of the post-colonial state. These secular tendencies were embodied in the way of life of the ruling elite and were enshrined in the colonial legal heritage and ethos. Islamic movements disagreed with 'compartmentalizing' Islam by likening it to the Christian practice of pushing religion into a corner or viewing it as a mere spiritual sphere and an individual responsibility. In view of that, Islam being a comprehensive religion, communal as well as personal, is not and cannot be apolitical. Its nature of completeness logically provides guidelines for the political, social and economic life of Muslim communities and states. In accordance with these lines of thought, Islamic activists belonging to different schools of thought questioned the legitimacy of state policies, particularly those regarding the role of Islam in the state and society. These activists formed organizations addressing their understanding of Islam and this phenomenon was called Islamism by Western scholars and researchers.

The reaction of post-colonial states to the activities of these organizations was undemocratic, brutal and violent. It was a denial of the right to freedom in all its forms such as physical, cultural, economic and political. As a result, like all the other dissident political organizations in the early 1970s, Islamic activists in Somalia were pushed to the unavoidable option of underground activities.[43] In the wider understanding of Islamic revivalism, many groups and organizations could be mentioned in Somalia. The most prominent of these organizations are Islah and Itihaad. All the other organizations largely fall under the ideology of one of these two organizations, which date back to the late sixties and early seventies. They are local and Somali by birth, but their methodology for advocating the harmonization of the indigenous culture and the laws of the communities and the state with the Islamic legal system and values, had its roots in the wider Islamic world. The Muslim Brotherhood in Egypt, the Wahabi School or Salafia in Saudi Arabia, and neo-Sufis in India could be considered their respective ideological affiliates. Though, all these movements share aspirations to bring Islamic values into the lives of their communities, their tactical approaches cover a very wide spectrum, from peaceful evolutionists to armed revolutionaries.[44] Also, their visions, strategies, and organizational structures are so diverse that it could be said only their activism and aspirations make them different from other Somalis. In practice, these organizations take on the colour of the societies around them – and in this context, a Somali flavor. This is even so within Somalia, as the

---

[43] The military government banned all political parties and social organizations, and all dissidents resorted to the underground option or exile.

[44] For instance, the Islah movement is considered evolutionary while *al-Itihad* was considered during 1992-97 as revolutionary. As widely observed, *al-Itihad* had been shifting towards more moderation since then.

movements reflect the cultural setting: pastoral, agricultural, urban and so on.[45] Moderate Islamic movements (*al-Wasadiyah wa al-Ictidal*) are all those peaceful organizations believing in evolutionary reformation of society through the educational process and the revival of Islamic values. In this category falls all Muslim brotherhood persuasions in particular Islah Movement. Extreme groups in their social approach (*al-Tadaruf wal-Guluwu*) include some branches of disenfranchised Al-Itihad organization and Takfir, which became armed revolutionaries and believe in exclusivity and absolutism.[46]

The moderate components of the Islamic movements are not isolated from their cultural heritage; in fact, they believe that their historical roots can be traced back to the early struggle of the Islamic scholars, the Ulama, to confront British, Italian and Ethiopian colonial invasions and their policies geared towards political domination and cultural influence on Somali Muslim society. The Dervish Movement of Mohamed Abdullah Hasan, the Sheikh Hassan Barsane resistance, the Biyamaal Revolt and other anti-colonial movements led by Islamic scholars could be considered as early Islamic revivalist movements.[47] In that sense, the modern revivalism of Islam is a continuous process, a progressive and anti-colonial resistance movement standing for the protection of the Islamic cultural heritage against the cultural hegemony of the other countries. Indeed, early Islamic scholars did at least succeed in protecting and maintaining Islamic faith in the face of the invasion of privileged Christian missionaries who were poised to create Christian minorities in Somalia. As documented in the colonial archives, these missionaries enjoyed financial, political and

---

[45] It has been observed that extremism (religious and political) is more entrenched in the culture of pastoralists or a strong nomadic culture, where moderation is mostly detected in the agricultural and urban locations.

[46] Yusuf Al-Qaradawi, *Priorities of the Islamic Movement in The Coming Phase* (Al-Dar; 1st edition, 1992), 27-60.

[47] These scholars were the intellectuals and leaders of the communities. They understood the dangers posed by the colonial powers and therefore called for armed resistance. There is no contradiction between being Islamists and being nationalists. This is the best intermarriage for mobilizing internal forces and effectively repulsing enemies.

moral support from the colonial powers as part of the overall colonial scheme of conquering and pacifying weaker nations. The Islamic movements strongly believe that their task is to continue the resistance of their forefathers in the ways corresponding to the magnitude of the threat that is facing Somali society. This new generation of Islamic activists are destined to deal with the growing external and internal threats and challenges facing Somalia.

The moderate Islamic movements consider themselves an embodiment of the continuing aspirations of the Somali national movement, which succeeded in bringing about political independence in 1960, but fell short of completing the expectations of the people in gaining economic and cultural independence.[48] The national movements, which used the rhetoric of nationalist ideology alone, also failed to maintain the unity of the Somalis. Therefore, the Islamic movements' position is that political independence alone was not sufficient to realize national goals after independence. In addition, they have focused strongly on the cultural aspect in the belief that reviving Islamic culture and safeguarding its values will create conducive environment for societal peace, economic development and strengthened national cohesion. Islam is also an effective element in curbing clannish alignments in society and creating trans-clan affiliations and groupings, a goal that the ideology of nationalism alone failed to achieve. Indeed, according to the Islamic movements, the ideology of nationalism has never been the only factor during the struggle for independence. Rather, it was coupled with the Islamic injunctions calling on the Muslim faithfuls to wage inexhaustible resistance (Jihad) against infidels, particularly if they were transgressors and occupiers. However, the new ruling elite trained in the colonial schools underestimated the Islamic factor in their nation-building programs after

---

[48] Of courses, extremists consider the fathers of Somali state to be the source of the Somali debacle, being secular and followers of the colonial ways.

independence. In the Somali situation, state policies that did not give adequate weight to the Islamic factor led to the collapse of the state institutions. It is absolutely proven that after 30 years of independence, only Islamic organizations and clan militia remain functional, as organized groups in Somalia. As a result, Islamic movements envisage that nation-building in Somalia requires not only a revival of the country's national consciousness and awareness, but also an appeal to the country's rich Islamic heritage, its tolerant and community-oriented values. They hope that appealing to and sowing these two elements, Islamic values and nationalism, will have enough innate strength to dislodge and weaken destructive political clanism and separatist tendencies from the psyche of Somali society.

Islamic movements also represent the re-awakening of the faith due to the improved comprehension of Islamic teachings by modern Somali scholars trained not only in the Islamic education centers and Islamic universities, but also in modern universities.[49] Traditional Islamic education centered on the spiritual aspect of Islam but fell short in explaining the totality of Islam; it was divorced from being the supreme guidance for modern state institutions. The new and revived understanding of Islam is that Islam is a complete way of life and is not confined to personal creed. In the views of the Islamic movements, Islam is the supreme guidance and reference for all aspects of life for Muslim communities. As such, the Somali state should therefore, apply and abide by Islamic law and protect Islamic values. Obviously, this view is contrary to the understanding of religion by the former Christian colonial powers, the founders of the collapsed Somali state, and most of the educated elite in the highest echelon of the political spectrum. This view of religion by the colonial powers was and

---

[49] Most Islamic activists are graduates from modern science universities. The reason may be that modern education offers Muslims better freedom to question and understand their identities and the world than the so-called Islamic universities, which have state employees controlling their curriculum and activities.

remains that religion and the state must be totally separated from each other since the modern state, according to their view, should be secular. Moreover, religion should be relegated to the domain of individual responsibility and religious non-governmental organizations.

The re-awakening of faith (*Tajdid al-Iman*) is a phenomenon that occurs whenever Muslims suffer an external threat such as colonialism and invasion and Islam is employed as an ideology of liberation (Jihad). Also, that re-awakeningtakes place whenever new charismatic preachers, organizations and brotherhoods appear and intensify the call for the renewal of the faith.In the history of Islam, this cyclical re-awakening of the faith has been occurring since the initial revelation before 6th century AD. In Somalia, waves of re-awakening of the faith occurred during the anti-colonial struggle and in the confrontation with the Marxist military regime (1969-1991). The new cycle of re-awakening of faith has created a new hope for the desperate and disenfranchised young generations of Somalis who have responded to the call that Islam provides salvation in this world and hereafter.

Moderate Islamic movements are neither anti-Western in sentiment, nor idealistically nostalgic, nor blind imitators of other nations' cultures and ways of life. Therefore, in international context, moderate Islamic movements are not directed against any foreign state, nor are they established to achieve sinister objectives. Their main focus is on internal Somali affairs, which require an enormous reformation of the collapsed state institutions. Somalia needs massive international support in all aspects of life in order to reassert itself as a sovereign state among other nations. Somalia also needs the understanding and support of its neighbors in order to reconstruct its statehood. Unless these requirements are achieved, regional peace and common security will not be achieved among the nations in the Horn of Africa. But it is a prerequisite that all states of the region should adhere to the principle of non-interference and cease their subversive activities and hegemonic strategies. Instead, regional cooperation should take its course in the region to foster economic and social development. Contrary to what some writers may entertain regarding "clash of civilizations",[50] genuine Islamic revivalism is in the interests of peace and security in the Horn of Africa. The essence of neighborhood feelings praised by the Prophet Muhammad (PBUH) particularly between Muslims and Christians, greatly enhances mutual cooperation.[51]

During the last four decades, moderate Islamic movements has been working under dictatorial rule where organizations are banned or in a situation of civil war, where law and order were the law of the jungle became the rule of life. Having survived these two stages of Somali history, Islamic movements are more mature and experienced and now play a vital role in the Somali affairs. Today, the influence of Islamic movements can be seen in every aspect of life of the Somali people. In business, in education, in the civil society movement, in the mass media, in political life, the values and ideals of Islamic movements are taking root in the social fabric of the nation. Islamic activists are taking an important role in the Diaspora communities and established organizations that propagate Islam, teach children the Qur'an and urge communities to frequent mosques and Islamic centers. This is simply because Islamic values are deeply rooted in Somali society and its modern revival, according to the modernist understanding, is just the continuation and revival of faith, not

---

[50] Samuel P. Huntington, "*The Clash of Civilizations?*", in " Foreign Affairs", vol. 72, no. 3, Summer 1993, 22–49.
[51] On caring the neighbour, Prophet Muhammad said: *"Angel Jibril advised me continuously to take care of the neighbour till I thought that Allah is to make him an inheritor."* Ethiopia is a neighbour to Somalia, however, historic conflict and sensitivities remain intact from both sides of the border. One of the Ethiopian scholar had expressed that sensitivities in his book. See Medhane Tadesse, *Al-Ittihad: Political Islam and Black Economy in Somalia: Religion, Clan, Money, and the Struggle for Supremacy over Somalia* (Addis Ababa: Meag Printing Enterprise, 2002).

creating innovations and discordance with the available and known doctrines of Islam.

The objectives of the moderate Islamic movement during the civil war focused on forsaking internecine wars, internal reconstruction and reorganization after the fall of the reign of tyranny, improving their image in the community by cooperating with other organizations and making local and national reconciliation one of their major priorities. The promotion of education and establishing institutions for that purpose were made priorities. Other main objectives were the intensification of the Islamic call and education in all regions, the promotion of civil society organizations and improving their image at the international level. In the field of national reconciliation, the Arta Peace Process in Djibouti in the year 2000 was the culmination of all reconciliation efforts since 1995.

Moderate Islamic movements strongly believe that they had a vital role to play in reviving Somali consciousness and nation-building. In addition to their role of reconciliation, education and social service, they are convinced that any viable national political organization needs the active participation of their members. Ironically, Islamic movements are not political organizations in their own right, nor are they planning to convert themselves into political parties. In reality, the Somali society of today is far beyond interacting with conventional political parties based on ideology rather than clan affiliations. Islamic groups are movements for the common good and are working very hard to bring about social reforms, which will pave way for the appearance of the national political parties. However, members of Islamic movements may participate in any organization of their own choice which they believe may bring good for Somalia. Members of the Islamic Movements are ready elements for reconstructing organizations of a national character. These members may play the role of "unifiers" in the segmented clans, where each clan has formed its own militia, political entity and social organization. Of course, extreme elements of Islamic movements are totally different from the above constructive vision and approach and always create social conflict and armed confrontations.

Conclusion

This paper focused on the Islamic factors that was undermined in the nation-building process. It brings out the role of Islam in the society and state formation and discusses how the post-colonial state diminished that role and undermined those values. It also traces the reality of modern Islamic movements as the most active trans-clan and ideologically motivated groups in the Somali society. Recovering the Somali state requires, among other things, reviewing its shared values and state structures and a prudent understanding of the concerns of the external stakeholders. Values shared by all Somalis are clanism, nationalism and Islam. Ideological reconciliation between these factors should be considered in the process of any actual political reconciliation in Somalia and nation-building.

Whatever hypothesis with respect to Somalia may be projected, the fact remains that Somalia is a Muslim clan-based society striving to re-establish its national state institutions. There are two dangerous tendencies in Somalia that hinder nation-building: denying clanism and opposing an increased role of Islam in nation-building. The radical nationalistic ideals when dealing with the traditional indigenous Somali ideologies, clanism and Islam, are still looming and prevalent. Moreover, the concerns of external powers and strong opposition to the increased role of Islam are also intact.

By the 1970s, modern Islamic movements emerged with both radical and moderate components to advance the Islamic cause in Somalia. Among three shared values of the Somalis, only political clanism carries the virus of divisiveness in society, while nationalism and Islam are agents for societal cohesion if not radicalized. Therefore, raising national consciousness and strengthening Islamic values are the necessary ingredients in containing political clanism. Any success of the future Somali nation-building depends on the skilful reconciliation of nationalism and Islam on one hand and accommodating clan attachments on the other. Moderate Islamic movements propagate conducive Islamic values for nation-building in the society such as supremacy of law, protection of public and private properties, supreme loyalty to the state, equality of all citizens and consultative form of governance (democracy). If moderate Islamism is not promoted and accommodated within the state apparatus in Somalia, the alternative will be the emergence of more extreme groups that may cause social conflict and regional security problems.

CHAPTER TWO

Transitional Justice in Islam: Concepts and conceptions

I
Islam and Transitional Justices:
Principles, Mechanisms and Historical Role in Somalia

II
Somali Conceptions of Transitional Justice:
Findings of Field Research in Mogadishu

I

Transitional Justice in Islam: Principles, Mechanisms and Historical Role in Somalia[1]

> The recompense for an injury is an injury equal thereto (in degree): but if a person forgives and makes reconciliation, his reward is due from Allah....But indeed if any show patience and forgive, that would truly be an exercise of courageous will and resolution in the conduct of affairs
> (The Qur'an 42-40-43)

Introduction

The practices associated with the field of Transitional Justice dates back to centuries, but its modern application has gone through four phases: the Nuremburg Tribunals after the end of World War Two in 1945; democratization process after the end of the Cold War in 1990s; mainstreaming Transitional Justice in the peace-building in the last two decades and finally accounting for local specificity and cultural sensitivities of Transitional Justice.[2] The current use of the term Transitional Justice was coined in 1995 and since then has influenced the legal, social and political discourse in the academia, civil societies, states in conflict, broken societies and international community.[3] The term Transitional Justice attracted many definitions, however, all of them agree in broad principle that Transitional Justice refers to the set of judicial and non-judicial measures and a set of approaches to address massive human

---

[1] This paper was produced as part of research project on Transitional Justice in Somalia commissioned by Max Planck Institute for Social Anthropology, Halle/Saale, Germany.
[2] Dustin N. Sharp, "Interrogating the Peripheries: The Preoccupations of Fourth Generation Transitional Justice" (Harvard Human Rights Journal / Vol. 26, 153-57) available from http://harvardhrj.com/wp-content/uploads/2013/05/V26-Sharp.pdf (accessed on May 15, 2016).
[3] Neil J. Kritz (ed.), *Justice: How Emerging Democracies Reckon with Former Regimes,* Volume I: General Considerations(United States Institute of Peace,1995).

rights violations.⁴ Transitional Justice measures promote civic trust, build peace, foster national unity, and strengthen the democratic rule of law through measures that ensure accountability.⁵ Transitional Justice mechanisms include four processes: a justice process, to bring perpetrators to justice; a reparation process, to redress victims of atrocities for the harm suffered; a truth process, to fully investigate atrocities so that society discovers what happened during the repression/conflict; and an institutional reform process, to ensure that such atrocities do not happen again.⁶ Classical Transitional Justice permits the implementation of hybrid processes and making use of local exceptionalities. Somalia being a Muslim society where gross violations of Human rights occurred for decades, Sharia can be explored as the basis for the application of Transitional Justice. Moreover, growing mass violations of the human rights and conflicts in the Middle Eastern Muslim societies necessitated the development of Islamic rooted Transitional Justice mechanism. The Islamic concepts of Transitional Justice is less developed in the Muslim majority countries and that is why it require more academic attention.

Transitional Justice attracted scholarly studies and is a growing field in Islamic sharia, being a comprehensive religion, has addressed concepts of Transitional Justice in its basic sources: the Qur'an and Prophetic traditions. For instance, the above stated verse (42:40-43) is one of the numerous verses in the Qur'an that lays the foundation of the concept of Transitional Justice. The vocabulary of "recompense for an injury is an injury," "forgiveness" and "reconciliation" are the

---

⁴ Among these definitions are UN definition in Annan, K., UN Secretary-General, *The Rule of Law in Conflict and Post-Conflict Societies* (NY: United Nations,2004), 4. Other definition include ofN.Roht-Arriaza and J. Mariezcurrna (eds.),*Transitional Justice in the Twenty-First Century: Beyond Truth Versus Justice* (Cambridge: Cambridge University Press,2006), 2.
⁵ Lavinia Stan and Nadya Nedelsky, *Encyclopaedia of Transitional Justice*, 235.
⁶ Clara Sandoval Villalba, "Briefing paper: Transitional Justice, key concepts, Processes and Challenges",2010, 3. Available from http://www.idcr.org.uk/wp-content/uploads/2010/09/07_11.pdf (accessed on June 11, 2016).

core Transitional Justice mechanisms. Moreover, establishing justice on earth is the supreme purpose of Islam and the rationale for revealed divine books and sent messengers, as expressed in the following Qur'anic verse:

> We sent a foretime our apostles with Clear Signs and sent down with them the Book and the Balance (of Right and Wrong), that men may stand forth in justice; ... (57: 25).[7]

Thus, the concept of justice in Islam is rooted in the divinely revealed laws termed as Sharia, which are obligatory and binding on all believers.[8] Accordingly, Muslims are required to obey Allah, His prophets and their leaders who follow Sharia principles. In case of disagreement and conflict, adjudication should be made in accordance with Sharia principles and guidance. This concept is straightforwardly expressed in the following Qur'anic verse:

> O ye who believe! Obey Allah, and obey the Messenger, and those charged with authority among you. If ye differ in anything among yourselves, refer it to Allah and His Messenger, if ye do believe in Allah and the Last Day: That is best, and most suitable for final determination.(4: 59).[9]

Transitional Justice, which deals with situations after mass violence, is not well developed in most Muslim majority countries.[10] Thus, this paper contributes to academic studies

---

[7] The main revealed books according to Qur'an are Tawrat (Torah), the book of Judaism, revealed to Prophet Moses; Zabur (Psalms) revealed to Prophet David; Injil (Gospel) revealed to Prophet Jesus; Suhuf Ibrahim (Scrolls of Ibrahim) revealed to Prophet Ibrahim; Suhuf Musa (Scrolls of Moses) revealed to Prophet Moses and the Qur'an, revealed to Prophet Muhammad. The revealed books are mentioned in the Qur'an. See Qur'anic verses (87: 18-19, 5: 44, 5: 46, 17: 55).

[8] See the Qur'anic verse "But no, by the Lord, they can have no (real) Faith, until they make Thee judge in all disputes between them, and find in their souls no resistance against Thy decisions, but accept them with the fullest conviction." (The Qur'an 4: 65).

[9] This verse is used wrongly by the authoritarian Muslim leaders to demand obedience from the people; even though they do not abide by the Sharia laws, which make it obligatory for Muslims to consult each other on their affairs. However, its true meaning may be to give loyalty to the institutions built on the Islamic principles and legitimate authorities elected though democratic process (*Shura*).

[10] See the United State Institute of Peace, Peace Brief 87, March 2011, 2. Exceptions include a truth commission convened in Morocco and the trials of Saddam Hussein and other Ba'thist

that aim to investigate Transitional Justice concepts and mechanisms based on the Islamic Sharia and its applicability in Somalia. Methodologically, it draws primarily on the two basic sources of Islam: The Qur'an and prophetic traditions besides other relevant references. At the beginning, the paper delineates theoretical framework on the basic concepts and classifications of Islamic Sharia. Secondly, it offers mechanisms of the Transitional Justice in Islam and its retributive and restorative system of justice. Thirdly, it explains historical role of Sharia in Somalia and the development of various schools of jurisprudence. Finally, conclusions are derived.

Theoretical Framework: The Islamic Shari'a

Islam is a comprehensive religion that provides a complete code of life and guidelines to follow in all spheres, including personal matters and collective societal issues. Therefore, Islamic Law covers a broad and comprehensive system of legislation in all aspects of life. It has distinctive characteristics and unique qualities, which allowed it to enjoy stability, growth, and relevance for over fourteen centuries. It is a divine law, and its application is part of obedience to Allah and submission to His will. It offers stability and permanence in principle and flexibility in application. It includes economic order, social organization and codes of civil and criminal laws. The personal aspects include the belief system, ritual worships, manners and values. The collective aspects include political, economic and social systems that offer general frameworks and norms.

Muslims in general agree on the personal aspects of Islam, such as the principles of faith, other pillars of Islam and the Islamic value system. However, many collective aspects that were sidelined during the colonial era and replaced by modern

---

leaders in Iraq. The current trials of the Mubarak regime and similar trials in Tunisia are also new developments.

European laws remain contentious. To rectify this anomaly that created conflict between the state and society, modernity and tradition, and Islamic values and Western values, various forms of Islamic movements emerged. They advocate the revival of Islam and comprehensive application of Sharia. Moreover, these movements adopted various strategies and tactics that include moderate and extreme ways. The role of these Islamic movements is growing, and they have wielded strong societal support, which makes Transitional Justice mechanism that complies with Sharia more relevant in the Muslim majority countries.

Shari'a: Basic Definitions and Classifications

Sharia literally means "way to water," signifying the source of life. To Muslims, it signifies the right way to Allah and to the eternal life in the hereafter. It is also broadly defined as "those doctrinal, practical and dispositional regulations which Allah had legislated through one of His messengers."[11] Moreover, its definition can be traced from the verbal Arabic noun *"Shari'a"* that appears in the following verse:

> Then we put thee [O Muhammad] on the (right) way of religion [Shari'a]: so follow thou that (way), and follow not the desires of those who know not (45: 18).

In addition, its derivative form appears three times: at (The Qur'an 42:13) in the form of single verb *Shara'a*; at (The Qur'an 42:21) in the form of the plural verb *Shara'u*; and at (The Qur'an 5:48) in the form of a noun *Shir'atan*.[12]

---

[11] Hanafi Jurisprudence, 1. See http://www.slideshare.net/IslamicBooks/hanafi-jurisprudence-fiqh-explained.

[12] *"The same religion has He established for you [shara'a] as that which He enjoined on Noah - the which We have sent by inspiration to thee - and that which We enjoined on Abraham, Moses, and Jesus: Namely, that ye should remain steadfast in religion, and make no divisions therein. ...* (The Qur'an 42: 13). Moreover *"What! have they partners (in godhead), who have established for them some religion [shara'u] without the permission of Allah. ..."* (The Qur'an 42: 21). Furthermore, *"To thee We sent the Scripture in truth, confirming the scripture that came before it, and guarding it in safety: so judge between them by what Allah hath revealed, and follow not their vain desires, diverging from the Truth that hath come to thee. To each among you have we prescribed a law [shar'atan] and an open way..."* (The Qur'an 5: 48).

According to the modern definition, *Sharia* is the comprehensive body of Islamic laws that should regulate the public and private aspects of the lives of Muslims through the excessive examination of the primary sources of Islamic laws: the Qur'an and the prophetic authentic traditions.[13] There are also two secondary sources: the consensus (*Ijma*) and the juristic analogy (*Qiyas*).[14] Moreover, there are complementary sources such as the concept of considering general welfare (*Istislah*) as basis for legislation[15] and customary practices of particular community (`Urf*).[16] Based on these basic, secondary and complementary sources, Islamic scholars have developed Islamic jurisprudence "Fiqh" to deal with the changing conditions of human interactions in space and time.

Therefore, Islamic jurisprudence is

> ... the science of extraction of practical religious regulations from their detailed sources. It is the practical implementation of Sharia through its human understanding.[17]

---

[13] The Qur'an contains 114 chapters (*suwar*) and 6616 verses (*ayat*). Moreover, Sunni Muslims consider six major collections of the prophetic Sunna as the most authoritative. These are *Sahih Bukhari* and *Sahih Muslim*, the two works considered the most authentic. Both of them contain approximately 7,000 unrepeated *ahadith*. Moreover, there are four other works such as *Sunan al-Nisai, Sunan abu Dawood, Jami al-Tirmedi*, and *Sunan abu-Majah*. See Ibn Hajar al-Asqalani, *al-Nukat Ala Kitab ibn al-Salah* (*Maktabah al-Furqan, Ajman*, U.A.E., 2 edition, vol. 1, 2003),153.

[14] The consensus is based on the Hadith, which says, "*My Community shall never agree upon misguidance, therefore, if you see divergences, you must follow the greater mass or larger group.*" See Sunan Ibn Majah (Chapter 2: 1303). The question of whose consensus is relevant is very contentious among scholars. For modern Islamic thinkers "*Ijma is not a matter of consensus of a number of experts or jurists. Its meaning and function should be worked out in relation to the legislative function in concrete political systems, where it may produce a workable relationship between the ideal and the real with maximum possible support and participation on the part of Muslim peoples*". See Abdul Hamid A. Abu Sulayman, *The Islamic Theory of International Relations: New Directions for Islamic Methodology and Thought* (Herndon, VA: The International Institute of Islamic Thought, 1987), 84. Also, see Wael Hallaq, "On the Authoritativeness of Sunni Consensus," International Journal of Middle Eastern Studies 18 (1986), 427–454.

[15] The role of "*Istislah*" or "*maslahah mursalah*" involves attaining what is beneficial, avoiding that which is harmful, preventing wrongdoing and dealing with the changing times and context.

[16] It is a custom of specific community which does not contradict Islamic text and the legal system but offers flexibility and widens its scope. For example, the value of the dowry differs from one community to another, and such customs are considered to fall within Islamic jurisprudence.

[17] See *Hanafi Jurisprudence* (Accessed on Jan. 28, 2012).

Because these regulations are interpretations of various scholars in different times and space, diverse methodologies were employed and different opinions and legal judgments were offered to varieties of issues. Process of deducing new Islamic laws is called *"Ijtihad,"* which enables it to regulate for fresh and contemporary issues and revisits previous scholarly judgments.[18] As a result, various interpretations of the Islamic Sharia were developed during the course of the Islamic history. There are four Sunni schools of jurisprudence called *"madhab (sig) and madahib (plu)*, namely, *Shafi'i, Hanbali, Hanafi and Maliki*, a number of *Shi'a* schools such *Ja'fari and Zaidi*.

The existence of these schools and continuation of the process of *Ijtihad* attests that Islamic jurisprudence is not static but rather dynamic, flexible and applicable in every circumstance in all times and spaces. This nature of the *Shari'a* demonstrates the soundness of its higher objectives and intents called *Maqasid al-Shari'a*, the philosophical basics of juridical theory of Islamic law. Islamic scholars have classified the entire range of *Maqasid into* three categories: The essentials *(Daruriyyat)*, complementary benefits *(Hajiyyat)* and the embellishment *(Tahsiniyyat)*. The essentials are necessary to normal order in society as well as to the spiritual well being of individuals. According to Imam al-Ghazzali:

> The objective of the Sharia is to promote the well-being of all mankind, which lies in safeguarding their faith (din), their human self (nafs), their intellect (`aql), their posterity (nasl) and their wealth (mal). Whatever ensures the safeguard of these five serves public interest and is desirable.[19]

---

[18] *Ijtihad* is an intellectual effort by Islamic scholars, individually and collectively, to derive rules or choose one from among various interpretations to use when legislating for changing conditions, provided the change does not contradict with the spirit of the Sharia. Ijtihad is what keeps the dynamism of the Sharia and its suitability for all spaces and times.

[19] M. Umer Chapra, *The Future of Economics: An Islamic Perspective* (Leicester: The Islamic Foundation, 2000), 118.

The complementary benefits (Hajiyyat)

supplement the essentials and refer to those interests that, if neglected, would lead to hardship but not to the total disruption of life's normal order. In other words, they are needed to alleviate hardship so that life may be free from distress and predicament.[20]

The embellishment (Tahsiniyyat)

refer to those interests that, if realized, would lead to refinement and perfection in the customs and conduct of people at all levels of achievement.[21]

The science of Islamic jurisprudence in the traditional literature is divided into *Ibadah* (devotional law) and *Mu'amalat* (transactional law), due to the simple fact that each has distinct primary objectives. For instance, the primary objective of devotional law is to regulate the rituals and direct individual worship of Allah. This includes prayers, fasting, Hajj and Zakat. On the other hand, transactional law regulates human activity in the spheres of economic, social and political sectors. It addresses many legal aspects like Criminal Law *(jinayat)*, Personal Law *(Al-nikah)* and Commercial Law *(al-bay'c)*. However, in the modern development, Islamic jurisprudence has attracted immense studies and its scope has been widened to include various fields in response to the growing and changing modern necessities of the time.

Generally, Islamic law classifies all human actions into two major categories: Ma'ruf (right and good) and Munkar (wrong and bad or evil). In that conception, communities and states have been commanded "to enjoy the right and forbid the wrong."[22] The right and good in Islam includes obligatory and

---

[20] Asyraf Wajdi Dusuki and Nurdianawati Irwani Abdullah, *Maqasid al-Shari`ah, Maslahah, and Corporate Social Responsibility* (The American Journal of Islamic Social Sciences), 24:1. available from http://kantakji.com/media/2699/0308914.pdf(accessed on June 13, 2016).
[21] Ibid, 33
[22] See the Qur'anic verse, *"The Believers, men and women, are protectors one of another: they enjoin what is just, and forbid what is evil: they observe regular prayers, practise regular charity, and obey Allah and His Messenger…"* (9:71). See also, *"Ye are the best of peoples, evolved for mankind, enjoining what is right, forbidding what is wrong, and believing, in Allah…"* (3:110).

recommended actions, while evil includes the discouraged and forbidden actions. In between the right and wrong, there is a permissible position where flexibility and freedom is given to the individuals. Therefore, all human actions are categorized according to the "quantum of actions," which has, at its center, the neutral and permissible position, with two degrees of goodness and evilness to either side.

Forbidden ← Discouraged ← Neutral → Recommended → Obligatory

Fig 2: Classification of Human Actions in Islam

For example, the obligatory category includes the five daily prayers, fasting and so on. Recommended categories, also called *"Sunna,"* include many activities that are rewarded if done with good intentions and not punished when they are not done. "Permissible" includes all behavior that is neither forbidden nor discouraged, neither obligatory nor recommended. Discouraged behavior is considered undesirable and constitutes minor sins. Forbidden behavior is explicitly prohibited and includes all sinful and criminal actions. Transitional Justice deals with the last category of forbidden types, in particular with criminal actions.

Mechanisms of Transitional Justice in Islam

The major mechanism of Transitional Justice in general are criminal prosecution of the perpetrators of the crimes, reparation of the victims morally and materially, institutional reform to prevent recurrence of serious human rights abuses and impunity and truth commissions or other means to discover the truth of the crimes. The mechanisms of Transitional Justice in Islam could be classified into three categories: criminal persecution, reconciliation and hybrid system. In the criminal persecution category, all crimes are classified into one of three types; namely, Hudud (Allah's boundaries), Qisas (retribution) and Ta'zir (discretionary punishment). On the other hand, reconciliation includes elements of truth-seeking/telling, compensation, repentance and forgiveness. Hybridity combines some elements of criminal prosecution and reconciliation and is the preferred option to avoid a culture of impunity, although it depends on the changing circumstances and societal context. This section explores these mechanisms, beginning with introducing how Islam envisions individual responsibility.

Islam and Individual Responsibility

Islamic criminal law is based on individual responsibility for crimes, and collective punishment is not allowed in general.[23] Qur'anic verses state that this responsibility is direct and personal. For instance, Allah says,

> That man can have nothing but what he strives for;" (53:39). In another verse, Allah says, "Whoever works righteousness benefits his own soul; whoever works evil, it is against his own soul: nor is thy Lord ever unjust (in the least) to His Servants. (41:46). Furthermore, Every soul draws the meed [consequence] of its acts on none but itself: no bearer of burdens can bear of burdens of another… (6:146).

Besides that individual responsibility, Prophet Muhammad (PBUH) explained personal responsibility for the crime, addressing the clan-based communities in which the culture of revenge killing is prevalent. The Hadith, narrated by Abu-Dawuud, states that "A soul is not held responsible for acts committed by his father or by his brother." This means that believers of Islam must avoid revenge killing based on communal fighting. Islamic jurisprudence in its various schools sets specific conditions for criminal responsibility with subtle differences. These schools consider crimes

---

[23] In Hanafi School of *"Qasama doctrine where the inhabitant of a house or a village can be held liable for financial consequence of homicide with unknown perpetrator committed in the house or the village."* See Rudolph Peters, *Crime and Punishment in Islamic Law: Theory and Practice from the Sixteenth to Twenty-First Century* (Cambridge University Press, 2005), 20.

Individual, non-transferable and based on [the] conscious intentional conduct of a person possessing his mental faculties who was not acting under extenuating circumstance.[24]

In cases where a crime has been committed, individuals and communities are urged to come forth and tell the truth of their responsibility of the crime. Such confession of culpability (al-I'tiraf) by the offender is the first positive step in any reconciliation process. The Qur'an articulates this point eloquently emphasizing to stand for justice regardless of race, religion, relationships and class. It is a universal principle of justice, as the Qur'anic verse says,

> O ye who believe! stand out firmly for justice, as witnesses to Allah, even as against yourselves, or your parents, or your kin, and whether it be (against) rich or poor: for Allah can best protect both…(4:135).

Truth-telling is fundamental in Islam, and the Qur'an says, "And cover not Truth with falsehood, nor conceal the Truth when ye know (what it is)." (2:42). Moreover, the prophet said, "You must be truthful, for truthfulness leads to righteousness and righteousness leads to Paradise".[25]

When the responsibility for a crime is established either through voluntary truth-telling or by means of criminal investigation, the process of Transitional Justice follows the line of retribution or compensation, reconciliation, forgiveness or some other settlement based on mutual agreement. To achieve the ultimate goal of justice and community cohesion, criminals must seek repentance and forgiveness from the

---

[24] See Abdelwahab Bouhdiba and Muhammad Ma'ruf Dawalibi, *The Different Aspects of Islamic Culture: The Individual and Society in Islam* (UNESCO, 1998), 302. There is also a difference for the age of maturity and for bearing responsibility among Islamic Jurisprudence schools. Hanafi School extends the age of maturity to 18 years, while other three schools confine it to 15 years.

[25] This part of Hadith narrated by Abdallah ibn Mas'uud who said: "The Messenger of Allah said: 'You must be truthful, for truthfulness leads to righteousness and righteousness leads to Paradise. A man will keep speaking the truth and striving to speak the truth until he will be recorded with Allah as a *siddeeq* (speaker of the truth). Beware of telling lies, for lying leads to immorality and immorality leads to Hellfire. A man will keep telling lies and striving to tell lies until he is recorded with Allah as a liar" (Sahih Muslim: 4721)

victims. This repentance and forgiveness may be complemented with some form of retribution and compensation.

Elements of the Criminal Punishment in Islam

Punishment is justified in Islamic Sharia by deterrence, retribution, and rehabilitation and to protect the society by incapacitating the offender. The legal framework of Islam has to protect the five universal objectives of Sharia *(Maqadid al-Sharia):* the life, the religion, the reason, the lineage and the property. All crimes fall in the category of crimes against Allah and crimes against human being besides being a transgression of Allah's boundaries. Punishments of these crimes are divided into Hudud, Qisas and Ta'zir.

Hudud Punishments in Islam

The Hudud punishments in general are not part of Transitional Justice; however, they are important to discuss here as part of the overview of the criminal law of Islam. Penalties for Hudud crimes are divinely prescribed by the basic sources of Islam: The Qur'an and the Prophetic traditions. They are the claims of Allah and thus, cannot be waived by a judge and authorities. It includes all forms of theft *(Sariqa)*, armed robbery *(Hirabah)*, illegal sexual intercourse *(Zina)*, false accusation of adultery *(Qadf)*, use of toxicants *(isti'mal al-khamr)*, apostasy *(Ridah)* and rebellion *(Baghy)*.[26] For these types of crimes, the Qur'an prescribes specific punishments, because they abuse and transgress one of the five universal objectives of Islam. For instance, to preserve life, the law of retribution is prescribed, which the following Qur'anic verses clearly states, "In the Law of Equality [Qisas]

---

[26] Detailed studies on *Hudud* in Islam and their punishments, see Muhammad Ata Alsaid, *The Hudud: The Hudud are the Seven Specific Crimes in Islamic Criminal Law and their mandatory Punishments* (Kuala Lumpur: Muhammad Ata al Sid Sid Ahmad, 1995).

there is (saving of) Life to you, o ye men of understanding; that ye may restrain yourselves" (2:179).

Moreover, Islam prohibits forceful conversion from one religion to another.[27] However, after accepting Islam voluntarily, there is the law of apostasy in order to protect Islamic belief. On this issue, classical Islamic scholars reached consensus on the punishment for apostasy in the light of their historical and political contexts, although the Qur'an does not prescribe clear cut punishment for this.[28] There are, however, many Prophetic traditions on this issue, such as the following:

> The blood of a Muslim who confesses that none has the right to be worshipped but Allah and that I am His Messenger cannot be shed except in three cases: in Qisas for murder, a married person who commits illegal sexual intercourse and the one who reverts from Islam (Apostate) and leaves the Muslims.[29]

Another prophetic tradition says, "Whoever changes his religion, kill him".[30] However, some contemporary legal scholars are revisiting this issue with great caution in the light of the new circumstances.[31]

Furthermore, to preserve reason, all types of intoxicants such alcohol and similar substances are prohibited, and punishment for their consumption is prescribed. The punishment for using intoxicants is 40 or 80 lashes because of the various narrations from the Prophet Muhammad and

---

[27] See the Qur'anic verse: "*Let there be no compulsion in religion: Truth stands out clear from Error: whoever rejects evil and believes in Allah hath grasped the most trustworthy hand-hold that never breaks…*" (2: 256).
[28] The cited verse for the punishment for the apostasy is the following: "*But (even so), if they repent, establish regular prayers, and practice regular charity,- they are your brethren in Faith: (thus) do We explain the Signs in detail, for those who understand. But if they violate their oaths after their covenant, and taunt you for your Faith, - fight ye the chiefs of Unfaith: for their oaths are nothing to them: that thus they may be restrained.*" (9: 11, 12).
[29] Sahih al-Bukhari, chapter 9: 17.
[30] Ibid., chapter 30: 17.
[31] For example, Dr. Ahmad Al-Raysouni,*a professor of principles of Islamic jurisprudence at Moroccan University*, is quoted saying, "*If Allah [the Most High] did not coerce His creation towards belief in Him, nor did He permit His Prophet to do so instructing him, then how could He allow, or order, the leaders of the Muslims to force one to remain as a Muslim or return to it under the threat of death?*" see http://www.suhaibwebb.com/islam-studies/islam-101/misconceptions/freedom-of-religion-and-apostasy-in-islam-by-dr-ahmed-raysuni; accessed on Jan. 31, 2012.

different opinions of the Islamic scholars which offers different numbers of lashes.³²

In addition, to preserve a person's lineage, the penalty for fornication and false accusation is enacted. For instance, on the punishment for fornication, the Qur'an says,

> The woman and the man guilty of adultery or fornication, - flog each of them with a hundred stripes: Let not compassion move you in their case, in a matter prescribed by Allah, if ye believe in Allah and the Last Day: and let a party of the Believers witness their punishment.(24:2).

On false accusations, the Qur'an says,

> And those who launch a charge against chaste women, and produce not four witnesses (to support their allegations),- flog them with eighty stripes; and reject their evidence ever after: for such men are wicked transgressors (24:4).

It is clear from these two verses that 100 and 80 lashes are, respectively, the punishment for fornication and false accusation. Moreover, the punishment of stoning to death pre-married adulterers is a consensus of the Islamic scholars based on numerous Prophetic traditions and practices common during the life of the Prophet Muhammad (PBUH).³³ However, proving a case of adulterous behavior was made so complicated (i.e. one must produce four credible witnesses who actually witnessed the intercourse) that proof became close to unattainable.³⁴

Finally, to preserve wealth, the punishment for theft and armed robbery according to the Qur'an is in the following verse:

---

³² Abu l-Hasan Ali b. Muhammad al-Mawardi, *al-Ahkam al-Sultaniyya wa al-wilayat al-Diniyya* (Cairo: Maktaba wa Matba'a Mustafa al-Babi al-Halabi, 1966), 228–229.

³³ There is no verse in the Qur'an for the punishment of stoning adulterers. New interpretation on this matter is emerging which articulates that stoning punishment has been relaced with other forms of punishments. see the interview of Sheikh Yusuf Al-Qaradawi on this subject on june 22, 2016. Available from http://m.arabi21.com/story/917157/

³⁴ See the Qur'anic verse, *"And those who launch a charge against chaste women, and produce not four witnesses (to support their allegations),- flog them with eighty stripes; and reject their evidence ever after: for such men are wicked transgressors"* (24: 4).

> As to the thief, male or female, cut off his or her hands: a punishment by way of example, from Allah, for their crime: and Allah is exalted in power. (5:38).

Moreover, armed robbery *(Hirabah)* refers to robbery with violence, and its penalty varies according to whether the robber killed or injured the victim or simply robbed (or threatened to rob) him or her. The Qur'an gives various options for punishments ranging from death penalties, crucifixion, cutting off hands and foot on the opposite sides and exile. The Qur'an says,

> The punishment of those who wage war against Allah and His Messenger, and strive with might and main for mischief through the land is: execution, or crucifixion, or the cutting off of hands and feet from opposite sides, or exile from the land: that is their disgrace in this world, and a heavy punishment is theirs in the Hereafter (5:33).

It is noteworthy to mention here that the crime of rape is not classified in the category of Zina (consensual adultery), but rather in the crime of armed robbery *(Hirabah)*.[35]

Although Hudud are crimes that infringe on the rights of Allah, some of them infringe on both the rights of Allah and the rights of individuals. For instance, thefts are crimes that involve taking away the properties of other individuals, and a settlement could be concluded between the two parties before coming to courts.[36] Moreover, false accusation of adultery is considered as violating the rights of the individual, and this could also be settled between the two parties.[37] Consequently,

---

[35] Rape is classified under *Hirabah* according to the opinion of the Islamic scholars such as Ibn Hazm, Al-Dasuqi, Ibn 'Arabi. Sayyid Sabiq described *Hirabah* as *"a single person or group of people causing public disruption, killing, forcibly taking property or money, attacking or raping women (hatk al 'arad), killing cattle, or disrupting agriculture."* See Sayed Sabiq, *Fiqh-us-Sunnah,10 Edition* (Mecca: Bab al- log, 1993), 450.

[36] See the Hadith of the Prophet: *"Forgive each other among you for Hudud offences (if committed). When an offence of Hudud reaches (informed to or tried by) me, it becomes enforceable."* See Al-Tibrizi, *Mishkat al-Masabih* Vol.2 (Dimashq: al-Maktab al-Islami,1961), 292.

[37] There are many opinions on this issue; however, Al-Mawardi supports the possibility of settlement. See Al-Mawardi, *al-Ahkam al-Sultaniyyah*, 219, 231.

Transitional Justice treats crimes committed against human beings and in this case individuals and communities have total discretion to seek either retribution or compensation. Therefore, Hudud punishments, which are limited to the rights of Allah, are out of Transitional Justice's mechanisms; whereas, crimes that touch on human rights are included within the sphere of Transitional Justice.

Qisas and Ta'zir Punishments

Qisas punishments deal with all forms of murder and injuries that were committed intentionally. The law of Qisas is mentioned in the Qur'an as giving life to the Muslims: "In the Law of Equality [Qisas] there is (saving of) Life to you, o ye men of understanding; that ye may restrain yourselves" (2:179).

Contrary to the Western Criminal Laws, Qisas crimes are dealt as civil cases, and four stakeholders are involved. These are the state (authority), the community (tribe, clan, family), the victims and perpetuators. The state has the full right to lay on additional punishments such as imprisonment, while the victim or his inheritors in case of his death has the final say on whether to choose the option of retribution or compensation. In this process, the two parts of the case are involved and their two families and communities. According to the teachings of Islam, retribution is applicable and permitted when the killing or injury was done intentionally, but accidental killing or injuring is excluded.

In the case of unintentional killings or injuries, blood money compensations (Diya) are applied. The following verse puts forth retaliation with equal measurement saying:

> We ordained therein for them: "Life for life, eye for eye, nose or nose, ear for ear, tooth for tooth, and wounds equal for equal." But if any one remits the retaliation by way of charity, it is an act of atonement for himself. And if any fail to judge by (the light of)

what Allah hath revealed, they are (No better than) wrong-doers (5:45).

Moreover, the next verse also offers a detailed ruling of juridical equivalence in retribution and the option of forgiveness and compensation by paying blood money.

> O ye who believe! the law of equality is prescribed to you in cases of murder: the free for the free, the slave for the slave, the woman for the woman. But if any remission(s) is made by the brother of the slain, then grant any reasonable demand, and compensate him with handsome gratitude, this is a concession and a Mercy from your Lord. After this whoever exceeds the limits shall be in grave penalty(2:178).

Qisas punishment is well known and applied in the traditional Somali system of justice. Both elements of retribution and compensation have been practiced among various communities. The same practice remains intact as part of customary law known as *Xeer* system. In particular, after the collapse of the state in 1991, the available system of justice was Islamic criminal laws, and it took the center stage beside *Xeer* system of laws. *Xeer* mostly emphasizes compensation and reconciliation whenever communal violence erupts. However, with the growth of the Islamic movements, retribution was widely used. Today, retribution as a form of justice is prevalent in the Transitional Federal Government, Puntland and Somaliland. It also prevalent in the regions under the control of *Al-Shabab* and *Ahlu-Sunna wa al-Jama*.[38]

The Ta'zir punishment includes all laws that Allah left for human beings to make their judgment in changing time, space and circumstances. It covers a wide range of punishments such as verbal reprimands, public exposure, corporal

---

[38] For example, the military court of the transitional government executed a soldier on Jan. 23, 20012 who had killed other soldier. See http://www.raxanreeb.com/?p=128871(accessed on Jan, 27, 2012). Moreover, *Qisas* executions routinely occur in Al-Shabab controlled regions of Somalia. See http://sonna.net/content/xarakada-al-shabaab-oo-xukun-qisaas-ah-ku-fulisay-nin-dil-horay-ugu-geystay%E2%80% (accessed on Jan.27, 2012). Ahal-Sunna also exercises *Qisas*. See http://www.kulmiyenews.com/?nid=1861(accessed on Jan.27, 2012).

punishment, imprisonment, exiling or even execution for serious cases.[39] Thus, the vast majority of punishments is discretionary in nature and is determined according to the society's local culture. Crimes may infringe on the rights of Allah, such as by breaking fast and not performing daily prayer. It may also be infringing on the rights of individuals (for example by insulting a person).

Making laws in areas not prescribed by Allah is left for the states and authorities. These laws, however, must be compliant with the Islamic legal framework and the universal purposes of Islam that balances the right of society with the right of the individuals. These two forms of punishment – Qisas and Ta'zir – are parts of Transitional Justice. Besides, the possibility for criminal persecution of the perpetrators, Islamic scholars such as Ibrahim Ibn Farhun have emphasized the importance of reconciliation, in particular when faced with certain types of conflict and cases. For instance, when the disputants are relatives or people of authority who are respected in the community, when there is a high possibility of increased animosity between the litigants and their families, or when the nature of the case is such that it is very difficult to make a decision.[40]

Restorative Transitional Justice: Reconciliation, Repentance and Forgiveness

Restorative justice is about restoring both the victim and perpetrator of the crimes back into harmony with the community. Unlike retributive mechanisms such as Qisas and Ta'zir which are applied through courts, restorative justice empowers the victims. The spirit of Islamic law accords restorative justice because it attaches values of reconciliation, repentance and forgiveness to the criminal punishments. Since

---

[39] One such crime is drug trafficking, which is punished in some Muslim countries (e.g. Iran) by the death penalty.
[40] Ibrahim ibn Ali Ibn Farhun, Abdallah Ali Ibn Salmun,*Kitab Tabşirat al-Hukkam fi Uşul al-Aqdiyah wa-manahij al-Ahkam*(Dar al-Kutub al-Ilmiyah, 1983).

the ultimate objective of the application of Sharia is to achieve a just society and harmony, it does not focus on adjudication alone but rather combines it with reconciliation. Furthermore, it should be noted that all Transitional Justice mechanisms in Islam are always linked with the spirit of piety and God's rewards in the hereafter. Therefore, a combination of restoration and retribution is applied to conflicts and crimes that occur between communities and individuals.

> The first step in the reconciliation process is acknowledgment of responsibility and confession by the aggressor, even if accompanied by an excuse for the incursion. In the Somali cultural context, this is critical for the success of traditional conflict resolution and is the first question to be presented before addressing other fundamental issues. The declaration of responsibility, 'I am an aggressor,' by the respective party is seen as representing more than a third of the path to a solution.[41]

Reconciliation: Primary Objective of Restorative Transitional Justice

Reconciliation is used as a restorative component of Transitional Justice that differs from criminal proceedings. It involves three approaches: religious, human rights and communal. Here, our objective is the religious approach, in particular the Islamic conception of reconciliation (*al-sulh*), which means to reconcile and make peace with the opponent. In the Somali language, the term is derived from the Arabic roots called "*Sulux and Mussalaxa*").[42] According to Sayyid, Sabiq, *sulh* means to settle any dispute.[43] It also means an agreement between two parties in the process of settling their disputes. The spirit of reconciliation commences with acknowledgement of the committed crimes, known in Somalia as "*dambi qirasho*", repentance "*tooba keen*" from the

---

[41] Inter-peace, *in Search for Peace: Somali Programme* (The Center for Research and Dialogue), 20
[42] Nasimah Hussin and Ramizah Wan Muhammad, *Sulh in Islamic Criminal Law*, 1
[43] Sayyid Sabiq, *Fiqh al-Sunnah*, *Vol.3* (Dar al-Diyan li al-Turath, Kaherah, 1990), 389.

perpetrators and forgiveness "*cafis*" from the victims.[44] It is a well-known conflict-resolution mechanism in the Somali society. In the traditional society, in cases of community conflict, there is either reconciliation or continued fighting, because there is no central authority or system of courts similar to the modern state system to adjudicate disputes. Its mechanism and processes are founded on forging a settlement based on compromise between disputants.

The Qur'an generally recommends reconciliation and promises great rewards of Allah for those who accept reconciliations and for those who are engaged in reconciliation and mediation between people. The following Qur'anic verse demonstrates the importance of reconciliation and its processes:

> If a wife fears cruelty or desertion on her husband's part, there is no blame on them if they arrange an amicable settlement between themselves; and such settlement is best; even though men's souls are swayed by greed. But if ye do good and practise self-restraint, Allah is well-acquainted with all that ye do (4:128).

The narrated prophetic tradition said:

> Should I inform you of something that is higher in virtue than fasting, praying and charity?' They said, 'Yes O Messenger of God.' Then the Prophet said, 'To make reconciliation between peoples that are in conflict.[45]

Moreover, the topic of reconciliation in Islam is included in the section of "Jihad" in the book of Prophetic tradition (*Sahih al-Bukhari*). Among the prophetic traditions cited here is the following: "To make reconciliation is a righteous act of charity."

---

[44] Erin Mobekk, "Transitional Justice in Post-Conflict Society – Approaches to Reconciliation, 2005", 262. Available from http://www.gsdrc.org/go/display&type=Document&id=1685 (Accessed on January 22, 2012).
[45] Nasiruddin al-Albani, Sahih Al-Ja"mi" al-Saghir, Hadith no. 436.

Further, the Prophet warns against resorting only to adjudication, which sometimes makes mistakes because of the eloquence of one of the litigants. The Prophet said:

> Allah's Apostle said: 'I am only a human being, and you people (opponents) come to me with your cases; and it may be that one of you can present his case eloquently in a more convincing way than the other, and I give my verdict according to what I hear. So if ever I judge (by error) and give the right of a brother to his other (brother) then he (the latter) should not take it, for I am giving him only a piece of Fire.[46]

Thus, the trial process is not the only truth-finding mechanism that will lead to substantive justice. It can be subverted by the imperfect nature of man; therefore, it should be avoided whenever possible.

However, in the case of communal violence or civil conflict, Islam offers comprehensive mechanisms and clear approaches. It emphasizes *"peace with justice"* as the ultimate goal, and reconciliation as the best mechanism to reach that objective. It also gives guidance on how to deal with aggressors and rejecters of the peace. It calls for the use of military intervention to ensure the compliance of the perpetrators to the ceasefire and negotiated settlement. This intervention force is even permitted to fight alongside the victims against the aggressors. There is no room for neutral positions between aggressors and victims as seen in the following Qur'anic verse:

> If two parties among the Believers fall into a quarrel, make ye peace between them: but if one of them transgresses beyond bounds against the other then fight ye (all) against the one that transgresses until it complies with the command of Allah; but if it complies then make peace between them with justice and be fair: for Allah loves those who are fair (and just) (49: 9).

---

[46] See translation of Sahih al-Bukhari, *Volume 9, Book 89, Number 281*.

One of the mechanisms of reconciliation is arbitration, which occurs when a third person selected by the parties is engaged to resolve their disputes either through conciliation or adjudication. The disputing parties use an arbitrator in order to work towards a settlement in case they fail to conclude a deal by themselves. Arbitration differs from reconciliation in two respects. Firstly, reconciliation is an amicable settlement that may be reached between the litigants with or without a third party, while in arbitration the appointment of a third party is indispensable. Secondly, the agreement of reconciliation is not binding unless it has taken place before the court, whereas, arbitration is binding without court intervention.

Repentance and Forgiveness

Repentance and forgiveness are directly linked to one another. Feelings of regret and guilt are natural reflections of sinning if the individual who has sinned has a pious conscience. After committing a sin, a person who fears Allah would feel a sense of despondency. He has to seek forgiveness, which is considered one of the signs of piety in Islam. In the Qur'an, Allah says,

> Say: O my Servants who have transgressed against their souls! Despair not of the Mercy of Allah. for Allah forgives all sins: for He is Oft-Forgiving, Most Merciful (39: 53).

Repentance is a good sign of true piety and faithfulness since human beings are inducible by various worldly means which leads to the transgression of Allah's boundaries and committing sins. It is only through repentance that one can wipe out those sins and gradually free oneself from the clutches of the ego. Therefore, repentance is the most noble and beloved form of obedience in the eyes of Allah, and He loves those who repent. Hence, the repenting person reaches the status of being amongst the beloved through his repentance.[47] Moreover, repentance brings about humbleness and a sense of submission to Allah. Allah says in the Qur'an,

> Those who invoke not, with Allah, any other God, nor slay such life as Allah has made sacred except for just cause, nor commit fornication; - and any that does this (not only) meets punishment. (But) the Penalty on the Day of Judgment will be doubled to him, and he will dwell therein in ignominy, - Unless he repents, believes, and works righteous deeds, for Allah will change the evil of such persons into good, and Allah is Oft-Forgiving, Most Merciful (25: 68-70).

Moreover, Allah also says,

> And those who, having done something to be ashamed of, or wronged their own souls, earnestly bring Allah to mind, and ask for forgiveness for their sins, - and who can forgive sins except Allah.- and are never obstinate in persisting knowingly in (the wrong) they have done (3:135).

Is any crime too big to be forgiven by Allah? The answer to this question can be found in the following sacred prophetic tradition "Hadith Qudsi":[48]

> Allah has said: 'O Son of Adam, so long as you call upon Me and ask of Me, I shall forgive you for what you have done, and I shall not mind. O Son of Adam, were your sins to reach the clouds of the sky and were you then to ask forgiveness of Me, I would forgive you. O Son of Adam, were you to come to me with sins as great as the earth, and were you then to face Me ascribing no partners to Me, I would bring you forgiveness nearly as great as it.

However, transgressions that infringe on the rights of human beings require their forgiveness, even though Allah

---

[47] Allah said: "For Allah loves those who turn to Him constantly and He loves those who keep themselves pure and clean" (2: 222)

[48] The difference between the normal prophetic tradition (*Hadith*) which is defined as a narration of the words or acts of the Prophet and *Hadith Qudsi* (or Sacred Hadith) is important. The later one is narration from the Prophet Muhammad where he relates what Allah has said (says) or did (does). It is different from the Qur'an which is completely words of Allah.

forgives all sins. The following case study demonstrates the extent of Allah's forgiveness in the case of sincere repentance.

Case Study 1: Repentance and Forgiveness

An exceptional example of repentance and forgiveness is given for a serial murderer as narrated in the following prophetic tradition:

> There was a man from a nation before you who killed 99 people and then made an inquiry about the most learned person on the earth. He was directed to a monk. He went to him and told him he had killed 99 people and asked if there was any chance his repentance would be accepted. The monk replied in the negative, and the man killed him [also to complete one hundred]. He then asked for the most learned man on the earth and was directed to a scholar. He told the scholar that he had killed one hundred people and asked if there were chances his repentance would be accepted. The scholar replied in the affirmative and asked, "Who stands between you and repentance? Go to such and such land. There [you will find] people devoted to the prayer and warship of Allah. Join them in worship and do not come back to your land because it is an evil place." So he went away and hardly had he covered a half of the distance when death overtook him, and there was a dispute between the angels of mercy and the angels of torment. The angels of mercy pleaded, "This man had come with repenting heart to Allah"; and the angles of punishment argued, "He never did a virtuous deed in his life." And there appeared another angel in the form of human being, and the contending angels agreed to make him an arbiter between them. The arbiter said, "Measure the distance between the two lands. He will be considered as belonging to the land to which he is nearer." They measured and found him closer to the land [land of piety] where he intended to go. So the angels of mercy collected his soul.[49]

Repentance has the following requirements: firstly, the individual must regret and confess his/her sin(s) directly to Allah, sincerely; secondly, he/she should repent of that sin(s)

---

[49] Imam Abu Zakaruya Yahya bin Sharaf An-Nawawi, *Riyad Us-Saliheen, chapter two*, 20 (Narrated by Abu-said al-Khudri and recorded by Sahih Muslim and Sahih Bukhari).

sincerely; and thirdly, he/she must intend to never do it again. To this basic processes, the Qur'an also adds that repentance should be proved by doing good deeds: "And whoever repents and does good has truly turned to Allah with an (acceptable) conversion" (25:71).

An additional requirement is attached to crimes committed against human beings that is forgiveness of these individuals

Case Study 2: Transitional Justice Mechanisms after the Conquer of Makkah

A lesson learned from the Conquest of Makkah, which is well recorded in the early history of Islam, offers a good example of Transitional Justice in Islam. Prophet Muhammad offers us an excellent example of amnesty, reconciliation and retributive justice after the mass violence. The city of Makkah was the place of birth of the Prophet Muhammad where his kinsmen and relatives settled and lived. He remained there for thirteen years after his appointment as the messenger of Allah experiencing various types of persecution from Quraish elites and some of his companions were murdered. Quraish tribe also attempted to assassinate him before he migrated to the town of Madina with his companions.

The Quraish tribe and its alliances were engaged in fierce and continual wars with the Muslims headquartered in the city of Madina and fought nearly 21 battles in 8 years.[50] In these battles, Prophet's companions and his close relatives were murdered at the hands of Makkans and their allies. After eight years, the Makkah capitulated peacefully and the Muslim army entered without substantial resistance. The Prophet advanced to the Ka'aba (the sacred Mosque of Islam in Makkah), destroying 360 (one for each tribe) idols immediately while reciting Qur'anic verse "And say: Truth has (now) arrived, and

---

[50] The most famous battles before the conquering of Makkah are Badr (624 AD, 2 Hijra), Uhud (625 AD, 3 Hijra), battle of trench (627 AD, 5 Hijra). Hijra is the Islamic calendar which starts from the migration of the Prophet from Makkah to Madina in 662 AD.

Falsehood perished: for Falsehood is (by its nature) bound to perish" (1 7: 81).

The prophet order Bilal bin Rabah, the famous black companion of the prophet to call the people to prayer and the people gathered around the Ka'aba.[51]

The Prophet gave a historic speech announcing the beginning of new era for the broken community, which was hostile to him for about 21 years. He said,

> There is no God but Allah. He has no partner. He has fulfilled His promise, granted victory to His servant and defeated the allies alone. O People of the Quraish, Allah has purified you from the arrogance of the Period of Ignorance and its flattering with ancestry. People are descended from Adam, and Adam was created out of mud.

Then he recited

> O mankind! We created you from a single (pair) of a male and a female, and made you into nations and tribes, that ye may know each other (not that ye may despise (each other). Verily the most honoured of you in the sight of Allah is (he who is) the most righteous of you. And Allah has full knowledge and is well acquainted (with all things) (49: 13).

Firstly, the Prophet declared general amnesty addressing the people: "O you people of Quraish! What do you think of the treatment that I am about to accord to you"? And they replied, "O noble brother and a son of a noble brother! We expect nothing but goodness." The Prophet said,

> I will say to you what my brother Prophet Yusuf said: "This day let no reproach be (cast) on you: Allah will forgive you, and He is the Most Merciful of those who show mercy" (12: 92)[52] ...Go your way, for you are freed ones.

---

[51] Bilal was born as a slave and was among the emancipated slaves and among early Muslims of Makka. He was known for his beautiful voice which he called people to the prayer.

[52] Prophet Yusuf (AS) was the son of Prophet Ya'qub (AS) and in the Bible he is referred to as Joseph son of Jacob. He was one of the youngest and possessed excellent character and manners. His brothers were jealous of the favour that he enjoyed in their father's eyes and planned to somehow get rid of him and threw him into the well. A caravan of traders passing by the well got

Secondly, the Prophet commanded the execution of a few persons exempting them from the general amnesty for their heinous crimes, and some of them were pardoned later.

The first comprehensive application of the Transitional Justice mechanism in the history of Islam was exercised by the Prophet Muhammad after conquering Makkah in 630 AD. The Prophet used four mechanisms; namely, criminal persecution, general amnesty, individual pardoning and institutional reform. After Conquering Makkah and experiencing mass conversion to Islam, the communities that had been at war had to be rebuild. In particular, early Muslim migrants (*al-Muhajirun*) who were forced to migrate from their homes due to the oppression and subjugation of the Makkah aristocracy had to come into new term of peace, reconciliation and wished to restore their cohesion and brotherhood. Subsequently, Prophet Muhammad applied four mechanisms of Transitional Justice. Firstly, he criminally persecuted five individuals because their heinous crimes were unpardonable.[53] Secondly, he pardoned three individuals after announcing their criminal persecution because of community intervention requesting their amnesty.[54] Thirdly, he proclaimed general amnesty to all the people of Makkah. Finally, and the most important, was the complete reform of the institutions of oppression based on the clan supremacy of Quraish. The new institutions were established based on the Islamic community "Muslim Ummah." This new institutions were built on the

---

him and sold him to some slave traders and was sold the king of Egypt and later was appointed as the minister of finance. This verse as narrates the Qur'an was his words when he was forgiving his brothers who threw his in the well.

[53] Those persecuted individuals were Abdul Uzza ibn Akhatal, Abdallah ibn Abu-Sarah (a former and close companion to the Prophet who committed treason and claimed apostasy), Maqyas ibn Sababah (a former Muslim who killed another Muslim and escaped to Makkah announcing his apostasy), Huwierith and the daughter of Akhtal (a poetess who had particularly irked Muhammad with her satires). See Safiur-Rahman Al-Mubarakpuri, *Ar-Raheeq Al Makhtum (The Sealed Nectar)* (Islamic University Al-Madinah Al-Munawwarah, 1995), 468.

[54] These pardoned individuals were Ikran bin Abijahal (fought Muslim army entering peacefully Makkah), Wahshi (the murderer of Hamza, the prophet's uncle) and Habbar (attacked the Prophets daughter, who died from the injury). See Ibid.

principles of Islam which is founded on the fact that all Muslims were equal citizens under the leadership of the prophet with the noble mission of establishing Allah's rule on earth. No supremacy of one race upon others and that all are brothers and sisters in Islam.

Islamic Transitional Justice and its applicability in Somalia

Somali people are Sunni Muslims who adhere to traditional Islam, which consists of Ash'ariyah theology, Shafiyah jurisprudence and Sufism. Sharia has been accepted and partially implemented in Somalia throughout its history. The traditional legal system is a combination of Sharia and Xeer (local customs), which vary slightly from community to community. In the traditional society, clan elders stand for the implementation of the local Xeer, while Islamic scholars are responsible for rendering religious aspects of law and related services. Therefore, at the community level, Somali people employ parallel legislations: the Sharia and local Xeer. However, with the dominance of colonialism, European laws were introduced, pushing aside many aspects of the indigenous laws at the state level, even though European law had failed to penetrate deeply into the societal space. Thus, three sources of laws are competing and cross-cutting each other in Somalia: Xeer, Islamic Sharia and secular European laws.[55]. These are:

(a) Interaction between Sharia and the State

At the national state level, secular laws dominated most aspects of life except in the domain of personal and family laws, where Sharia remained functional and Xeer also played

---

[55] These laws are not mutually exclusive. For instance, many elements of Xeer are compliant with Islamic Sharia while many modern European laws introduced in Somalia were to a certain extend considering the Islamic faith of the Somali people.

an important role.[56] The role of Sharia was gradually diminished in the Somali state. For instance, the two constitutions adopted in 1960 and 1979 agree that Islam is the religion of the state. In the first constitution of 1960, Somalis were to be governed in accordance with the general principles of Islamic Sharia (1:3). It also affirmed that

> The doctrine of Islam shall be the main source of laws of the state (50) and laws and provisions having the force of law shall conform to the Constitution and to the general principles of Islam (94:1).

Moreover, the constitution of 1960 states that

> Every person shall have the right to freedom of conscience and freely to profess his own religion; however, it shall not be permissible to spread or propagandize any religion other than the religion of Islam (29).[57]

Even though the constitutional principles were not fully implemented in the first nine years, they affirmed the indispensable role of Sharia in the state. Conversely, the Military regime that took power in 1969 adopted socialism and marginalized Islam by adopting a number of secular legislations that contradicted Islamic laws. These include the adoption of socialism and dictatorial rule, the curtailment of the citizens' freedom, the nationalization of private properties, the prohibition of women's dress code (Hijab), the abolition of Diya-paying system and the adoption of secular family law.[58] Moreover, in the second constitution of 1979, which was

---

[56] Abdurahman Abdullahi, "Women, Islamists and the Military Regime in Somalia: The Family Law and its Implications". In Markus Hoehne and Virginia Luling (eds.) *Milk and Peace, Drought and War: Somali Culture, Society and Politics* (London: Hurst & Company, 2010),137–160.

[57] After the assassination of Mr. Merlin Grove of Mennonite Mission in Somalia in July 1962 by Yasin Abdi Ahmad Ibrahim, propagating other religions in Somalia was prohibited.See Somali Constitution of 1960, article 29, which states, "Every person shall have the right to freedom of conscience and freely to profess his own religion; however, it shall not be permissible to spread or propagandize any religion other than the religion of Islam." For detailed information, see Abdurahman Abdullahi, "The Islamic Movement in Somalia: A Historical Evolution with the Case Study of Islah Movement" (A PhD thesis submitted to McGill University, 2011), 22.

[58] See Ibid.

developed after ten years of the military rule, secularization was evident to accord with the ideology of socialism. It only offered simple lip service to Islam and reconfirmed that "Islam shall be the state religion" (1: 3).

(b) The Role of Sharia after the Collapse of the State

After the collapse of the state in 1991, national secular laws disappeared from the society, and a combination of Xeer and Sharia took the center stage, reverting Somalia to the pre-colonial state of affairs. In particular, with the growth of the Islamic movement and its increased role in the society, Islamic Sharia conquered more public spaces. This drastic shift had shown its strong presence in the drafting of the Transitional Charter in the National Reconciliation Conference held in Djibouti in 2000. This charter is the most Islamized in the history of Somalia. Besides reiterating the status of Islam as it was set down in the first constitution of 1960, it included one important additional provision: this important article states that

> The Islamic Sharia shall be the basic source for national legislation and any law contradicting Islamic Sharia shall be void and null (The Transitional National Charter of 2000, article 4: 4).

This provision offers Islamic Sharia absolute and ultimate reference for all laws in Somalia. The Transitional Federal Charter that was adopted in 2004 backs away from the Islamic articles established in the Charter of Djibouti conference of 2000 because of the strong foreign influence.[59] It just reaffirms that

> Islam shall be the religion of the Somali Republic (The Transitional National Charter of 2004, article 8: 1) and that the

---

[59] The Somali Reconciliation Conference held in Kenya in 2004 was dominated by Ethiopia and its allied Somali armed groups. The charter that was adopted reflected this domination and indicates marginalization of the Somali civil society. It diminished the role of Islam and omitted some articles that had been adopted in 2000 during Djibouti Peace Conference.

Islamic Sharia shall be the basic source for national legislation (The Transitional National Charter of 2004, article 8: 2).

Although the national agenda for comprehensive application of Sharia was never implemented, various communities had attempted to create some sort of justice mechanism based on Islamic Sharia. As a result, various Islamic courts that were administered and supported by specific sub-clans opened in many locations in the southern part of Somalia. In particular, Mogadishu has experienced an Islamic court system (1991-2001) in Medina District, in the eastern part of Mogadishu under the control of Ali Mahdi Mohamed (1994-1997) and finally the formation of many Islamic courts in the various districts of Mogadishu. Some of these courts were later politicized and unified under the Union of Islamic Courts in 2006.[60] These clan-based Islamic courts applied some elements of Sharia in haphazard ways, focusing mainly on the punishment aspects of Sharia. The model of applying Sharia elements of criminal law initiated over different stages during the civil war has continued in the areas controlled by armed opposition of Al-Shabab, which controls large swaths of southern and central Somalia.[61]

At the state level, the role of Islamic Sharia was reaffirmed in 2009 when the Somalia's parliament unanimously approved the implementation of Sharia across the country.[62] The unanimous adoption of Sharia in the parliament is part of the battle between the state and the armed opposition of Al-Shabab, who both aim to win the hearts and minds of the population. The majority of the Somali population offers its support and renders legitimacy to whomever implements Sharia. However, there is no consensus among Somali Islamic

---

[60] See Cedric Barnes, SOAS and Harun Hassan, *The Rise and Fall of Mogadishu's Islamic Courts* (Chatham House, 2007), 2.
[61] Roland Marchal, "The Rise of a Jihadi Movement in a Country at War: Harakat Al-Shabab al-Mujaheddin, 2011".
[62] Somali Parliament approved the application of Sharia in Somalia in April 2009. Available from http://www.smh.com.au/world/somalia-adopts-sharia-to-counter-militias-20090419-abdl.html (accessed on 31 Jan, 2012).

scholars on how to approach Sharia implementation. Moreover, the call for application of Sharia is not accurate and the right notion is the call for completion of the application of Sharia since many elements of Sharia had been in the process of implementation in Somalia throughout its history. The process of Sharia provisions should begin with the establishment of the appropriate institutions and mechanisms to produce comprehensive studies on the status of Sharia application in Somalia. In the preparatory phase should be included programs such as raising public awareness about the Islam and the harmonization of indigenous culture and state laws with the Islamic legal framework and moral values. The completion of the application of the Sharia should be viewed as a national project and be conducted as an orderly process that avoids any hasty and slap-dash implementation. The attempts that have been made so far are generally deficient and lack such mechanisms.[63] Despite this deficiency, the process has resolved many outstanding issues, responded to the community needs for adjudication and improved security.

The following table (1) indicates the evolution of the role of Sharia in the Somali constitution making processes. It shows the ups and downs and the fluctuating role of Sharia in two periods in which "secular" nationalists rose to power: the military regime (1969-1991) and the regime of President Abdullahi Yusuf (2004-2008).

---

[63] Abdurahman Abdullahi, the Application of Sharia Law in Somalia, available at http://www.hiiraan.com/comments2-op-2009-mar-the_application_of_shari_a_laws_in_somalia.aspx, accessed on February 24, 2012

Somali Constitutions and Charters (1960-2012)	The Role of Islam in the Constitutions and Charters	Remarks
The first Constitution of Somali Republic of 1960.	"Laws and provisions having the force of laws shall conform to the Constitution and to the general principles of Islam" Article 94:1	Except personal law, all other laws did not conform to the constitutional provision and colonial legal system remained intact.
Military regime abolished the constitution and ruled the country through ordinances. There were no legislative body.	The military regime adopted socialism and forced secularism. The regime diminished the role of Islam and persecuted Islamic scholars	An example of forced secularism is abolishing many Islamic laws and execution of the Islamic scholars in 1975 for their opposition to the secular family law.
Constitution of 1979 is the constitution of the military regime.	It was an expression of socialism and Islam was mentioned as a lip service	It was against Islamic principles and values
Draft Constitution of 1989 was aimed to abolish socialism.	This draft constitution was an indication to change the course of socialism.	
Transitional National Charter of 2000 was adopted during National Reconciliation Conference in Djibouti in 2000.	This charter had a provision which states: "any law contradicting Islamic Shari'a shall be void and null".	It was not implemented because of the weakness of the government
Transitional National Charter of 2004 was adopted during National Reconciliation Conference in Kenya in 2004.	This charter removed the Islamic provision of the charter of 2000. In 2009, the parliament unanimously adopted Islamic Shari'a	It was not implemented because of the weakness of the government

Table 1: The historical role of Sharia in the Somali Constitutions and Charters

(c) Introduction of Multiple Schools of Jurisprudence

There are no apparent variations of Sharia applicability inside Somalia except for minor jurisprudence issues, which crosscuts local customs of various communities. However, it is noteworthy that local customs that do not contradict with the spirit of Islam could be incorporated in the jurisprudence. Besides these minor issues, variations can be observed between traditional jurisprudence school and modern development of Islam which have growing influence in the society. The modern development of Islam consists of three main persuasions which had appeared on the scene after independence in 1960 introducing other jurisprudence schools. This modern development of Islam was influenced by similar persuasions in the Muslim world and by Somalia's interaction with it. The major movements are the Salafia movement, the Muslim Brotherhood and the Tablighi Jama'a. Although these persuasions advocate for the implementation of Sharia in the modern Muslim state and society, they nevertheless, differ in their approaches and in the kind of societies they aspire to establish. Understanding these persuasions and their particular jurisprudence schools is very important to clearly present the possibilities of Transitional Justice based on the Sharia law with subtle different interpretations.

Traditional Islam follows Shafiyah jurisprudence, which is one of the four major Sunni schools of jurisprudence and rooted in the methodology and teachings of Abu Abdallah al-Shafi'i (767–820).[64] Al-Shafi'i provided a framework for deducting Islamic laws that permits independent and locally based legal systems. The four Sunni legal schools kept within the general framework and methodology that Shafi'i initiated. The Somali people mainly adhere to the Shafi'i school that was historically introduced through its connection with Yemen Islamic education centers.[65] Moreover, Somalis combine Shafiyah jurisprudence with Sufism, which appeared in the Islamic urban centers when Muslims indulged in luxurious lifestyles under the influence of other cultures. Its roots are argued to be linked to the practices of Prophet Muhammad and the early generations of companions and followers.

---

[64] Muhammad ibn Idris al-Shafi'i, *Islamic Jurisprudence: Shafi'i's Risala*, trans. by Majid Khadduri (Baltimore: The Johns Hopkins Press, 1961).
[65] The historic town of Zabid in Yemen was the center of Islamic learning where most of the famous Somali scholars were educated. For example, Mawlanaa Abdirahman bin Mohamud (d. 1874), who is the founder of Ahmadiyah branch of Rahmaniyah was educated in Zabid. See Abdurahman Abdullahi, The Islamic Movement in Somalia, 62.

However, its systematization into organized brotherhoods didn't appear until the eleventh century.

Abu Hamed al- Ghazali (1058–1111) was the famous scholar who attempted to combine Sufism and Islamic jurisprudence in his works.[66] He argued that Sufism originated from the Qur'an and is compatible with Islamic thought. In Somalia, Sufi Islam has long been the most important form of religious identification in the country. Its tremendous influence is exercised through its two main brotherhoods: Qadiriyah and Ahmadiyah.[67] The modern manifestation of Sufism has appeared recently under the name of "Ahl-Sunna wa Al-Jama" as a reaction to the desecration of the tombs of the prominent Islamic scholars by Al-Shabab.[68]

The Salafia persuasion appeared in Somalia in second half of the twentieth century and grew exponentially in the 1980s.[69] The terminology of Salafia is highly contentious and is used differently by various schools and scholars.[70] However, the group who identifies with Salafism places principal importance on preaching idealized *Tawhid* (monotheism). It was introduced to Somalia as part of the rising influence of Saudi

---

[66] *The Revival of the Religious Sciences (Ihya ulum al-din)* is the famous work authored by Al-Ghazali which combines fiqh and Sufism. This work is one of the great works and was published widely by many publishers and was translated to many languages.
[67] There are two main Sufi orders in Somalia: Qadiriyah and Ahmadiyah. Each Sufi order has its local offshoots. Qadiriyah has two main branches, Zayli'iyah and Uweysiyah. Zayli'iyah was founded by Sheikh Abdirahman al-Saylici (1815–1882), while Uweysiyah was founded by the spiritual master Sheikh Aweys ibn Ahmad al-Barawe (1846–1907). Axmadiyah also has three offshoots in Somalia: Rahmaniyah, Salihiyah, and Dandarawiyah. Rahmaniyah was founded by Maulana Abdurahman ibn Mohamud (d. 1874). Salihiyah has two branches: a southern branch introduced by Sheikh Muhammad Guled al-Rashidi (d. 1918) and a northern branch by Sayyid Mohammad Abdulle Hassan (1856–1920). Dandarawiyah was introduced by Sayyid Adan Ahmad and has a limited following in northern Somalia. See Abdurahman Abdullahi, The Islamic Movement, 52.
[68] On desecration of Sufi tombs, see article available from http://allafrica.com/stories/201003231408.html (accessed on 03 Jan., 2012).
[69] Sheikh Nur Ali Olow (1918–1995) was a pioneer and prominent scholar who relentlessly preached methodology of Salafism in Somalia for 60 years (1935–1995).
[70] As a general rule, Muslim scholars accept and follow the understanding and methodology used by the first three generations of scholars to interpret Islam, and also look to them as their role models. In this sense, all Muslims cherish and adore Salafism; however, there are many groups that claim to belong to a particular school of "Salafia." Detractors of this school call them Wahabiyah, linking them to the teachings of Muhammad Ibn Abd al-Wahhab (1703–1792), an Islamic scholar highly popular in Saudi Arabia and other Gulf States.

Arabia in the global politics, and it spread into Somalia through students who graduated from Saudi Islamic universities who were taught Hanbali jurisprudence. Moreover, Somali migrant labor force during the economic boom of the 1970s also adopted Hanbali jurisprudence which they have experienced during their stay in Saudi Arabia.[71] Many graduates of the Saudi Islamic universities were employed by Saudi Islamic institutions to spread Salafism in Somalia. These graduates were provided with enormous resources such as ample Islamic literature, new spacious mosques and other incentives like scholarships and trainings to their followers. As a result, Hanbali jurisprudence spread rapidly in Somalia. Historically, Hanbali Jurisprudence came into prominence under the teachings of its greatest exponent, ibn Taimiyah (1263–1328) and later through the teachings of Sheikh Muhammad Abd al-Wahhab (1703–1792). Hanbali Jurisprudence was founded by Ahmed Ibn Hanbali (780–855) and its adherents are famous for their strenuous conflict with the adherents of Shafiyah jurisprudence in many insignificant aspects of jurisprudence.

The Muslim Brotherhood (MB), founded in 1928 by Hassan al-Banna in Egypt, reached the Horn of Africa in 1933.[72] However, in 1953 the Muslim Brotherhood ideology was introduced in Mogadishu, the capital city of Somalia, through Egyptian teachers and then via Somali students who graduated from the Sudanese, Egyptian and Saudi universities. The MB, promoting Muslim unity among various groups, adopted the slogan, "We should unite upon that which we agree, and excuse each other in that which we disagree".

In this context, followers of MB methodology avoid divisive Islamic discourses on doctrinal matters and legal

---

[71] Approximately 250,000 Somalis have migrated to Gulf countries after the Somali/Ethiopian war of 1977/78. See David Laitin and Said Samatar, *Somalia: Nation in Search of a State* (Boulder: Westview Press, 1987), 145.

[72] Abdallah Aqil, *Min I'lam al-Da'wa wa al-Harakah al-Islamiyah al-Muasirah* (Dar al-Tawzi wa al-Nashr al-Islāmyah. Qāhira, 2000), 380, quoted from "Jaridat al-Ikhwan al-Muslimun", 24/6/1933.

aspects within its society. Indeed, its main agenda is to create an atmosphere of collaboration between various Islamic groups and organizations for the advantage of the bigger goals: the promotion of Islam in the society, and its application at the state level. Therefore, the MB respects Shafiyah jurisprudence since the traditional jurisprudence is Shafiyah, MB promotes to follow it.[73] However, it does not create conflict against other schools of jurisprudence; it is flexible and tolerant to all groups.

The Tablighi Jama originated from the Indian subcontinent where it emerged in 1926. This Jama does not focus on political reform and is generally a quietist movement constituting of a large group of Islamic preachers in Somalia. The Jama uses a simplified approach of calling for Islam by sending a group of people to various cities, villages and locations to propagate Islam. The procedures of the call for Islam started with calling people to the congregation prayers in the mosques and then inviting them to stay and listen to their Islamic message after prayers. Their message includes advocating six main principles: One-ness of God (*Taw'hid*), five daily ritual prayers (*Salah)*, knowledge and remembrance of God (*'Ilm and dikr*), respect for every Muslim (*Ikram i-Muslim*), commendation of intention and sincerity (*Ikhlas i-niyah*) and sparing time (*Tafriq i-wiqt*).[74] The Jama have succeeded in influencing the uneducated masses because of their simplicities, community spirit and openness. However, in Somalia, the Jama have introduced Hanafi jurisprudence, which is prevalent in the Indian subcontinent. The Hanafi jurisprudence was founded by Abu Hanifa an-Nu'man (699–

---

[73]Hassan al-Banna, *The Message of Teachings*, article 7, says, "Any Muslim who has not reached the level to understand the different branches of Islamic jurisprudence may follow one of the four great Imams of this religion." The full text is available from http://web.youngmuslims.ca/online_library/books/tmott/index.htm#understanding (accessed on Jan. 20, 2012).
[74]See Jan A. Ali, *Tabligh Jama'at: A trans-national movement of Islamic faith regeneration* (European Journal of Economic and Political Studies. IJIPS-3, (SI), 2010), (103–131), 112.

767) and was developed to a large extent by Abu-Yusuf and Muhammad al-Shaybani (749/50–805[75]

Islamic Persuasions	Schools of Jurisprudence (Madhab)
Traditional Sufi Islam (Qadiriyah and Ahmadiyah)	Shafi'i Jurisprudence
Muslim Brotherhood (Islah, Wahdah, Ikhwan (Aala-Sheikh)	Tolerant to all jurisprudence schools, although prefer Shafi'i Jurisprudence.
Salafia (Academic Salafism, political Salafism "Al-Itihad, Al-Itisam," Jihadi Salafism "Al-Shabaab" and neo-Salafia "La-jama'a."	Claim non-affiliated to schools of jurisprudence while propagating Hanbali Jurisprudence and are intolerant of some aspects of Shafiyah.[76]
Tablighi Jama	Adhere to Hanafi Jurisprudence and are tolerant to other jurisprudences.

Table 2: Islamic persuasions and their jurisprudence schools

To sum up, Somalia adheres not only to the traditional Shafi'i school of jurisprudence but also other schools of jurisprudence are active such as Hanbali and Hanafi schools. In the areas where Salafia persuasions are strong, such as Puntland and some regions of Somaliland, Hanbali jurisprudence is prominent. On the other hand, in the central regions and in southern Somalia, traditional Islam and Shafi'i schools of jurisprudence are very strong. Therefore, any implementation of Sharia in Somalia – and in particular Transitional Justice mechanisms and processes – should consider the multiple schools of Islamic jurisprudence. As a result, the best approach may be to use comparative jurisprudence instead of one particular school.

---

[75] Al-Shaybani is considered the father of Muslim International law. He is a preeminent scholar of Hanfi School of jurisprudence and a disciple of Abu-Hanifa and Abu-Yusuf.
[76] Salafia in Somalia *"introduced some aspects of Hanbali jurisprudence, mixing it with other jurisprudences under the pretext of not following a specific school of jurisprudence."* See Abdurahman Abdullahi, The Islamic Movement, 28.

Conclusion

This paper has examined Transitional Justice Framework and mechanisms from an Islamic perspective. Methodologically, it relies mainly on the primary sources of Islam: The Qur'an and Prophet Traditions. At the beginning, it offered an overview of the theoretical framework on the Islamic Sharia, its basic concepts, its scope and classifications. Then, it explores Transitional Justice mechanisms of Islamic Sharia examining various punishments such as Hudud, Qisas and Ta'zir. It became evident that most Hudud punishment does not belong to the Transitional Justice mechanism, whereas Qisas, and Ta'zir as indispensable components. Elements of restorative justice such as reconciliation, repentance and forgiveness were also investigated and a case study of an exceptional case of repentance and forgiveness was presented. Also, a case study of comprehensive Transitional Justice mechanism applied by the Prophet Muhammad is produced by studying the incident of conquering Makkah in 630 AD. Finally, this paper explores interactions between Sharia and the State and the growing role of Sharia after the collapse of the state. It also discussed the impact of Islamism in introducing various schools of jurisprudence which entails using comparative Islamic jurisprudence.

Finally, the application of Transitional Justice is indispensable after the long conflict and unaddressed gross violations of human rights since 1969 in Somalia. This is very important to reverse the culture of impunity and to restore individual responsibility for the crimes instead of communities and clans. Islamic Sharia provides both retributive and restorative mechanisms applicable in Somalia. It is acceptable to the overwhelming majority of population and offers the best option if combined with traditional customs prudently.

II

Conceptions of Transitional Justice in Somalia: Findings of Field Research in Mogadishu

Introduction

Before the emergence of the independent Somali state in 1960, violence within and between Somali clans were typically resolved by traditional authorities using conflict resolution mechanisms based on customary law (Xeer) combined with Islamic Shari'a. These mechanisms were administered without reference to the modern concepts of Transitional Justice and Human Rights (HRs) found in secular and international law. However, in the process of state-building, low intensity violations of human rights perpetrated by the state security apparatus occurred with impunity. The intensity of violations increased in the early 1980s with the rise of armed confrontation between opposition movements and the Somali state.[1] In these new circumstance, the nature of human rights violations and the accountability of their perpetrators extended beyond the prerogatives of the traditional authorities. All sides in the conflict were guilty of committing gross violations of HRs, including the targeting of civilian populations because of their clan affiliation. Following the collapse of the state in 1991, the motives, nature, and actors changed significantly. Clan-based armed militias fought each other from corner to corner of the country, causing havoc and committing gross violations of HRs against civilian populations. Those violations were not limited to the actions of Somali non-state actors—i.e, warlords, Al-Itihad, Union of Islamic Courts and Al-Shabab—but also implicated external actors: the United Nation Operations in Somalia (UNOSOM (1992-1995),

---

[1] Early armed factions were Somali Salvation Democratic Front (SSDF), Somali National Movement (SNM), United Somali Congress (USC) and Somali Patriotic Movement (SPM).

Ethiopia's military, African Union Mission in Somalia (AMISOM), and others.[2]

Strange enough, despite the many violations of HRs taking place in Somalia, 'Transitional Justice' was not incorporated as part of the international plan for assisting the Somali peace-building process.[3] Many victims of the civil war felt bitter over what they perceived as the indifference of the international community to the gross violations of human rights committed by known individuals. Moreover, it seemed to many Somalis that the culture of impunity was encouraged by the international community which privileged perpetrators of violence for high political positions in various transitional governments while ignoring their human rights records.[4] Such defective approaches were very much evident in the policies of UN agencies and even in the paucity of academic literature on the subject of Transitional Justice for Somalia.

This paper was part of a larger research project on the conception of Transitional Justice in Somalia and Ethiopia's Somali Region.[5] The rationale behind this research emanates from a deep conviction that understanding the views of the local population on the acceptable modalities of Transitional Justice for resolving their grievances is a necessary precondition for restoring faith in the system and averting inappropriate top-down or externally driven Transitional

---

[2] UNOSOM was led by the United States and was accepted by the UN and made possible through United Nations Security Council Resolution 794. On the evening of 4 December 1992, US forces landed in Mogadishu. AMISOM is the regional peacekeeping mission in Somalia launched in 2007 by the African Union with the approval of the UN. Other countries include Eritrea and some European fishing companies, as well as those international companies which dumped nuclear waste within Somalia's territorial marine border.

[3] For instance, the mandate of the African Union Mission in Somalia does include a Transitional Justice component. See Margherita Zuin, "A Model for Transitional Justice for Somalia," *PRAXIS, The Fletcher Journal of Human Security* (Vol XXIII), 2008.

[4] Somali warlords participated in all political reconciliation conferences. While alleged HRs violations were examined as one of the criteria for participation, many of these warlords still remain as members in the Somali parliament.

[5] "Transitional justice in protracted conflict: local and Diaspora conceptions of retributive and restorative justice between *sharia*, customary and human rights law in Somalia and Ethiopia's Somali Region." Project proposal submitted to the Deutsche Stiftung Friedensforschung, Max Planck Institute for Social Anthropology, Halle, 2010, 6.

Justice mechanisms in the future. The findings are based on field research undertaken from June 2012 to October 2012 in Mogadishu. The focus of the inquiry was to discover prevailing public opinion of Transitional Justice through sample interviews; it sought to identify the most 'acceptable' mechanisms from the menu of available Transitional Justice approaches ranging from local customary law, Sharia, to national and international law. In addition, the paper offers a brief summary of HRs violations in south-central Somalia since 1991 and provides accounts of the personal traumas and coping mechanisms experienced by Somalis during the civil war. Finally, the paper analyzes the responses of the interviewees to discover the main conceptions of Somalis about Transitional Justice Mechanisms.

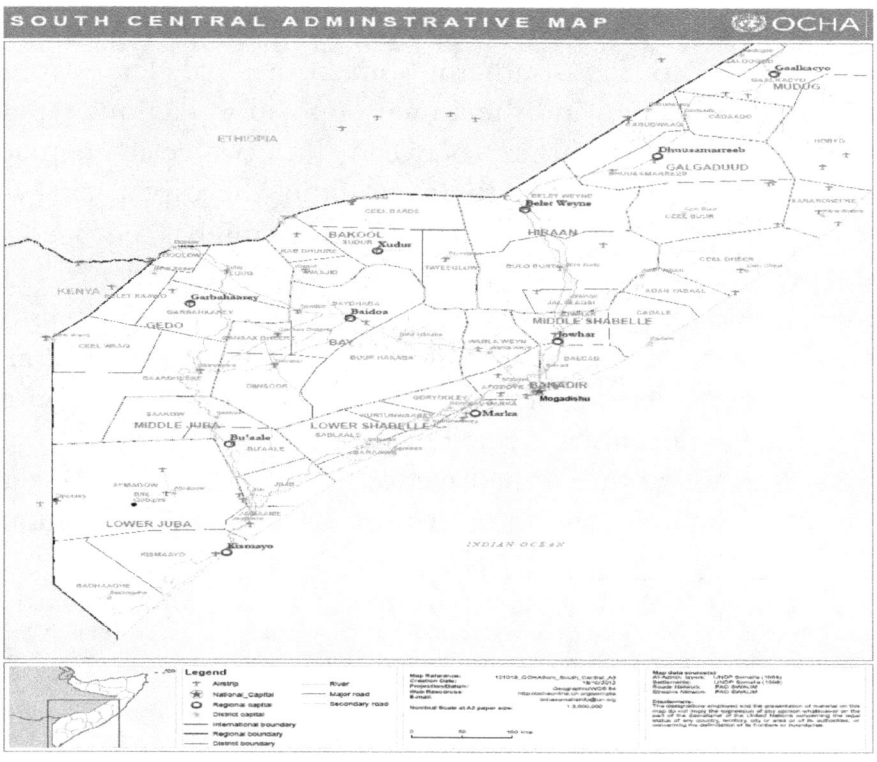

The Map of Southern Somalia

History of Mass Violence in South-Central Somalia

This brief historical background to the mass violence in Somalia confines its scope to the period after 1991 and examines the role of Somali non-state actors, Somali state apparatus and military interventions by external actors. However, it is important to recognize that substantial violations of HRs began under the Military regime which took power in Somalia in 1969. State violations including torture, extra-judicial detentions, collective punishments, clan cleansing, mass executions, and internal displacements which occurred in the 1970s and 1980s have not yet been fully documented or addressed in literature.[6] Nonetheless, the real agony of Somalia began with the total collapse of the state. On January 26, 1991, President Mohamed Siyaad Barre fled the Villa Somalia presidential palace and retreated with his supporters into the southern Somali regions. The conflict between the regime and the armed opposition factions rapidly transformed into warfare between the two clan families: Darood and Hawiye.[7] At the same time, the capital city was engulfed in utter mayhem as unbridled militias engaged in plundering, looting, and killing of civilian residents. The political and military leadership of the United Somali Congress (USC)—part of the coalition which overthrew the Barre government lost control of its militia as they vied for control of strategic locations including the seaport, airport, and Villa Somalia against other armed factions. In this anarchy, all state property such as factories, historical monuments, national

---

[6] The terminology of clan cleansing has been applied most recently in Kapteijn's study of the mass killings in 1991-2. However, even before the collapse of the regime, government forces targeted specific clans for collective punishment. See Lidwien Kapteijns, *Clan Cleansing in Somalia* (Philadelphia: University of Pennsylvania Press, 2013).

[7] Although both the Barre government and the opposition USC played to clan loyalties before 1991, the transformation of the conflict into an all-out Hawiye vs Darood war appears to date to April 1991, when allied forces comprising all Darood clans attempted to recapture Mogadishu. These forces advanced to the outskirts of Mogadishu, and the USC was caught in panic and mayhem launching a counter offensive to throw them out at all costs. See Terrence Lyons and Ahmed I. Samatar, *Somalia: State Collapse, Multilateral Intervention, and Strategies for Political Reconstruction* (Washington DC: Brooking Occasional Papers, 1995), 22.

archives, administrative offices, and social service sites including schools, universities, and hospitals were ransacked and gradually destroyed. Moreover, private houses, businesses, land, farms, and livestock were also captured and plundered. Nothing was spared from destruction. Comparable behavior of pillaging and preying on the peaceful civilian population was witnessed from the Somali Salvation Democratic Movement (SSDF), Somali Patriotic Movement (SPM) and Somali National Front (SNF) militias in their push and pull fighting with USC forces. Hassan Cali Mire, a veteran Somali scholar describes these occurrences succinctly as though "all the pent-up frustrations of three decades of postcolonial independence exploded into the ugly rise of fratricide, which has made the barbaric killing of innocent members of other kin communities a worthy goal."[8]

Within two days of the old regime's collapse, on January 28, a provisional government was announced, and Ali Mahdi Mohamed was designated as the interim president. This precipitate decision by the civilian wing of the USC in Mogadishu (the so-called Manifesto Group) pre-empted the Mustahil accord which had been agreed to by the SNM, SPM and USC- General Aidid factions.[9] The Mustahil stakeholders were swift to rebuff the new government. General Aidid considered the formation of the interim government to be a betrayal of USC goals and a return of the former regime through the back door, while the civilian USC charged the Aidid faction with seeking a return to military rule. As a result, the previously divided USC further polarized into two antagonistic armed camps which mobilized along clan lines:

---

[8] Hassan Ali Mire, "On providing for the future," in Ahmed Samatar, ed., *The Somali Challenge: From Catastrophe to Renewal?* (London: Lynne Rienner, 1994), 22.
[9] The three armed factions SNM, SPM, and the USC-Aidid wing were bound by the Mustahil agreement in June 1990 to form an alliance. Moreover, this agreement was consolidated in October 1990 and rejected any negotiated settlement with the regime. However, the civilian USC in Mogadishu were furious with General Aidid and the possible return of military rule in Somalia. It seems that this difference precipitated the hasty formation of the interim government

the Ali Mahdi camp and the General Aidid camp.[10] At the same time, the SPM and SSDF formed a new coalition of Darood and allied with Mohamed Siyaad Barre's supporters in Gedo and Kismaayo. The alliance mobilized its combined military forces against the fractured USC and assaulted Mogadishu on April 9, 1991.[11] The country was carved up by competing armed factions which were almost exclusively clan-based.

Meanwhile, in northern Somalia, opponents of the old regime, predominantly though not exclusively Isaaq, were threatening a separation of the North from the South. Even though separatist sentiments in the north were already strong, the public in the North was newly enraged by the USC's unilateral decision to form a government in Mogadishu. As a result, under public pressure, the Somali National Movement (SNM) unilaterally revoked the act of Union of 1960 and declared the independent state of Somaliland on May 17, 1991.[12]

Back in Mogadishu, the appointment of the interim government triggered a bitter feud between rival Hawiye clan factions and power contenders. Consequently, in September 1991, when all efforts for peaceful political agreement were exhausted, severe fighting broke out between the two USC factions in Mogadishu.[13] The fighting continued for about 100 days, destroying most parts of the city and causing an estimated 20-30,000 deaths through military causalities and

---

[10] The two contesting leaders Ali Mahdi and Aidid belonged to two Hawiye sub-clans: Mudulood and Madar-kicis, respectively, and clan mobilization was used for the power struggle.

[11] See Lyons and Samatar, *Somalia: State Collapse*, 22.

[12] In the Grand Conference of Northern Peoples "Shirweynaha Beelaha Waqooyiga" held in Burco in May 1991, secession of Somaliland was not originally on the table. The SNM leadership was negotiating for a new model of governance with the USC-Aidid faction in Mogadishu. Mark Bradbury writes: "*secession was not in the agenda of the SNM central committee*" in the Burco Conference. See Mark Bradbury, *Becoming Somaliland* (London: Progresso, 2008), 80. See also, John Drysdale, *Whatever Happened to Somalia?* (London: HAAN Publishing, 1994), 25.

[13] General Aidid declared a military coup and a toppling of the Ali Mahdi government. See Hussein Abdi Osman, "*Malaf al-Sarā' beyna 'Ali Mahdi wa 'Aidīd*" (unpublished paper submitted to the Horn of African Centre for Studies, Mogadishu, 1993).

civilian starvation.[14] The humanitarian relief supplies could not reach starving people, as it was hijacked by the warlords and their militias who exchanged most of it for weapons. By the end of 1991, the fighting had divided Mogadishu with a green line between the two USC factions. The United Nations (UN) mediated a cease-fire agreement in March 1992 and reduced the magnitude of the conflict to some extent.

The struggle between the Somali National Front (SNF) and the USC faction of General Mohamed Farah Aidid for control of the southern coast and hinterland brought devastation to the grain-producing region between the rivers of Shebelle and Juba, spreading famine throughout southern Somalia. All attempts to distribute relief food were undermined by systematic looting by militias. The epicentre of famine, the town of Baidoa which had exchanged hands between various militias many times, became the theatre for the conflict, and a massive number of deaths occurred in the Bay and Bakol regions. It was estimated that more than 300,000 died and more than a million people suffered severely in 1991 and 1992.[15]

In January 1992, as international concern over the Somali debacle was growing, the UN supported the U.S. decision to send a peacekeeping force to Somalia. US forces landed in Mogadishu in December 1992, leading to a coalition of willing nations in accordance with UN Resolution 794, adopted on December 3, 1992. The aim of the intervention was to help create a secure environment for humanitarian efforts in Somalia. "Operation Restore Hope" consisted of a multinational force of more than 37,000 troops from 22

---

[14] See Mohamed Sahnoun, "Somalia: the Missed Opportunities," (paper delivered to the United State Institute of Peace, 1994), 11.
[15] The total cost of lives was never fully tallied. Lewis provides a statistic of 300,000 See I.M. Lewis, *A Modern History the Somali: Nation and State in the Horn of Africa*, Revised/Fourth Edition (Columbus: Ohio University Press, 2003), 265. See also Kenneth Rutherford, *Humanitarianism under fire: The US Intervention in Somalia* (Kumerian Press, 2008), 38; and Ahmed Samatar, ed., *The Somali Challenge*, 3.

nations (24,000 troops from US and 13,000 from other countries).¹⁶ However, the mission was aborted on October 3–4, 1993 when a fight erupted between peacekeepers and General Aidid's militia, which resulted in the death of 24 Pakistanis, 19 US soldiers, and 500–1,000 Somalis.¹⁷ For that reason, the UN withdrew from Somalia on March 3, 1995, leaving the country "in a state of violence and anarchy."¹⁸ Notwithstanding widespread criticism of UN operations at the time, the ramifications for Somalia were on the whole positive. The UN mission relieved famine, weakened the warlords, promoted civil society organizations, and encouraged business ventures in the private sector¹⁹ The culmination of these developments was a change in national reconciliation strategy which recognized a greater role for civilian leadership. One outcome was the National Reconciliation Conference, held in Arta, Djibouti in 2000, which incorporated a wide spectrum of civil society actors after 10 years of failed warlord-driven conferences.²⁰ Arta produced a Transitional National Government (TNG), which gave some promise of restoring civilian governance in Somalia and reconciling the warring factions.

Unfortunately, in the aftermath of 9/11 and the Bush administration's proclamation of a 'Global War on Terrorism' (GWT), Somalia was listed among the states that were potential havens for terrorism.²¹ The first victim of the Global

---

[16] Ibid.
[17] The number of Somali deaths was highly controversial. For instance, Rutherford reported 500 deaths and 700 wounded. See Rutherford, *Humanitarianism*, 160. Other sources provide a number of 500–1000. See Luke Glanville, "Somalia Reconsidered: An Examination of the Norm of Humanitarian Intervention", *Journal of Humanitarian Assistance*, available from http://www.jha.ac/articles/a178.pdf (accessed on June 19, 2010), 11.
[18] The World Bank, "Conflict in Somalia, drivers and dynamics, 2005", available from
http://siteresources.worldbank.org/INTSOMALIA/Resources/conflictinsomalia.pdf (accessed on June 31, 2010).
[19] This author was a Somali living in Diaspora who went back to Somalia during the UNOSOM period to work in the humanitarian field.
[20] Abdurahman Abdullahi, "Penetrating Cultural Frontiers in Somalia: History of women's political participation during four decades (1959–2000),"*African Renaissance* 4:1 (2007), 34–54.
[21] "On 23 September 2001, less than two weeks after the 9/11 terrorist attacks in the U.S., President George W. Bush signed Executive Order 13224, which blocked the assets of 27

War on Terrorism was the Transitional National Government (TNG), which erstwhile international supporters suspected of having too many Islamists in its ranks.[22] Moreover, the TNG proved dysfunctional due to low capacity of leadership and opposition from warlords who had been marginalized by the TNG government. The warlords found support from Ethiopia and from Western intelligence agencies concerned about the Islamist leanings of the TNG. International efforts to establish another government led to a new round of peace talks in Kenya, known as the Eldoret/Mbagathi conference. The conference was sponsored by IGAD (the Intergovernmental Authority on Development) but was dominated once again by warlords and their allies. With the strong backing of Ethiopia, the conference concluded by endorsing another 'Transitional Federal Government' (TFG) in 2004. The TFG unsurprisingly failed to secure popular support in Somalia, especially in the south As such, personal squabbles among assembly members and government ministers, lack of governance capacity, and rampant corruption paralyzed the TFG and thwarted efforts to restore state institutions. The TFG had to govern from the inland town of Baidoa because of its unpopularity in the capital, Mogadishu, where local warlords vied with a growing Islamic Courts movement..

---

organisations and individuals linked to terrorism. Tenth on the list was a little-known Somali organisation, *al-Itihaad al-Islaami* (AIAI)". See International Crisis Group, *Somalia's Islamists* (Africa Report N°100 – 12 December 2005), available from http://www.crisisgroup.org/~/media/Files/africa/horn-of-africa/somalia/Somalias%20Islamists.ashx. Also, see Abdurahman Abdullahi, "Recovering the Somali State: the Islamic Factor," In *Somalia: Diaspora and State Reconstitution in the Horn of Africa*, edited by A. Osman Farah, Mammo Mushie, and Joakim Gundel (London: Adonis & Abby Publishers Ltd, 2007), 196-221, 196. However, on August 27, 2002, US removed al-Barakat from its designated terrorist list. See Terrorist Financing Staff Monograph, Al-Barakaat Case Study: *The Somali Community and al-Barakaat*, available from *http://www.9-11commission.gov/staff_statements/911_TerrFin_Ch5.pdf (accessed on August 25, 2010),* 85.

[22] Somali Reconciliation in Djibouti in 2000 was a civil-society driven process, and ideological and clan differences were acknowledged in the inclusive approach. As \a result many Islamists became members of the parliament and Islam was accepted as the ultimate reference for the laws of the land..

The United State counter-terrorism operations offered covert financial and political support to the warlords who established an "Alliance for the Restoration of Peace and Counter-Terrorism,"[23] with the aim of uprooting Mogadishu-based Islamists. However, the undertaking provoked an unprecedented upsurge of Islamic rage in Mogadishu under the Union of Islamic Courts (UIC) leadership, and the US-backed warlord programme was aborted and dissolved. The political environment of Somalia changed dramatically with the outright victory of the UIC over the warlords. In June 2006, the UIC assumed uncontested control over Mogadishu and many of the surrounding regions. But once again popular hopes for peace and stability under a UIC administration were dashed with the impasse of peaceful dialogue in Sudan and the renewed escalation of civil war in which the Ethiopian military participated with tacit US support. The UIC was defeated on Christmas Eve 2006, and a new round of resistance against Ethiopia began with various forces pursuing their own political agendas.

After the defeat of the UIC, various forces opposed to the Ethiopian occupation and/or to the TFG regime gathered in Asmara, the capital city of Eritrea, and an Alliance for the Re-liberation of Somalia (ARS) was formed in September 2007. International and regional diplomats encouraged reconciliation between the TFG and ARS, and a meeting in Djibouti in 2009 ultimately produced a new Transitional Government which combined former TFG and ARS supporters. However, the hasty reconciliation process sponsored by the United Nations proved ineffective, and the new government depended heavily on protection from the African Union Mission in Somalia (AMISOM). At the same time, Al-Shabab, an extremist group ideologically affiliated with Al-Qaida, used popular discontent with the central government to seize control of large portions

---

[23] The alliance consisted of eight Mogadishu based warlords. See "Somali warlords hold 'secret anti-terrorism' talks with US agents: witnesses", *Agence France Presse*, February 28, 2006.

of southern Somalia and even extended its terrorist attacks to Uganda, threatening other African countries which were contributing troops to the security mission in Somalia.

In the course of these changing political alliances and international interventions, many war crimes and human rights violations were perpetrated by all parties. The chart below summarizes the various phases of the conflict following the collapse of the state in 1991, each of which produced HR violations against the people in South-Central Somalia.

---

1. 1991-1992: the collapse of the state and outbreak of the civil war and famine causing 20.000-30.000 deaths in Mogadishu and 300.000 deaths in Bay and Bakol famine.

2. 1992- 1995: Intervention forces combining Unified Task Force (UNITAF) and The United Nations Operation in Somalia (UNOSOM). This operation caused the death of 24 Pakistanis, 19 US soldiers, and 500–1,000 Somalis.

3. 1995–2001: inter-clan conflict and marauding militia belonging to various warlords.

4. 2001–2006: The beginning of the GWT, emergence of Union of Islamic Courts (UIC) and its conflict with Mogadishu Warlords.

5. 2007–08: Ethiopian military intervention, UIC resistance, the AMISON, US counter-terrorism operations and war with Al-shabab.

6. January 2009 and after: Continuation of conflict between AMISOM and Somali military and Al-Shabab.

Table 3: Chronology of mass violations of HRs after the civil war (1991-2009)

Conceptualizing Transitional Justice

Transitional Justice has been defined in different ways by different scholars, and different conceptual approaches have evolved over time. Early scholars narrowly defined Transitional Justice in the process of laying the foundations of international human rights law. These early attempts were exemplified in the legal developments associated with the trials of Nuremberg and Tokyo after World War II. The second generation of scholars focused mostly on the development of restorative mechanisms as well as innovative tribunals.[24] During these two periods, **Transitional Justice** was approached from a Western legal perspective, and alternative approaches from the southern hemisphere were not considered relevant. Recent scholarship, however, has moved towards a more comprehensive perspective which seeks to account for cultural variations in the understanding and application of judicial principles. Naomi Roht-Arriaza, for example, writes:

> The universe of Transitional Justice can be broadly or narrowly defined. At its broadest, it involves anything that a society devises to deal with a legacy of conflict and/or widespread human rights violations, from changes in the criminal code... to tackling the distributional inequities that underlie conflict.[25]

It is worth comparing Roht-Arriaxza's definition with those developed by international organizations such as the UN. **The United Nations defines Transitional Justice as**

> The full set of processes and mechanisms associated with a society's attempts to come to terms with a legacy of large-scale past abuse, in order to secure accountability, serve justice and achieve reconciliation.[26]

Another definition adopted by the International Center for Transitional Justice **reads that**

> Transitional Justice refers to the set of judicial and non-judicial measures that have been implemented by different countries in order to redress the legacies of massive HRs abuses.

---

[24] These restorative mechanisms included truth commissions, official apology and reparations, as well as innovative tribunals, including the International Criminal Tribunals for the Former Yugoslavia and Rwanda, as well as hybrid courts like the Special Court for Sierra Leone.
[25] Naomi Roht-Arriaza, ,'The new landscape of transitional justice,' in," in Naomi Roht-Arriaza and Javier Mariezcurrena, eds., *Transitional Justice in the Twenty-First Century* (Cambridge University Press, 2006), 2.
[26] Annan, K., UN Secretary-General, *The Rule of Law in Conflict and Post-Conflict Societies*(NY: United Nations, 2004), 4.

These measures include criminal trials, truth commissions, reparations programs and various kinds of institutional reforms.[27]

All these definitions emphasize the fact that Transitional Justice implies a particular set of approaches dealing with the legacy of gross HRs violations and concur that alleged perpetrators of mass atrocities, war crimes and crimes against humanity should not be given impunity.

However, the argument here is that the forms of Transitional Justice which should be applied in a country like Somalia must take into account the local context, which includes considerations of which factors to put a community at peace with itself and prevent the recurrence of violence. Most communities utilize some type of customary law which is accepted and respected by the individual members of the community. In Muslim countries like Somalia, Islamic jurisprudence has also influenced notions of peacemaking and restorative justice. Thus, multiple legal systems consisting of customary law (Xeer), Sharia law, national laws and International law are available in Somalia.

Conception of Transitional Justice in the Traditional Xeer

The traditional legal system as it has evolved in Somalia is a combination of Sharia and Xeer (local customs). In most traditional settings, clan elders oversee the implementation of the local Xeer, while Islamic scholars are responsible and called upon for rendering religious judgments related to criminal acts and civil disputes. At the community level, then, Xeer and Sharia constitute parallel and interlocking systems of legislation. Sharia law is familiar to most Somalis, though its application in combination with Xeer varies from community to community. Most Somalis are Sunni Muslim who adhere to

---

[27] See this definition from http://icTransitional Justice.org/about/transitional-justice (accessed on June 11, 2013).

traditional Islam, which consists of Ash'ariyah theology, Shafiyah jurisprudence and Sufism.[28] This gives them a widely shared set of Islamic practices and concepts which serve to unify a culture which otherwise is prone to fragmentation along clan lines. During the colonial era, European laws were introduced, pushing aside many aspects of the indigenous laws at the state level, even though European law had failed to penetrate deeply into the societal space. Therefore, three crosscutting sources of laws are competing with each other in Somalia: Xeer, Sharia and secular European laws.[29]

Somali customary law provided both restorative and retributive justice mechanisms. Communal (inter- and intra-clan) violence was not resolved through formal courts, but was settled by what we would call today an Alternative Dispute Resolution (ADR) body made up of Traditional Elders. The role of the elders was and is to seek ways of repairing damages caused by clan violence, including bodily harm and material damages. Through application of traditional Xeer and often tedious deliberations between traditional elders from both sides of the conflict, decisions are made on how to redress injustices through compensation and other restorative mechanisms. In the Somali clan system, the individual is not separated from his/her clan in dealing with violence and crimes. Thus, the basic concept of resolving conflicts emanates from the collective responsibilities of the clan members, which attribute only limited culpability to the individual perpetrator. This notion, of course, diminishes individual responsibility for a crime and may encourage

---

[28] The Ashariyah theology was founded by Abu al-Hassan Al-Ashari (873-935) in reaction to the extreme rationalism espoused by the school of Mutazilah, one of the early theological schools in Islamic theology. The Shāfiīyah School of jurisprudence is also one of the major four Sunni schools of jurisprudence and rooted in the methodology and teachings of Abū-Abdallāh al-Shāfiī (767–820). Sufism appeared as a reaction against luxurious lifestyle that grew prevalent in the Islamic urban centers when Muslims became powerful and wealthy and plunged under the influence of other cultures.

[29] These laws are not mutually exclusive. For instance, many elements of Xeer are compliant with Islamic Sharia while many modern European laws introduced in Somalia took account of the Islamic faith of the Somali people.

impunity within society. Restorative justice practices which derive from custom in Somalia include forgiveness, payment of blood money (Diya), and other penalties for injuries.

Conception of Transitional Justice in Modern Somalia

Justice is a concept of moral rightness and its understanding differs to some extent from society to society depending on their cultural values. This does not mean however, that there are no universally accepted justice principles which are shared across cultures. In exploring conceptions of traditional justice within the Somali population, it became evident that there is no agreed upon terminology for Transitional Justice in the Somali language. Only three entries for Transitional Justice in the Somali language were found in the Google search engine,[30] suggesting that the notion is not a familiar one in Somali popular discourse. This observation indicates that the modern concept of Transitional Justice is not well articulated in the Somali mass media or even in Somali's academic circles.

To further explore this notion, I posted a question on my Facebook page requesting readers to come up with Somali terminology for Transitional Justice.[31] More than 50 individuals participated in the discussion and proposed 13 different terminologies.[32] Analyzing and short listing these terminologies, it was discovered that "*cadaalad*" (justice), which

---

[30] Moxamed Cali Xarakow. "Cadaaladda Xilliga kala-Guurka". Available from http://www.hiiraan.com/op4/2012/july/25249/cadaaladda_xilliga_kala_guurka.aspx (accessed on August 6, 2013). Also see Abdi Gadiid, "Yaan laga Tegin Cadaaladda Danbiilayaasha ma yaro". Available from http://www.qubanaha.com/2012/08/16/yaan-laga-tagin-cadaaladda-dambiilayaasha-ma-yaro-faalo-xiiso/(*accessed on August 6, 2013*).

[31] See replies of the participants available fromhttps://www.facebook.com/abdurahman.baadiyow (posted in September 4, 2013). The question was posed as follows: 'A form of justice called in English language "Transitional Justice" and in Arabic " al-Cadaala al-intiqaaliyah" is dispensed in the countries where civil wars and gross violation of human rights occur. There is no definitively agreed terminology for Somali language. Can you propose a Somali terminology for TRANSITIONAL JUSTICE? Can you find such terminology from Somali poetry?'

[32] *Garbax iyo xaalmarin, 2. Waddadii caddaalada, 3. Garsoorka marxaladda kalaguurka, 4. Wadadii Cadaalad Raadinta, 5. Caddaaladda kalaguurka, 6. caddaalad ku meelgaar ah, 7. Xaq- xeerin, 8. Xeerka Kala Guurka, 9. Garsooridda kumeel gaarka, 10. Ka-Gudbidda Gaboodfalka, 11. Xaq uraadin xasuuq dhacay, 12. Garsoor kumeel gaar ah, 13. Is-xaqsiin.*

is borrowed from the Arabic "al-'Adalah," is commonly accepted and fairly widely used. The Somali term *"garsoorka"* coined from the compound words *"gar"* which means "something right" and *"soor"* meaning "to provide" was also proposed by several respondents. The term *"garsoor"* literally signifies "providing rights to someone" and is often applied to magistrates and judges; in fact *"garsoore"* is the terminology coined by Somalis to refer to judge and jurist. However, in Somali discourse the words *"cadaalad"* and *"garsoor"* are often used interchangeably by the public and in the mass media, which also employ the English words justice, law and judge.[33]

If we accept the generic term *"cadaalad"* as the most appropriate translation of "justice", it is more difficult to find a Somali equivalent for 'transitional'. In the Somali language, *"kalaguurka"* (transition or change) and *"kumeelgaarka"* (interim, provisional, temporary and transitory) are possible candidates.[34] The term *"kumeelgaarka"* is probably less suitable here since it connotes a notion of "interim" or "provisional" justice), while *"kalaguurka"* appears closer to the concept of 'transitional'.[35] However, to clarify the meaning in Somali, it is necessary to add *"xilliga"* which means "the time of". Therefore, the phrase *"xilliga kalaguurka"* (the time of transition) provides a more nuanced meaning. Putting these concepts together, we devised a Somali terminology for 'Transitional Justice' --*"Cadaaladda Xilliga Kalaguurka"*—which was used in the Somali interviews for this research. Somalis are already familiar with the well articulated form of resolving conflicts known as reconciliation (*Dib-u-Heshiisiin*), which is one of the important components of any Transitional Justice process.

---

[33] http://www.thefreedictionary.com/justice
[34] http://www.yourdictionary.com/temporally
[35] The meaning of 'transition' according to http://www.merriam-webster.com/dictionary/transition is 'passage from one state, stage, subject, or place to another'. In similar fashion, the Somali term of "kala-guurka" indicates passage from one situation to another.

In the current Somali context, there is no clear national policy for pursuing Transitional Justice and no specific institutions established for that purpose. The Provisional Federal Constitution (PFC) stipulates support for HRs and fora Human Rights Commission. Article 4 of the PFC affirms the state's commitment to the promotion of HRs and the rule of law, while article 39 outlines procedures to redress violations of HRs. Article 41 mandates the establishment of an independent HRs Commission.[36] Thus, there is growing awareness in Somali legal and political discourse about the importance of Transitional Justice, even if there are not as yet any mechanisms in place for that purpose at the national level.

Conception of Sharia among Somalis

Islamic Sharia has a long history in Somalia, and while its implementation has been partial and uneven throughout the country, most Somalis have a familiarity with its general precepts. Recent calls by various Islamic movements for a more extensive application of Sharia appear to be a reaction to the secular tendency of the modern Somali state and its perceived failures. This trend is manifested in the constitutions of Somaliland and Puntland, as well as in the Provisional Federal National Constitution. It is worth noting that Somalia has produced three national constitutions (1960, 1979 and 1989), two charters (2000, 2004) and one Provisional Constitution (2012), and all of but one of them explicitly acknowledges Islamic principles as the ultimate foundation for the laws of the land. (The only exception was the constitution of the military regime enacted in 1979).[37] While it

---

[36] Somali Provisional Constitution Available from http://unpos.unmissions.org/LinkClick.aspx?fileticket=RkJTOSpoMME=(accessed on 12 September, 2013.)
[37] In the first Constitution of 1960, see articles (1:3, 50, 94 and 29). The national Charter of 2000 included two important additional provisions in articles (2 and 4) which prohibits adoption of any law contradicting Islam or propagating other religions in Somalia. Also, see article 2 of the provisional Federal Constitution of Somali Republic.

is important to keep in mind the historical importance of Sharia in the doctrinal and constitutional discourses of Somali religious and legal elites, our attention here is focused on conceptions of Sharia among non-experts of Islam as reflected in our sample of interviews.

Somali cosmology has been influenced historically by the Islamic Sharia, including its concepts of justice. These concepts are addressed in the basic sources of Islam: the Qur'an and prophetic tradition, and the science of jurisprudence *(Fiqh)*. For instance, the following well-known verse from the Qur'an offers an Islamic conception of justice:

> The recompense for an injury is an injury equal thereto (in degree): but if a person forgives and makes reconciliation, his reward is due from Allah...But indeed if any show patience and forgive, that would truly be an exercise of courageous will and resolution in the conduct of affairs (42:40-43).

This verse is one of many in the Qur'an which can be considered as laying a foundation for the concept of Transitional Justice. The Islamic vocabulary of "rewarding evil by evil", "forgiveness", "reconciliation" and "patience" represent concepts which also stand at the core of contemporary Transitional Justice mechanisms. For Muslims, these notions are rooted in the divinely revealed laws termed as Sharia which are obligatory and binding on all believers.[38] One model of the application of Transitional Justice in Islam can be inferred from the events following the Prophet Muhammad's conquest of Makah (the holy city in Saudi Arabia). In dealing with his defeated enemies, the Prophet deployed four mechanisms: general amnesty, criminal persecution, individual forgiveness and institutional reforms.[39]

---

[38] The Qur'anic verse *"But no, by your Lord, they shall have no faith until they make you (O Muhammad) judge in all their disputes and find in themselves no resistance against your decisions and accept them with full submission."* (4:65).

[39] Abdurahman Abdullahi (Baadiyow), "Islam and Transitional Justice: Principles, Mechanisms and Historic Role in Somalia". A paper produced as part of research project on Transitional Justice in Somalia commissioned by Max Planck Institute for Social Anthropology, Halle/Saale,

How does the contemporary Somali public conceptualize Sharia? Most of our interviewees had a rather simplistic understanding of Sharia, taking a legalistic perspective that confined it to "Hudud Punishments". Hudud is that part of the Islamic law ordained by Allah which prescribes proper behaviour and invokes punishments for serious crimes as a means of deterrence. Interviewee (#27), for example, states: "To apply Shari'a, women should wear Hijab (Islamic code of women's dress); alcoholic beverages and gambling should be prohibited; women should stay at home and care for the children; women should not sit in the parliament". While Muslim scholars from various legal schools have provided various interpretations of the classical Islamic texts using distinct legal methodologies, the mechanism of "Ijtihad" (diligent independent reasoning) still remains intact as a means to review and adopt new laws. The issue of women's political role, for example, is considered one of the controversial issues in Islam; in Somalia, the debate has been influenced by the patriarchic culture typical of many pastoral societies.

One interviewee (#21) expressed the following general conception: "For me Sharia is simply to follow the Qur'an and traditions (sayings and actions of the Prophet Mohammad), while another (#11) stated: "Shari'a means to stone adulterers, to give alms, to pray and to fast during the month of Ramadan and make pilgrimage". This interviewee combined "Hudud" punishments with performing the four essential pillars of Islam. One of our Facebook respondents explained that "Sharia is not to begin amputating limbs of the poor, sick, hungry and ignorant people. So, public education is a prerequisite prior to the implementing of Sharia". Another Facebook commentator considered that Sharia is not anything except to prevent aggression, to detain the aggressor, to help

---

Germany, 2013. Available http://www.scribd.com/doc/132832431/Islam-and-Transitional-Justice-Edited1-Doc. (accessed on June 14, 2013), 19-20.

victims of the aggression and to do so, we must have executive power". Thus, most of the interviewees' conceptions were fixed on specific elements of Sharia, notably, those associated with Hudud punishments in one way or another. Clearly absent from our limited sample was a comprehensive view of Sharia as a guide for regulating all human activities in the realms of morality, values, social relations, economic activities and politics. While Islamic law may have a crucial role to play in the establishment of Transitional Justice mechanisms for Somalia, it is important to recognize that the general public's understanding of Sharia is not monolithic and is frequently limited to notions of 'punishment.'

Research Note and Methodology

The survey research for this study was conducted in Mogadishu, where one can find individuals from all over South Central Somalia who were either victims, perpetrators or bystanders of the massive HRs abuses since 1991.Three well qualified research assistants were recruited, two from Mogadishu and one from Baidoa region. They were selected for their diverse clan affiliations and their familiarity with the various clans and regions in Southern Somalia. The author held a day-long familiarization and planning session with them on March 17, 2011. Together we designed the survey and divided the tasks equally: each researcher was to interview ten persons representing different age groups, genders and educational backgrounds. The team began working in the month of April and produced the first collection of data by the end of the month. On May 2, we met to review the preliminary findings and to begin the analysis. We discovered the need for more interviews, to increase the number of females and the number of respondents above the age of 40. To include participants who had more direct involvement in the civil war-- "the big fish", as we called them-- we used innovative interview methods e.g, inviting them for a dinner and engaging them in open and friendly discussions.

Our research objective was to document and analyze prevailing knowledge about past mass violence and gross HRs violations and to survey ideas about dealing with that violence among Somalis in Somalia. The population of interest for the study consisted of adults who were present in south central Somalia between 1991 and 2010. The sample was initially set at 30 individuals designed to encompass and give due consideration to gender, age and clan membership. On average, study participants were 35 years old. 60% had informal and 40% had formal education. The majority of participants (70%) were male.

The individual interviews used a predesigned set of questionnaires developed and agreed upon by the participating researchers. The core questions include personal background, experiences of injustice and/or violence that the interviewee had either been exposed to or witnessed directly, and their understandings of the reasons for that violence and its consequences The interviewees were also asked to comment on what steps had been taken to deal with the violence by legal or customary proceedings. Finally, each interviewee was requested to express his/her personal opinion on how to deal with the experienced injustice and asked to select from a menu of four available systems of justice: Somali customary law (Xeer) and/or Sharia and/or national law and/or international law.[40] Individuals selected for interviews had to fulfill the following three conditions. First, they had to be present or proximate to one or several of the events either as a victim, perpetrator or bystander. Second, they had to be old enough to have some memory of one of the events. Finally, they needed to be aware of what happened after the event. The interviews were conducted in the Somali language using the

---

[40] See questionnaires of the research in the attached appendix

"one-to-one" approach to collect confidential individual case histories.

This research benefited from the 'place-based approach' to Transitional Justice presented by Shaw and Waldorf.[41] Transitional Justice Practices work under assumed universal conceptions based on expectations that truth telling leads to reconciliation, prosecutions bring closure, and rendering of justice prevents the recurrence of violence. But because of different cultures and traditions, local responses to Transitional Justice may contest international and/or national laws and norms and offer different priorities. Thus, localizing Transitional Justice means to explore Transitional Justice mechanism preferred by the ordinary people and to propose more locally responsive approaches to social reconstruction after mass violence. In this approach, local preferences do not automatically or necessarily oppose national or international norms; multiple systems may come together in a particular locality which then can be taken as a starting point to engage complexities regarding Transitional Justice– e.g. contradictions between various conceptions of justice held by the people in a given place and by international actors working in that place. By applying a place-based approach, the research can also take into account local variations in Xeer or Sharia applications within Somalia, thereby providing a more nuanced approach to Transitional Justice.

Horrible Memories of Injustice and/or Violence/Conflict

This section provides translated narrations from Somali language to English of selected interviewees to demonstrate various Human Rights violations experienced and crimes committed in selected regions of Somalia. Most of these crimes involved indiscriminate murder, assassination, rape and revenge killing. The atrocities experienced and their associated

---

[41] Rosalind Shaw & Lars Waldorf (eds.), *Localizing Transitional Justice: Interventions and Priorities after Mass Violence*. (Stanford University Press, 2010).

memories caused wide range psychological, behavioral and medical problems in individuals, in addition to the social, economic and political implications for the clans or communities involved. Psychological problems include post-traumatic stress disorder, depression, anxiety disorders and psychotic conditions. Moreover, exposure to trauma can lead to sleep disorders, sexual dysfunction, chronic irritability, physical illness and a disruption of interpersonal relations. Although most interviewees expressed their experiences with some form of trauma, there were no institutions which offered therapeutic treatment, so traumas were dealt with mostly through traditional coping mechanisms.[42] Some of these traditional mechanisms derived from an Islamic cosmology based on the belief that disastrous events are the will of God. Consequently, Muslims must accept whatever happens to them and seek the help of Allah through supplications, without eschewing other available medical and social assistances.[43]

The concept of trauma is not well known to majority of Somalis, as both our field research indicates. In a recent study conducted in a Somali community in the UK attests:

> Out of 92 people interviewed 52.1% did not know the understanding of Post-traumatic Stress Syndrome although many were sufferers. It was also apparent that people suffering from mental health were not being supported and in fact were being stigmatized in the community resulting in many sufferers hiding their problems. 50% of sufferers did not receive any treatment.[44]

---

[42] There are numerous traditional coping mechanism employed in Somalia. Among the most important is the reciting of Qur'anic verses by traditional Islamic scholars which offer solace to the victims and their kin. . In addition, various forms of supplication by relatives and friends typically constitute a part of these traditional means of coping.

[43] See Qur'anic verse which says: "*No calamity befalls on the earth or in yourselves but is inscribed in the Book of Decrees, before We bring it into existence. Verily, that is easy for Allâh. In order that you may not grieve at the things that you fail to get, nor rejoice over that which has been given to you. And Allâh likes not prideful boasters.*(57:22-23)

[44] Northampton-Shire Somali Community Association, "Dhaawac ama Waxyeelo Maskaxeed", a Report on Post-Traumatic Stress in the Somali Community in Northampton and their experiences of Health Service, 2008. Available from http://www.nmhdu.org.uk/silo/files/post-

Let us now look at a sample of the testimonies gathered from our 30 respondents: One of the most painful narrations (#1) was obtained from a former member of the United Somali Congress (USC) militia, who exposes a tale of a father inheriting a sex slave from his son. He said: "I was one of the early members of USC militia who started guerrilla war against the Somali government. I fought from the Somali-Ethiopian border until we captured Mogadishu. During the civil war everything was destroyed and surviving militia members were desperate and unemployed. Most of the former militia members died in the war and survivors among them were scattered. In April 1994, I decided to visit the house in which I heard that one of my former colleagues lived, in the old district of Mogadishu-Hamarweyne. I was desperately in need of his financial assistance. When I knocked at the door of his residence, suddenly a chained Caucasian Banadir woman in her 20s opened the door.[45] Surprisingly, the lady was chained from her legs in a way that she cannot go beyond the door, but she can move around inside the house. I asked her where is my friend Ali? She replied in a whisper: He died a few months ago in the war in Bay Region. Then, she began to tell her story. She said: 'after the outbreak of the civil war in Mogadishu in early 1991, I was abducted by the brother of your friend who was a member of the USC marauding militia. He used me as his wife, but in reality I was his sex slave. After his death, his brother inherited me and I was his sex slave too.' Suddenly, while she was talking to me, I heard a noise in the house that indicated somebody is inside. I asked her who is now with you? She replied that she was inherited by the father

---

traumatic-stress-disorder-in-the-somali-community-northampton.pdf (accessed on August 5, 2013), 47.
[45] The Benadiri people traditionally lived in the Mogadishu districts of Shangani and Hamarweyne, in Marka, and in Barawa. They are reputed to be the early founders of Mogadishu and trace their mixed origins to Arab, Persian, and Cushitic people. They can often be identified by their lighter skin, in comparison with the majority of other Somalis. See Lee Cassanelli, *The Benaadir past: essays in southern Somali history* (Philadelphia: University of Pennsylvania Press, 1973).

of the two former 'husbands'... 'And he is taking care of me...' I was shocked and never imagined such incidents could occur in a Muslim country like Somalia. I quickly left the house".

Indiscriminate killing and house grabbing was reported by another former USC militiaman (interviewee #5) who was among those who entered and captured Mogadishu from the government forces in 1991. "One day, I met a former colleague of mine who was very active in the militia of USC in its early formation in Ethiopia. The time was 1994 when Mogadishu civil war had receded. I had not seen my friend after we entered Mogadishu in late 1990. I asked him: my friend how have we benefited from USC struggle? "Maxaad ka faaidaysatay halgankii USC"? We started sharing stories after stories and finally he took me to a beautiful two story building and showed me around. His family and relatives were living there. It was a well furnished house which most likely belonged to a wealthy family or high ranking government official. He told me: look my friend, I have benefited from our struggle, this house. This house belongs to me forever, he said with confidence. I asked: "my friend where is the owner of this house? They will return one day and reclaim their house". Then, he grabbed my hand and took me to the corner of the garden of the house and showed me the dry bones of dead human bodies. Then he said: "These were the mother and her 6 children who lived in this house. Their father was killed in the early days of the civil war and when I took over the house, I killed all the family members. "My friend!' he said: "For sure nobody is alive to reclaim this house."

Interviewee (#4) reports on the atrocities of the Al-Shabab insurgency, the militant Islamist group who controls large swathes of territory in the southern part of the country. The worst violence he experienced occurred when an explosion shocked the truck in which he was travelling in 2009 on the road between Afgoye and Marka.⁴⁶ He said: "Nine persons were injured including myself. I was injured badly and parts of my body had been completely removed. The area of the explosion was under the control of Al-Shabab and the most likely perpetrators were Al-Shabab militia. The injured individuals were all unarmed innocent people including three women and five men. We could not explain the true reason for committing such atrocities. The injured individuals were taken to Mogadishu Hospitals. Nothing could be done about those responsible for the violence."

Interviewee (#10) recalled a revenge killing among clans, a well known tradition in Somalia. She is a widow explaining how her husband was executed. "My husband was murdered between Garbahaarey and Buur-dhuubo in the Gedo Region in 1997.⁴⁷ Al-Itihad, an Islamist militant group, took control of Gedo region after the collapse of the state in 1991 and established their version of Islamic compliant administration.⁴⁸ However, they were surprisingly defeated by an alliance of clan militia and Ethiopian defense forces. Some sub-clans supported Al-Itihad and others opposed them. Thus, after their defeat, clan militia allied with the Ethiopian forces began to target clan members who supported Al-Itihad. My husband was from a clan that supported Al-Itihad, and therefore, he was targeted for revenge killing. My husband was travelling from Garbaharey to Buur-Dhuubo and the truck he was travelling with was stopped at a checkpoint and searched by the enemy clan militia. He was taken into custody and executed for revenge killing. The killing of my husband then instigated a fight between his clan and the clan of the militia

---

⁴⁶ Marka is a historical coastal town and the regional capital of Lower Shabelle, located about 110 km southwest of Mogadishu. Afgoye is a town and district of Lower Shabelle region which is located 30 km west/southwest of Mogadishu.
⁴⁷ Garbahaarey is the capital town of Gedo region in Somalia and Buurdhubo is one of its districts.
⁴⁸ Duale Sii'arag, "*The Birth and Rise of Al-Ittihad Al-Islami in the Somali Inhabited Regions in the Horn of Africa*", 2005. Available from http://wardheernews.com/articles/November/13__Alittihad_Sii'arag.html (accessed on August 5, 2013)

that shot him. My husband was a well respected and famous person and his murder was considered a great humiliation to his clan. Therefore, according to clan tradition, he should be revenged. The clan of my husband initiated a plan for his revenge and finally found two innocent individuals who belonged to the enemy clan and shot them in cold blood in the town of Buur-dhuubo. The conflict was exacerbated and many other individuals were murdered for revenge killing. Finally, the conflict was controlled and the two clans resorted to solve their conflict through traditional Xeer system."

Interviewee (#13) recounts his witnessing of killing and rape. He said: "my brother was killed and his wife was raped in front of me and my young brothers in Singale, located in Lower Juba in 1993. Our story begins when my elder brother evacuated me, his wife, the two young brothers and our mother from Kismayo town because of fear of war flaring there. The road we were travelling was muddy and it took us many days. Unfortunately, our car was broken at Singale and our supplies of food and water finished. My elder brother tried his utmost to get supplies and sent a message to relatives in Kismayo. The next night, while we were waiting someone to rescue us, a car loaded with militia came to us and we were very much delighted thinking they came to save us. However, after asking us some questions they recognized what clan we belonged to and began to threaten us pointing their guns towards us. They shouted, 'do not move' and dragged the wife of my brother away. When my brother started to resist they simply fired five bullets in his chest and raped his wife. They did not fire on us because the rest of us were children. My age was 14 years and the other brothers were younger than me. They left us, but they came back after a few hours and took the car and all our belongings. The unconscious wife of my brother was left alone in the nearby jungle; we were scared and remained there alone. In the next morning, individuals from our clan arrived and we were saved from imminent starvation.

No action was taken to deal with this atrocity even though the perpetrators were identified."

Interviewee (#6) tells about her husband who was murdered while attempting to halt fighting between two of his relatives' militias. She said: "My husband and I married in 2007 and had three children, two boys and one daughter. The daughter was born after the death of my husband and she also died after three months. My husband died while trying to mediate the fight between two close relatives' militias. He was intentionally shot by one of militias. My husband was a driver of Lorries and was well known in the central regions of Somalia. Five days before his death, he left us to travel as his routine work requires.. My last contact with him was the Tuesday morning he was murdered; I heard the news of his death in the afternoon. I was shocked and traumatized. I loved my husband so much and was not expecting to have orphans to raise alone. Anyway, it was the will of Allah and we have to accept and be patient."

Interviewee (# 8) speaks on his personal experience of intrigues, involving his clan and others during 2004. He narrated that he unintentionally killed a boy who worked for his family. He said: "In the beginning he was injured and I took him to the hospital and he died there. It took many nights before I could sleep. I was shocked and traumatized. My clan invited the clan of the murdered boy and we could not convince them that it was an unintentional killing and therefore, they have to accept blood money (Diya). This incident occurred after the emergence of clan-based Islamic courts. Thus, after some days I was detained by one of the Islamic courts and incarcerated. This court belonged to the clan of the murdered boy. I was in the prison for 6 months during which militia belonging to the clan of the dead boy kept trying to take me out of the prison to kill me. Finally, the court offered a verdict that it was a case of premeditated murder and that I had to be executed. My clan considered the ruling of the court to have been motivated by clan attachment to the murdered boy. In the night before the morning of my scheduled execution, a militia belonging to the clan of my mother attacked the prison and took me out. The clan of the boy announced a war against my mothers' clan. After skirmishes in which 4 persons were injured, the two clans agreed to imprison me again and to restart new negotiations. However, I fled to Beledweyne and I lived there for a year. I came back to Mogadishu during Court Union time in 2006 and after many assassination attempts, I decided to flee Mogadishu to Diaspora and I came back in 2012."

Interviewee (#3) witnessed a road robbery and indiscriminate killings. He said: "The road between Mogadishu and Kismayo is a very harsh road. In 2003 I travelled this road from Mogadishu to Kismayo. In the village called "Haramka" in the night, armed militia belonging to the clan residing in this area attacked us. They rained us with indiscriminate firing for quite some time. Most of the people in the truck were either killed or injured. The militia have searched each and every person and confiscated all the money, watches, mobile phones, and other materials. In addition, they dragged out two passenger girls and raped them not far from us. One of the two girls became unconscious for about a day. After they left us, we continued our journey and reached the town of Jilib where we buried our dead and received preliminary healthcare service."

Interviewee (#21) reported the murder of an international employee of one of the NGOs. He said: "A logistic officer working for MSF (Belgium) in Mogadishu in December 2011 murdered two international staff who were running MSF program in Mogadishu. This NGO employed more than 300 persons and ran many programs such as dispensaries and hospitals. As a result, the program was completely closed and MSF was evacuated from Mogadishu. I and the murderer belong to the same sub-clan, our clan elders tried to persuade government officials not to jail the killer because he is a Muslim, and the victims were non-Muslim.[49] However, the killer was kept in custody for months and justice was not administered. The community lost its healthcare service and employees lost their jobs."

Analysis of Research Findings

The following is the summary of findings from the interviews of 30 individuals. Categorizing types of violence, the research discovered that 17/30 interviewees reported that the type of violence they experienced/witnessed are murder/target killings/random killings/caught in crossfire. The second category of violence was rape and forced marriage which 4/30 respondents witnessed. Exploring who was directly responsible for the violence, findings demonstrate that marauding clan militias were identified by 8/30 interviewees. On the other hand, 7/30 respondents considered Ethiopian forces who intervened in Somalia in 2006 to be accountable for crimes, while 11/30 respondents believe that Al-Shabab insurgency was primarily responsible for the violence and crimes. Government soldiers were seen as less responsible: only 4/30 in our sample point the finger towards them. While the data suggest that Al-Shabab were the prime cause of violence and Ethiopian forces next in order. Inreality, the findings most likely reflect the fact that the majority of interviewees belonged to the younger generation who witnessed violence primarily during the phases of the Islamic Court Union in 2006 and the subsequent Ethiopian intervention.[50] Also, the data allow us to affirm that gross

---

[49] There is disagreement among Muslim jurists on what to do when a Muslim kills a non-Muslim. According to Abu Hanifa, if a Muslim deliberately kills a non-Muslim, the killer Muslim is killed. The following verse of the Qur'an demonstrates that equality of humanity. *"...if anyone slew a person - unless it be for murder or for spreading mischief in the land - it would be as if he slew the whole people: and if any one saved a life, it would be as if he saved the life of the whole people...*(5:32)." But there are other scholars like Imam Shafi'i, Imam Malik, and Imam Ahmad who advocate that a Muslim who kills a non-Muslim should not be killed., The latter conception is more prevalent in Somalia.

[50] Islamic Court Union was the association of clan-based Islamic Courts in Mogadishu which militarily reacted against the alliance of the warlords in 2006 and defeated them. The Union

violations in the period of 1991-2000 mostly involved clan militias belonging to various warlords. Other mass violence in that decade occurred between Al-Itihad Islamic organization and various clan militias in addition to sporadic Ethiopian incursions in the border regions with Somalia. While intervention of the multinational forces of UNISOM (1992-1995) also presumably caused gross violations of HRs, notably in its confrontation with General Aidid's militia in October 1993, none of our interviewees reported on that episode. Subsequent investigations reveal that the ordeal left 18 Americans dead and 70 wounded, while Somalis suffered casualties estimated around 3,000 (deaths and injuries). Indeed, this battle was immortalized in the famous "Black Hawk dawn" film.[51]

Responding to the question regarding reasons behind mass violence, half of the respondents (15/30) consider the civil war to be the real cause while 9/30 believe lawlessness and lack of government institutions explain the violence. These statistics indicate that violence is largely perceived to be motivated by contending clans and their militia groups, while substantial numbers see conflict as the result of an absence of law enforcement institutions to deal with public disorder and of government mechanisms to resolve conflict. Not surprisingly, 27/30 respondents concurred that these acts of violence, whatever their primary causes, were not being addressed through available customary or Shari'a law let alone state or international laws. As a result, the conflict continues to cause enormous psychological, social, and economic hardship, with implications that remain in the memory of victims. For instance, 12/30 respondents reported forcible loss of

---

comprised divergent ideological forces and later broke up into various groups. One of their components is Al-Shabab, which is currently affiliated with al-Qaida in Somalia.
[51] Black Hawk Down is a 2001 American war drama directed by Ridley Scott. It is an adaptation of the 1999 book of the same name by Mark Bowden, which chronicles the events of the Battle of Mogadishu, a raid integral to the United States' effort to capture General Mohamed Farah Aidid.

properties and claimed that there are no reliable institutions or court system to which they have recourse. The losses are not confined to consumable goods, but also include irremovable properties such as houses, agricultural firms and land with valuable natural resources. Many of these properties belong customarily to certain clans (including minority clans) but remain nowadays in the hands of powerful militias of other clans. This phenomenon is equally prevalent in Mogadishu. The implication of loss of property is huge and complex. One consequence of the lack of secure property rights is that most of the families and individuals displaced from their homes in Mogadishu still fear to return to their homes which have been occupied or confiscated by individuals belonging to other clans and communities. This situation creates mistrust among various communities and makes it harder for them to participate freely in the process of state reconstruction.

Apart from loss of property, 7/30 interviewees reported loss of dignity as a result of rape and forced marriages. Loss of dignity can be an unbearable burden, especially for Muslim women in more conservative Muslim countries. Most of the cases are not reported for fear of shame and social stigma. For example, the annual human rights violation report compiled by Peace and Human Rights Network in Mogadishu reported only six rape cases.[52] A woman who is a victim of rape is socially stigmatized and may not be considered suitable for marriage, or she may lose her marriage because of the shame culture in the traditional Muslim societies. This shame may even be transmitted to the victim's family and children, constituting a lifelong stigma for the woman and a source of ongoing hostility and never-ending revenge between the families involved.

In responding to the question of how best to deal with the past violence that has been experienced by Somalis, 21/30

---

[52] See Peace and Human Right Rights Network (PHRN),Annual Report from July 2010- June 2011, submitted on September, 2011.

respondents answered they are prepared to forget and forgive and to accept some form of compensation for lost relatives and properties; while 6/30 interviewees were adamant in choosing not to forget and strongly believe in retribution for the perpetrators of their agony. The widespread willingness to deal with past violence with forgiveness may be related to the deep Islamic influence in the cosmology of the people, as reflected in the Qur'anic verse cited earlier in the paper:
"… but if a person forgives and makes reconciliation, his reward is due from Allah…" (42:40-43).

On the other hand, revenge killing is an established element in Somalia's clan culture based on common responsibility of the clan for committed injuries. This culture emanates from the common security pact among clan members which mandates their responsibility to protect their members. From this point of view, clans collectively pay blood money (Diya) as a compensation for the damages/ injuries and lives lost. Diya is part of Somali customary law and is sometimes condoned by Islamic jurists as an alternative to revenge killings or perpetual feuds. At the same time, the influences of both urban culture and modern Islamic education have begun to erode the strong pastoral 'revenge culture', as is evident in the responses of our interviewees.

On the necessity of personal accountability for the violence/injustice, half of the interviewees (15/30) responded positively. This is another indication of the growing public attention to 'modern justice' norms resulting from exposure to Islamic jurisprudence, urban culture, and even the awareness programs of numerous civil society organizations and peace movement groups.[53] On the other hand, 6/30 of the respondents declared that they do not believe in personal accountability and continue to favor collective responsibility of

---

[53] Since 1992, various human rights organizations and many civil society organizations have been exploring options for transitional justice in Somalia The best known in Mogadishu are Ismail Jumale Human Rights and Elman Human Rights.

the clan members for the crimes committed. If our sample is representative of the population, it indicates that the pastoral clan culture is weakening in the urban city of Mogadishu even though most of its population had been displaced by the civil war.

On the question of who should be active stakeholders in the process of addressing past injustices and instances of violence, the role of clan elders topped the interviewee's opinions (11/30) whereas, the role of the Islamic scholars received 6/30 votes. Thus, 17/30 respondents saw local stakeholders as the most likely agents for promoting Transitional Justice. On the other hand, 9/30 assigned a primary role to the national government and only 4/30 saw the International community as a viable stakeholder. When asked which relevant legal norms come to mind when thinking about the issues of Transitional Justice, Sharia gets 15/30 while customary law gets only 3/30. While we might conclude from the data that a total of 18/30 of the interviewees prefer local solutions, it seems that the narrowing role of customary law and the widening preference for Islamic Sharia reflects the impact of modern Islamic movements in Somalia which have been actively advocating Islamic Sharia and have grown to prominence since the collapse of the state in 1991.[54]

Turning to our original question about Somalis' familiarity with the concept of Transitional Justice, our survey indicates that 21/30 respondents were not familiar with the term, and only 6/30 claimed to have heard about it. The statistics certainly does not show that Somalis are unfamiliar with the core ideas of retributive and compensatory justice, nor that they are uninformed about some of the mechanisms which

---

[54] Modern Islamic movements in Somalia have been active since the 1960s and are affiliated mostly with theEgyptian Muslim Brotherhood and the Salafia of Saudi Arabia. The two most prominent organizations within these movements are Islah and Al-Itihad (Itisam).. For more information, see Abdurahman Abdullahi, *The Islamic movement in Somalia: a historical evolution with a case study of the Islah Movement (1950- 2000)*. A PhD thesis submitted to McGill University, 2011. Available http://digitool.library.mcgill.ca/R/?func=dbin-jump-full&object_id=103487&local_base=GEN01-MCG02 (accessed on August 5, 2013).

various countries have implemented to deal with human rights violations in their recent past. As we have seen, elements of retributive and restorative justice are well articulated in Islamic law and also entrenched in the Somali customary law. And most Somali respondents were familiar with the International Criminal Court for Rwanda in Arusha, Tanzania and with the South African Truth and Reconciliation commissions, both of which have been widely covered in the Mass media. In a question about tailoring known Transitional Justice mechanisms from Rwanda and South Africa to the Somali context, 10/30 respondents preferred the Rwanda option while 6/30 regarded the South African Truth and Reconciliation Commission as more relevant for Somalia. (Even though these responses seem to be at variance at with our data showing that 18/30 interviewees preferred traditional options over imported ones, it is worth noting that both the Rwanda and South African Transitional Justice mechanisms incorporate elements of traditional justice alongside modern international and national laws.

> One way to interpret the data, then, is to conclude that while ordinary Somalis may not be aware of Transitional Justice as a holistic approach or familiar with the terminology of contemporary international law, they are quite conversant with the logics behind the various options which Transitional Justice theory and practice offer. Our survey also reveals that there are different understandings of the causes of past violence depending on the gender and generation of the interviewees. 15/30 respondents felt there were significant differences in how men and women, old and young viewed past violence, while only 9/30 believed that were no substantive differences.

We suspect that different understandings between genders may be related to the level of education which is generally much lower for women compared with men.[55] On the other hand, different understandings between generations may be correlated with the higher levels of education in the new generation and with their growing interest and connections with modern social media.[56] The implications of these differences in perception will need to be taken into account by those seeking consensus on how best to implement a Transitional Justice approach in Somalia.

Conclusion

This research was conducted in Mogadishu in 2012. The research used 30 selected individuals to discover variations in ways of understanding and addressing HRs violations that occurred in South Central Somalia after the collapse of the state in 1991. These violations intensified in six periods. The first period (1991-1992) followed the collapse of the state and outbreak of civil war which resulted in more than 300,000 deaths, hundreds of thousands of injuries, and loss of countless properties. The second period (1992-1995) witnessed the international intervention of United Nations Office for Somalia and was followed by a third period (1995-2001) characterized by low intensity conflicts among various warlords. The fourth period from 2001-2006 saw the launch of a Global War on Terrorism and the emergence in Somalia of the Union of Islamic Courts. Fear of Islamist radicalism prompted the Ethiopian military intervention (2006-08) and the subsequent rise of local resistance movements, including the appearance of Al-Shabab. Finally, the fifth period (2009-present) has seen the continuation and occasional

---

[55] According to the 2006 Somalia Multiple Indicator Cluster Survey, the adult literacy rate for women is estimated to be 26% (compared to 36% for men, and 31% overall). Available from http://www.so.undp.org/docs/Gender_in_Somalia.pdfv (accessed on August 6, 2013).

[56] As of 2012, Somalia has around 186 internet hosts. There were about 106,000 online users in the country in 2009. Available from https://www.cia.gov/library/publications/the-world-factbook/geos/so.html (accessed on August 6, 2013). Moreover, more than a million Somalis, most of them part of the younger generation, live in the Diaspora and use social media extensively.

intensification of the conflict between African Union Mission for Somaliaand Somali forces on one side and Al-Shabab insurgents on the other.

The findings of the research demonstrate that the overwhelming majority of the gross HRs violations that occurred in South-Central Somalia involved murder(including target killings as well as random killings by armed militias), violence against civilians by armed gangs, and rape. 27/30 of those interviewed agreed that these incidents of violence against civilian population have not been addressed and that the forcible loss of properties remains unresolved. However, the majority of Somalis are ready for peace and reconciliation and are prepared to forget and forgive and to accept some compensation for the loss of lives and properties. Furthermore, even though the Somali clan culture of collective responsibility for crimes remains intact, this research shows that more than half of the respondents believe in individual responsibility for the crimes which have been committed. For addressing past injustices, our interviewees gave precedence to traditional stakeholders over modern ones (national and international actors) and to some form of Sharia legal system over exclusive reliance on customary law (Xeer) or international law. However, the most common popular conception of Sharia is legalistic and focused on Hudud punishments. Our survey showed that modern understandings of Transitional Justice are limited among the general population and mostly confined to small educated elites in Somalia. The lack of Somali terminology for Transitional Justice testified to the paucity of public debate on the issue. Finally, most elements of modern Transitional Justice approaches can be found in internally accepted norms of Somali customary law and Islamic Sharia, and a place-based approach has the potential to reconcile multiple forms of law as they deal with issues of Transitional Justice.

CHAPTER THREE

History of the Islamic Movements: Phases, Moderation and Militancy

I
Historical Phases of the Islamic Movements

II
Islamic Moderation in the War-torn Somalia:
The Views of Islah on the Contemporary Issues

III
Militancy of the Sufi Orders in the History of Somalia

I
Somalia:
Historical Phases of the Islamic Movements

Introduction

The historical evolution of Islamic movements in Somalia have attracted less academic interest in the research communities.However, existing modest literature addresses Islam from the margins of history, through orientalist and secularist discourses, and security perspectives. Nonetheless, scholarship on Islam in Somalia has slightly improved since the collapse of the Somali state in 1991 and increased role of the Islamic movements afterwards. In particular, in the post-9/11 security studies literature, analysis of the armed Islamic groups have grown; albeit lacks in-depth historical background. This essay offers a general road map of the modern historical developments of Islam within the context of general history of Somalia. It draws on the PhD thesis by the author which provides unique historical analysis of the evolution of the Islamic movements.[1] This paper divides this historical development into four phases: the Islamic revival (1800-1950), the rise of the Islamic consciousness (1950-1967), the beginning of the Islamic awakening (1967-1978), and the emergence of the Islamic movements (1978-..). These historical phases are not mutually exclusive and demonstrates continuity and change. They are dynamic, crosscurrent, and overlap each other. This essay summarizes these four phases and the Islamic organizations that played major roles in each historical phase.

---

[1] Abdurahman Abdullahi, "The Islamic Movement in Somalia: A Historical Evolution with the Case Study of Islah Movement (1950-2000)" (PhD thesis, Institute of Islamic Studies, McGill University, 2011). This thesis was published in 2015 by Adonis & Abby Publisher under the title *"The Islamic Movement in Somalia: A Study of Islah Movement, 1950-2000".*

Literature Review

Current literature on the rising Islamic movements sprang up as part of the security studies that grew exponentially after 9/11, which was an academic campaign to discover what is termed as the threat of "Islamic fundamentalism".[2] Indeed, Western scholarship on Islamic movement has increased in the two historical periods in which Somalia was engaged in a conflict with Western powers. The first period was the years of Jihad against British colonialism, waged primarily by Sayyid Mohamed Abdulle Hassan in the British protectorate of the northern Somalia (1900-1921). Colonial scholarship showed particular interest in the study of this anti-colonial movement and produced ample literature on this topic. Among these works, two colonial works have particular relevance to the study of this movement: Douglass Jardine's work *The Mad Mullah of Somaliland* and Italian author Francesco Caroselli's book *Ferro e Fuoco in Somalia*.[3] Moreover, nationalist historiography followed suit to immortalize national symbols and offered special attention to the armed resistance against colonialism represented by the Darawish Movement of Sayyid Mohamed Abdulle Hassan. In this venue, the works of Said Samatar and Abdi Sheikh-Abdi are paramount.[4] Comparatively, nonviolent Islamic works that majority of the Islamic scholars were engaged received less Western academic interest except few anthropological works.[5] Moreover, there are some historical chapters on individual Sufi scholars produced by B.

---

[2] See Karim-Aly Kassam, "The clash of Civilization: The selling of Fear", available from https://dspace.ucalgary.ca/bitstream/1880/44170/1/Islam.pdf (accessed on February 14, 2011).

[3] These two works are: Douglass Jardine, *The Mad Mullah of Somaliland* (London: Herbert Jinkines, 1923) and Francesco Carosseli, *Ferro e Fuoco in Somalia: VentiAnni di LotteContro Mullah e Dervisc* (Roma: SindicatoItalianoArtiGrafiche, 1931).

[4] See Abdi Sheik Abdi, *Divine Madness: Mohammed Abdulle Hassan (1856-1920)* (Zed Books Ltd., London, 1993). Also, Said Samatar, *Oral Poetry and Somali Nationalism: The Case of Sayyid Mahammad Abdille Hasan* (Cambridge: Cambridge University Press, 1982).

[5] I. M. Lewis, *Saints and Somalis: Popular Islam in a Clan-based Society* (Lawrenceville, N.J.: Red Sea Press, 1998).

G. Martin, Said Samatar, and Scott Reese.[6] Therefore, as a general trend and a common denominator among all these scholarship, history of Islam and its role are marginalized, unless recognized as posing a security threat to the Western powers.

Exceptions to the above-stated trend are works in the Arabic language, authored by Islamist scholars. Four works could be placed at the top of these literatures. Two of them were authored by Ali Sheikh Ahmed Abubakar, the third by Ahmed Jumale "Castro", and the fourth by Hassan Makki. Ali Sheikh's first work *Al-Da'wa al-Islamiyah al-Mu'asira fi Al-Qarni al-Ifriqi* is a good introduction to the Islamic call in the Horn of Africa. The work offers historically in-depth overviews and challenges to Islamism that include secularism, illiteracy, tribalism, and policies of the military regime in Somalia. The second book *Al-Somal: Judur al-Ma'asat al-Rahina* seems complementary to the first book and focuses on the Islamic awakening and its encounter with the military regime. This book is unique in that it provides a detailed description of the execution of Islamic scholars in 1975 because of the Family Law confrontation between the regime and Islamists. It also provides the reaction of the Muslim world to the execution of the Muslim scholars. In addition to that, it offers an Islamist critique of the above-mentioned secular Family Law. Moreover, Ahmed Jumale describes the history and development of Islamic scholars in the Banadir region where Mogadishu is located. His PhD thesis is a useful source on the history of Sufi orders.[7] On the other hand, Hassan Makki produced an indispensable work as a PhD thesis "*Al-Siyasat al-*

---

[6] Bradford G. Martin, "ShaykhUways bin Muhammad al-Barawi, a Traditional Somali Sufi," in *Manifestations of Sainthood in Islam*, ed. G. M. Smith and Carl Ernst (Istanbul: ISIS, 1993), 225-37. Reese, Scott S., *Urban Woes and Pious Remedies: Sufism in Nineteenth-Century Banaadir (Somalia)* (Indiana: Indiana University Press, 1999). Said Samatar, "Sheikh Uways Muhammad of Baraawe, 1847-1909: Mystic and Reformer in East Africa," in *the Shadows of Conquest: Islam in Colonial Northeast Africa*, ed. Said S. Samatar (Trenton, NJ: The Red Sea Press, 1992), 48-74.

[7] Mohamed Ahmed Jumale "Castro", "DawrUlamaJunub al-Somal fi al-Da'wa al-Islamiyah (1889-1941)" (PhD diss., University of Omdurman, Khartoum, 2007).

Thaqafiya fi al-Somal al-Kabir (1887-1986)." This work is a very useful source of the cultural history of Somalia, in particular, it traces cultural competition between Arabic/Islamic and Western education, covering all Somali-inhabited territories of the Horn of Africa.

A similar academic interest with the emergence of Islamic Jihad by Sayyid Mohamed Abdulle Hassan in the first quarter of the twentieth century is noted after 9/11 and the declaration of Global War on Terrorism. In this period, many research centers have been producing occasional reports and briefings on Somalia as being a possible haven for terrorists. Somalia also appeared in the headlines of major newspapers, TV networks, radios, and electronic communications. The academic interest experienced an unprecedented growth and numerous papers and articles were published in many languages; of which these four works particularly stand out. These works were authored by an Ethiopian scholar Tadesse Madhene,[8] an Israeli Intelligence Officer Shay Shaul,[9] an American scholar Andre le Sage,[10] and Norwegian scholar Stig Hansen.[11] These works are in the field of security studies and counter-terrorism measures and focus on Al-Itihad and Al-Shabab, even though some background studies were made on other organizations.

Shaul Shay's book *Somalia between Jihad and Restoration* focuses on Somalia as a possible haven for terrorist organizations. The book examines Islamic movements in Somalia with a special focus on Al-Itihad and its connections with Al-Qaida, Hassan al-Turabi of Sudan Islamic Movement, and Iran during the USA intervention in Somalia in 1992-1995. The last chapters are dedicated to the rise and the fall of

---

[8] MedhaneTadesse, *Al-Ittihad: Political Islam and Black economy in Somalia: Religion, Clan, Money, Clan and the Struggle for Supremacy over Somalia* (Addis Ababa: Meag Printing Enterprise, 2002).
[9] Shaul Shay, *Somalia between Jihad and Restoration* (New Brunswick: Transaction Publishers, 2008).
[10] Andre Le Sage, "Somalia and War on Terrorism: Political Islamic Movements & US counter Terrorism Efforts" (PhD thesis, the Jesus College, Cambridge University, 2004).
[11] Stig Hansen, *Al-Shabab in Somalia: The History and Ideology of a Militant Islamist Group, 2005-2012* (London: Hurst and Co., 2013).

the Islamic Courts, the Ethiopian intervention, and its aftermath. This analysis of the challenges of the Islamic Courts and potentiality of Al-Qaida terror in Somalia concludes with remarks on ways to prevent the emergence of a radical Islamic state that harbors terrorism in the Horn of Africa. This work is mainly descriptive and lacks academic depth and analysis.

On the other hand, Tadesse Medhene authored the book of Al-Itihad: Political Islam and Black Economy in Somalia, the first comprehensive academic analysis of its kind in the Islamist movement after 9/11. The author provides a brief background of Islamism in Somalia during Siyad Barre rule (1969-1991) and moves on to examine extensively the role of Al-Itihad during the civil war and its interaction with the UN interventions in Somalia. It offers special attention to the issue of the ideological, political, and economic foundation of Al-Itihad that weakened the warlords. The last chapters deal with the Djibouti Peace Process in 2000 and the role of the international and regional actors. The author also offers policy guidelines for future actions to thwart the takeover by Islamists in Somalia. However, the timing of this research, its author, sources, and the main thesis call for suspicion of this study's motives. Tadesse wrote from the Somali opposition's perspective supported by Ethiopia; this opposition conferred on Ethiopia to mobilize their agenda against the Transitional National Government (TNG). The major theme of the book is that Al-Itihad is the umbrella terrorist organization shared by all Islamic organizations and that the TNG was built by Al-Itihad. Therefore, the TNG, as a product of terrorists, should be opposed and replaced by other national institutions with the support of the international community. The recommendations of the author were implemented later in Kenya in 2004 by establishing the Transitional Federal Government (TFG) headed by the former warlords who befriended Ethiopia. However, the consequence of this policy was disastrous and caused deteriorated security in the Horn of Africa.

Moreover, Andre le Sage's *Somalia and the War on Terrorism* undertook a field research on Islamism and counter-terrorism in Somalia. The author carried out his research in Mogadishu, where he met various local actors such as warlords, Islamic movement leaders, traditional elders, and members of traditional Sufi orders. In particular, he focused on Islah, Itihad, Islamic charities, Hawala-business, and the Islamic Courts. Providing an in-depth analysis of the Islamic movements, he concluded that political Islam is not monolithic, and doctrinal differences and competition exist between the various Islamist movements. Le Sage is credited with predicting the rise of Al-Shabab, a new derivative of Al-Itihad, and warning against it. Considering his dissertation as an initial study and admitting various limitations, he provided a number of recommendations such as continuing research and monitoring, opening dialogue with the moderate Islamists, and addressing social strains that push the population toward extremism. However, this moderate voice did not receive attention during the Bush administration which was entangled with the war on terrorism.

Furthermore, Hansen's work on Al-Shabab is the first comprehensive book on the militant Islamist group. The author examines the development of Al-Shabab chronologically in four stages. The first stage was initial formative period of 2005-06 as part of the Union of the Islamic Courts which had taken control of the capital Mogadishu after defeating the warlords in 2005. The second stage was the period of insurgency against Ethiopian occupation in 2007-2008. The third stage was the period 2009-2010 after the defeat of Somali government supported by Ethiopia and Al-Shabab took control of large territory in the southern Somalia. The fourth stage started in 2010 when Al-Shabab lost vast territory to the African Union Forces

(AMISOM) in collaboration of Somali National Army. This book's in-depth analysis and description of the Al-Shabab is valuable contribution to the subject matter.

There are also many other valuable researches on this topic; for instance, relevant papers include Roland Marshal's study titled "Islamic Political Dynamics in the Somali Civil War" that outlined the general developments of the ongoing Islamic revival in Somalia.[12] As one of the early studies, the paper has some errors and misconceptions, which does not belittle its merit and academic value. Also, Adam Hussein's paper "Political Islam in Somali History" offers a brief historical survey on the development of the Islamic movement and the four possible options of its future development. The study recognizes the inevitable role of moderate Islamism and criticizes counter-terrorism policies.[13] Moreover, the International Crisis Group (ICG) produced a unique study of Islamist movements in Somalia, classifying them into three categories: Jihadist Islamism, political Islam, and missionary activism. This report also offered a brief background of the Islamic movements.[14] Furthermore, Hansen and Mosley authored a research paper "The Muslim Brotherhood in the Wider Horn of Africa."[15] The study explored the general question of whether the Muslim Brotherhood in the region could act as a partner in the quest for development and peace in the Horn of Africa. It includes a historical section on the Islah Movement and its developmental organizations. Finally, the work of Afyare

---

[12] Roland Marchal, "Islamic Political Dynamics in the Somali Civil War," in *Islamism and its Enemies in the Horn of Africa*, ed. Alex De Waal (Indiana University Press, 2006), 114-146.
[13] Hussein M. Adam, "Political Islam in Somali History," in *Milk and Peace, Drought and War: Somali Culture, Society and Politics*, ed. Markus Hoehne and Virginia Luling (London: Hurst & Company, 2010), 119-135.
[14] International Crisis Group, "Somalia's Islamist" (African Report No. 100, December 12, 2005), available from http://www.crisisgroup.org/en/regions/africa/horn-of-africa/somalia/100-somalias-islamists.aspx (accessed on 22 June, 2010).
[15] StigJarle Hansen and AtleMesoy, "The Muslim Brotherhood in the Wider Horn of Africa" (Norwegian Institute for Urban and Regional Research (NIBR) Report 2009), 33.

Elmi "Understanding the Conflagration" produces an informative chapter on the role of Islam and Islamic awakening in the peace building in Somalia. Writing from an insider's perspective, Elmi concludes with strong statement of inevitability of an Islamist movement's rule in Somalia.[16]

Phase One: The Islamic Revival (1800-1950)

Islamic revivalism began in the 19th century and dealt with the emergence of various Sufi brotherhoods. Sufi orders, with their symbolical activities and closeness to people's culture, contributed greatly to the revival of Islam in the masses, using innovative mobilization techniques. The most popular techniques are called *Dikri* in which religious poems (*Qasaaid*)are composed and chanted in a chorus and in an artistic manner, blessing people, reciting the Qur'an for the sick and diseased, annual remembrance of deceased parents (closer and distant), the commemoration of the birth of the Prophet (*Mawliid*), visiting the blessed sheikh's tombs *(Siyaaro)*, etc. These techniques create collectiveness and a sense of belonging and mutual support for the adherents of the Sufi orders. They also create a web of trans-clan networks in society, diluting clan polarization and segmentation.

Although Sufism had existed and had been practiced since early Islamic history, most of the organized brotherhoods emerged in the eleventh, twelfth and thirteenth centuries AD. For instance, Qadiriyah was founded by Sheikh Abdulqadir al-Jeylani (1077-1166). In Somalia, the advent of Sufism has been recorded since the early fifteen century with the arrival of 44 Islamic scholars under the leadership of Sheikh Ibrahim Abu-Zarbai in 1430. Nevertheless, its renewal and reform as an organized movement was noted from the last quarter of the nineteenth century to the middle of the twentieth century.

---

[16]Afyare Abdi Elmi, *Understanding the Somalia Conflagration: Identity, Political Islam and Peace building* (London: Pluto Press, 2010), 72.

Indeed, Said Samatar wrote, "These years between 1880 and 1920 can be described as the era of the Sheikhs in Somali history."[17] Revival is an important dimension of the historical experience of Muslims; Sufi reformation entailed shifting from individual Islamic activities to institutionalized orders.[18]

Traditional Sufi orders have mainly taken peaceful approaches to socio-religious reforms through Islamic propagation and spiritual revitalization.[19] As such, they dominated religious life, reaching out to populations in the urban and rural areas alike, most of whom had identified with one of the Sufi orders by the nineteenth century. Sufi sheikhs, besides their complementary role in running community affairs, established Islamic commonwealth centers (Jamaacooyin) whose dwellers gave their allegiance only to their Sufi masters/sheikhs. Moreover, in contradiction to conventional historiography that considers Sufi orders to be mainly apolitical, many leaders of the Sufi orders and their disciples became the supreme leaders of their communities. In this way, clan allegiances and loyalties were diluted and at times transformed into ideological loyalties. Occasionally, both religious and secular authorities are combined in one leader creating a strong Sufi master or sheikh. Moreover, most of the Islamic education centers were located in settlements on agricultural areas and around water wells and many of these settlements were later transformed into villages, towns, and cities. In this way, Sufi orders transformed pastoral society to settled communities engaged in agriculture and/or trade.[20]

---

[17] Said Samatar, *Oral Poetry and Somali Nationalism: The Case of Sayyid Mohamed Abdulle Hassan* (Cambridge: Cambridge University Press, 1982), 97.

[18] Scott Steven Rees, *Patricians of the Banadir: Islamic Learning, Commerce and Somali Urban Identity in the Nineteenth Century* (PhD thesis submitted to the University of Pennsylvania, 1996), 306.

[19] The nature of peacefulness of Sufi Orders may be interrupted because of external provocations, such as colonialism in the case of many scholars, exemplified by Sayyid Mohamed Abdulle Hassan, and internal doctrinal conflicts, such as the conflict between Baardheere Jama'a and Geledi Sultanates and current fighting between Al-Shabab and Ahl al-Sunna wa al-Jama'a.

[20] David Laitin and Said Samatar, Somalia: Nation in Search of a State (Boulder: Westview Press, 1987) 45.

The two main Sufi orders in Somalia are Qadiriyah and Ahmadiyah and each of them has its local offshoots.[21] Qadiriyah was brought to western and northern Somalia in the early sixteenth century by Abubakar b. Abdallah al-Aidarusi (d. 1502) from Hadramout in Yemen and its two branches are Zayli'iyah and Uweysiyah.[22] Zayli'iyah was founded by Sheikh Abdirahman al-Zayli'i (1815-1882), who was based in Qulunquul near the town of Dhagahbur in the Somali State of Ethiopia. Uweysiyah was founded by the spiritual master Sheikh Aweys ibn Ahmad al-Barawe (1846-1907). The Ahmadiyah Brotherhood was founded by Ahmad Ibn Idris al-Fasi (1760-1837) and has three offshoots in Somalia: Rahmaniyah, Salihiyah, and Dandarawiyah. Rahmaniyah is founded by Sheikh Abdirahman ibn Mohamud (d. 1874) instead of Sheikh Ali Maye Durogba who is mistakenly considered the founder of the Order. Salihiyah has two branches: southern branch introduced by Sheikh Mohamed Guled al-Rashidi (d.1918) and northern branch by Sayyid Mohamed Abdulle Hassan (1856-1920). Dandarawiyah was introduced by Sayyid Adan Ahmed and has a limited followership in northern Somalia.[23]

Scholars of Sufi brotherhood led the initial Somali reaction to the rule of the colonial powers. The historiographical speculation that the Salihiyah order was anti-colonial while the Qadiriyah order remained acquiescent and even collaborated with the colonizers has no historical basis. The well-known historical fact is that "Sheikh Aweys promoted resistance to the European colonizers in German-occupied Tanganyika and

---

[21] Most scholars fail to distinguish between the original Sufi order and their later derivatives. Sometimes these Sufi orders are said to be three, making Salihiyah a separate order from Ahmadiyah and also neglecting the existence of the Rufaiyah Order. See Laitin and Samatar, *Somalia: Nation*, 45.
[22] See Mohamed Abdallah Al-Naqira, *Intishar al-Islam fi SharqIfriqiyahwaMunahadat al-GarbiLahu* (Riyadh: Dar al-Marikh, 1982), 160.
[23] Cabdirisaq Caqli, *Sheikh Madar. AsaasahaHargeysa* (biographical work on Sheikh Madar written in Somali Language, no date or publishing house).

even Uganda and eastern Congo."[24] Evidences shows that Qadiriyah's encounter with colonialism was circumstantial and prudent, and the narrative that focuses on singular approach or prioritizes militancy over peaceful means of struggle is simply myopic. These approaches should be seen as complementing each other, depending on the situations in which available options are evaluated. Movements who encountered colonialism through armed resistance operated in different territories and include both Qadiriyah and Ahmadiyah. For instance, Sayyid Mohamed Abdulle Hassan who belonged to Salihiyah order of Ahmadiyah offshoot led a Darawish Movement for roughly 21 years (1900-1921), against British, Italian, and Ethiopian forces. Moreover, Lafole massacre (1896), where disciples of Sheikh Ahmad Mahdi who belong to the Qadiriyah order, were accused for anti-colonial activities and retaliated by the Italians. The Biyomaal revolt (1896-1908) led by Macalimiin (Islamic teachers) continued resisting colonization for 12 years and ultimately networked their resistance with the northern one of Darawish Movement, demonstrating the unity of purpose and nationhood. Moreover, revolts led by Sheikh Hassan Barsane (d.1926) and Sheikh Bashir (d.1945) demonstrate their uncompromising attitude towards colonial programs. Unfortunately, most of these movements had been suppressed by 1924, and their leaders were marginalized, oppressed, eliminated and excluded after the colonial domination of Somalia. On the other hand, Somali Islamic scholars confronted colonialism both in armed and non-violent means. Those scholars who opted for violent means have been recorded widely in the Somali history and immortalized, while peaceful and non-violent scholars and activists were neglected and marginalized in the historiography.

With the suppression of the Islamic scholars, new approaches were used to confront colonial influence. It

---

[24]Lewis, *Saints*, 36.

included establishing initial civil society organizations and later political parties. The first civil society organization, the Somali Islamic Association, was founded in Aden in 1925 by the Somali activist Haji Farah Omar.[25] Other organizations that appeared in the Northern Somalia include Khayriyah, the Officials' Union and the Somali Old Boys Association (SOBA). The emergence of the civil society organizations in the Southern Somalia were delayed comparatively with the northern Somalia and appeared on the scene during the Second World War under the rule of the British Military Administration (BMA). Early organizations included *Jamiyat al-Kheyriyah al-Wadaniyah* (Patriotic Beneficiary Union), founded in 1942,[26] the Somali Youth Club (SYC), founded in 1943, and Native Betterment Committee (NBC), founded in 1942.[27] On the other hand, modern political developments of Somalia began in the early years of the Second World War after the 1941 defeat of Italian Fascism in the Horn of Africa and the establishment of the British Military Administration (BMA) in most parts of the Somali territories. The BMA, although completely destroyed existing small economic projects and infrastructures, brought an improved political environment by abolishing the "restrictions of the Italian regime on local political associations and clubs."[28] This new policy encouraged the development of the political consciousness of the Somalis after many of them had participated in the two wars: the Italian–Ethiopian War of 1935 and the Second World War

---

[25] See SaadiaTouval, *Somali Nationalism: International Politics and the Drive for Unity in the Horn of Africa* (Cambridge: Cambridge University Press, 1963), 65.
[26] Mohamed Mukhtar, *Historical dictionary of Somalia* (African Historical Dictionary Series, Lanham: MD: Scarecrow Press, 2003), 106. Also, Salah Mohamed Ali, *Hudur and the History of Southern Somalia* (Cairo: Mahda Bookshop Publisher, 2005), 340.
[27] AbdurahmanAbdullahi, "Non-state Actors in the Failed State of Somalia: Survey of the Civil Society Organizations during the Civil War (1990-2002)." *DarasatIfriqiyah*, 31 (2004): 57-87. See also Salah Mohamed Ali, *Hudur*, 361.
[28] I. M. Lewis, *A Modern History*, 121. The destroyed or removed projects include the railway line connecting Mogadishu, Afgoye, and Villagio Della Abruzi; Afgoye Bridge; salt production machinery in Hafun; and Maggiajan and Kandala mines. See PoaloTripodi, *The Colonial Legacy in Somalia: Rome and Mogadishu: from Colonial Administration to Operation Restore Hope* (London: Macmillan Press, 1999), 45.

(1939-1954). As a result, the Somali Youth Club (SYC), a pan-Somali youth organization, was formed on 15 May 1943 in Mogadishu. From its founding members of 13 men, this club grew into a political party in 1947 and was renamed as the Somali Youth League (SYL). A comparable rise in the political consciousness appeared in the British Somali Protectorate and similar nationalist party was established in the name of the Somali National League (SNL) in 1951.

Phase Two: The Rise of the Islamic Consciousness (1950-1967)

Islam and Somaliness were harmonious terms used to signify pan-clan and anti-colonial ideologies to resist Christian colonialism and growing westernization. With the total colonial domination by 1930s, Islamic scholars were marginalized from leadership role and the new elites created in the colonial system were steadily taking over national leadership. During this period, Islamic education and understanding of Islam's comprehensive scope was very limited. In particular, consciousness of the political aspect of Islam that aims at creating a state and society based on definitive references to the Islamic principles was not developed yet. The common vision and strategic priority of the Somali people before independence was centered on the liberation of the country from the colonial yoke. Indeed, Islamic consciousness was in high alert because of its role in championing Muslim cause in the Horn of Africa and due to Somalia's geographical location at the Christian-Muslim converging lines. Moreover, as a strategic region connecting the oil-rich Arabian Peninsula with the Suez Canal and the Indian Ocean attracting European colonialism and Cold War superpower rivalry, both Islamic and national consciousness were continuously provoked.

Thus, both national and Islamic identity and consciousness were intertwined in the historical development of Somalia, offering supra-clan identity to the traditional society. What these two ideologies have in common is to inculcate in the people rejection of foreign domination and its uncompromising resistance. Thus, Islamic and nationalistic slogans were used to mobilize the masses for anti-colonial campaigns to liberate the nation. Modern nationalists and Islamic scholars worked collectively and national ideology was compounded from nationalism and Islam. The evidence of unity of purpose and struggle is that Islamic scholars were recognized as national heroes, namely, Imam Ahmed Gurey, Sayyid Mohamed Abdulle Hassan, Sheikh Hassan Barsane and Sheikh Bashir.[29] Another factor that prompted the development of the nationalistic and Islamic consciousness was religious antagonism between Somali Muslims and Christian colonizers during the struggle for the independence. Moreover, Christian missionary activities in the Muslim society had provoked resentment in the society. Furthermore, rising Islamic consciousness was specifically linked to the development of modern education in the Arabic language and connections with the Arab/Islamic world. Within local, regional, and international dynamics, Islamic consciousness began to emerge and grow.

The development of the Islamic consciousness should be seen as a historical evolution and a range of responses to the challenges from specific tensions. It was concurrent with the growing nationalism in the second half of the twentieth century. They provided a supra-clan identity in a traditional society and shared in being indistinguishable from anti-

---

[29] Two national heroes that were given special position in the Somali History were Imam Ahmed Gurey (Garan) and Sayyid Mohamed Abdulle Hassan. Imam Ahmed fought against Ethiopian and Portuguese intervention forces, representing Christian superpowers of that time, from 1531 until he was killed in 1543. Ahmad's war with Ethiopia is described in detail in the *Futuh al-habaša* ("The Conquest of Ethiopia"), written in Arabic by Ahmad's follower *Shihab al-Addin Ahmad ibn Abdulqadir*.Sayyid Mohamed fought against Ethiopia and Britain in 1900-1921. References on Sayyid Mohamed are many; however, two academic works stand out: Abdi Sheik Abdi, *Divine Madness: Mohammed Abdulle Hassan (1856-1920)* (Zed Books Ltd., London, 1993), and Said S. Samatar, *Oral Poetry and Somali Nationalism: The Case of Sayyid Mahammad Abdille Hasan* (Cambridge: Cambridge University Press, 1982).

colonial resistance ideologies. However, with the introduction of a modern education system and competition between Western education in the Italian and English languages and modern education in Arabic in the 1950s, the trends of westernization and Arabism began to emerge. The culture of westernization, carrying with it secularization of the state and society, and Arabism, delivering the Islamic consciousness, nationalism, and anti-colonialism, were fiercely competing with one another. In the 1950s, the Egyptian regime and the Muslim Brotherhood were promoting Arab nationalism and Islamism, respectively. Egyptian cultural influence on Somalia gained momentum in the 1950s and 1960s within the Cold War politics and mutual strategic cooperation between Somalia and Egypt.

Specifically, two broad sets of factors had contributed to the growth of Islamic consciousness in the 1950s and 1960s. The first set contributed to the increased capacity of the society and its resilience in withstanding the torrent ideas of westernization and western modernization. These factors included the introduction of the Egyptian system of schools, the formation of early Islamic organizations, the provision of scholarships to Somali students in the civil and military higher institutions in Egypt and other Arab countries, and other cultural means. These developments had created a new Arabic-speaking Somali elite, political leaders, and Islamic scholars who were against westernization and secularization and lobbied for Arabism and Islamism. Some of these scholars were influenced by the Muslim Brotherhood ideology and the Salafism of Saudi Arabia and introduced them to Somalia. The second set of factors was involved in provoking the Islamic consciousness. They included the activities of Christian missionaries. The earliest missionaries were French Catholic Mission in British Somaliland (1891-1910), the Roman Catholic Church in Mogadishu (1904-1991) and the Swedish Overseas Lutheran Church in Kismayo (1896-1935).

Furthermore, the Mennonite Mission and the Sudan Interior Mission joined the Christian venture in the 1950s, with the return of Italy as the UN trusteeship administrator.

After independence in 1960, within the local, regional, and global context of the Cold War, regional competition, and transformation of the Somali society, the Islamic consciousness was gradually growing along with the growing westernization of the elites. The manifestations of this growth were the appearance of modern Islamist scholars educated in Arab universities and marginalized in the job market and the proliferation of Arabic schools, books, newspapers, and libraries. Nevertheless, in the first nine years of independence, there were no tangible conflicts between Islamic scholars and the new elites, with the priorities of the entire nation seemingly focused on consolidating the independence and pursuing the "Greater Somalia" project. Islamic scholars of these years became the pioneers of a new era of the Islamic awakening, in which Islamic activities took new dimensions.

Finally, the harmonious Somali society where tradition and modernity coexisted, the state and Islam were not in direct conflict, and tolerance and dialogue were exercised, began to falter. The growth of the Islamist elites and their rejection of marginalization led to increased Islamic activities and eventual establishment of more robust organizations. At the same time, westernization and secularization were also growing. Thus, the gap between the two camps gradually widened.

Phase Three: The Beginning of the Islamic Awakening (1967-1978)

The awakening of Islam started to take shape after Somalia's independence in 1960 and emerged strongly after 1967. It was as an outcome of the cultural divide promoted by multi-curriculum education programs, in Arabic, Italian, and English, and links with conflicting actors in the Cold War atmosphere. The split of the elites into non-Islamist and

Islamist factions slowly began to emerge, challenging social cohesion and the unifying aspects based on race, religion, and national aspiration. The roots of this division can be found in the clash between the nature of the state and nature of the society. The post-colonial nation-state was nationalistic, hierarchical, centralized, and quasi-secular, while the society was clannish, egalitarian, decentralized, and Islamic. In these strained conditions, the society as a whole was torn apart by the elites who gravitated towards competing ideologies such as liberal Western democracy, Socialism, and Islam. Although they possessed a strong cultural foundation, the weaker and less developed elites during this time were Islamists.

The bifurcation of the elites and their development, as illustrated in the figure (1), demonstrates the four types of elites in Somalia. The traditional elites consist of clan elders and Islamic scholars, who constitute traditional leaders. Modern elites consisting non-Islamist elites and Islamist elites, the two super-structural elites created mainly through modern education.[30] As the diagram indicates the dynamics of Islam (traditional and modern), clan (represented by elders) and the state (represented by secular elites) is the most challenging issue in Somalia.

---

[30] Islamist is an activist in realizing objectives of the Islamic movements which includes wide range of activities such as promoting Islamic beliefs, prescriptions, laws, or policies that are held to be Islamic in character. On the other hand, non-Islamists signify majority of the Muslims who are neither secular nor Islamic activists, some of whom are not even practicing Islam or even pretending to be secular nominally.

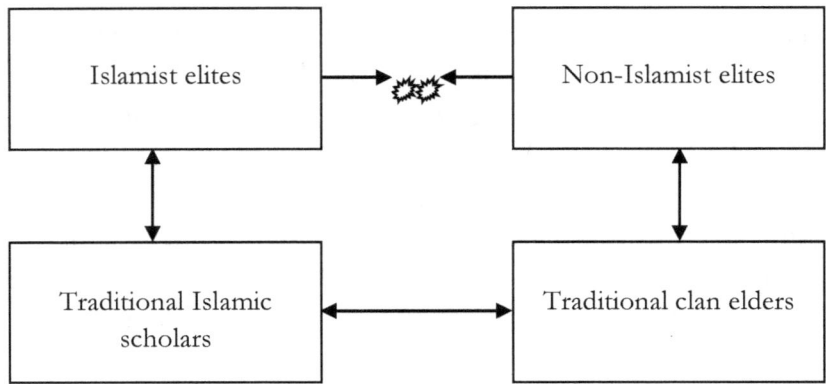

Fig 3. Development of the elites in Somalia

The relations between the traditional elites are cordial and collaborative in order to maintain community cohesion, however, non-Islamist elites and the Islamist elites are antagonistic because of their different position on the nature of the state. Non-Islamist elites, the inheritors of the post-colonial state, resolutely covet to retain the status-quo of the nature of the state whereas Islamists advocate zealously for its Islamization.[31] The free choice of the citizens through democratic process and peaceful resolution of the elite conflict is blocked by the non-Islamist elites who rely primarily on the support of the western powers. The consequence of this policy is severe and breeds extremism in the name of Islam and curtails moderate Islamism in general.

Consequently, in 1967, the country was in search of a new ideology, having been embarrassed by malpractices in liberal democracy; thus, socialism and Islamism were luring. Socialism was promoted by the socialist countries, and thousands of the Somali students were offered scholarships and indoctrinated in those countries. These students became later the elites that challenged the workings of liberal democracy. On the other hand, Islamists were not happy with

---

[31] For detailed description of the elite development and their relations refer to AbdurahmanAbdullahi, "Tribalism, Nationalism and Islam: The crisis of the political Loyalties in Somalia (MA thesis, Islamic Institute, McGill University, 1992), 92-101.

the entire secular tendency of the nation-state and opposed the growing leftist ideology, as well as the liberalist malpractices. They were also dissatisfied with the state policy on Islam that remained very similar to the inherited colonial approach based on the existence of two separate spaces; public and private. Islam which Islamists advocated for as comprehensive and applicable to all aspects of life was relegated to the private realm. They were not satisfied with Islamic window dressing such as establishment of a Ministry of Religious Affairs and occasional gesture of the politicians during Islamic festivities.

In 1967, after the pitiful of political and social harvests of the first years of independence, Abdirashid Ali Sharmarke was elected President of Somalia, and he appointed Mohamed Ibrahim Igal as the Premier. The new regime adopted two new policies that enhanced the fragmentation and conflict in the Somali society. In the domestic front, the regime planned to curb budding democracy by sowing dictatorship through transforming the ruling SYL party, the only political party in the country. This new trend was supported by Western countries and conservative Arab regimes, in particular Saudi Arabia which offered considerable financial assistance.[32] The goal of this undertaking was to curb the Soviet influence in Somalia and to reverse previous policies geared towards the Eastern blocks initiated by Dr. Abdirashid Ali Sharmarke in 1963. Therefore, the regime initiated policies intended to encourage the fragmentation of other parties. Consequently, more than 60 clan-based parties competed for 123 seats in the parliament during the 1969 election. As planned by the state, all Members of Parliament from the small, clan-based parties

---

[32] Saudi Arabia offered a loan of $50 million to Somalia designated to cover the election expenses in support of the SYL regime. See Mohamed Sharif Mohamud, "*Faslun fi al-Alaqat al-Somaliayah al-Saudiyah*", 2010 (Somali-Saudi relations), available from http://arabic.alshahid.net/columnists/8598 (accessed on February 6, 2010). This number seems exaggerated even though Mohamed Sharif insists that $50 million loan is true in my interview with him in Mogadishu on June 27, 2015.

were absorbed within the SYL after the election.[33] In the process, the National Army was implicated in rigging the election to dent its nationalistic image and weaken its credibility. At the same time, the Somali masses became utterly dismayed with the government because of widespread corruption, economic stagnation, rampant unemployment, and clan fighting caused by the rigged election. This state of affairs was characterized by Cabdalla Mansuur as "democracy gone mad."[34]

The second step taken by the regime aimed at changing national policies on "Greater Somalia" was the foundation of the Somali foreign policy. Since independence, Somalia supported Somali liberation movements in the Northern Frontier District (NFD) in Kenya, Western Somalia in Ethiopia and French Somaliland (Djibouti) as missing three parts of "Great Somalia".[35] The new policy was to improve the relations with the Western countries and to curb Soviet influence in Somalia embodied, in their technical support for the Somali army. Prime Minister Igal undertook the soft foreign policy approach of détente which was aimed at alleviating Somalia's political, military, and economic ailments. He established congenial neighborly relations with Kenya and Ethiopia and restored the severed relationship with Britain in 1962. Somalia broke diplomatic relations with Britain "when the special British NFD Commission determined that, despite the fact that the majority of the Somalis in the region wished to join the Somali Republic, Britain should grant Kenya independence and announced that Kenya will decide on the

---

[33] In 1969, all MPs joined the SYL except one person, the former Prime Minister Abdirisaq Haji Hussein.
[34] Abdalla Mansur, "Contrary to a Nation: The Cancer of Somali State'" in Ahmed, Ali Jimale (ed), *The Invention of Somalia* (Lawrenceville, NJ, Red Sea Press, 1995), 114
[35] NFD is the region in Kenya populated by the Somali people, while Western Somalia or Ogaden is a Somali territory annexed by Ethiopia. Both parts have Somali populations and are in the Horn of Africa. They had been divided by the colonial powers and then reclaimed by the Somali state as part of the "Greater Somalia."

matter."³⁶ The new Somali foreign policy was welcomed by Western powers and Somalia's neighboring countries but was perceived as a sell-out for the cause of Somali nationalism by domestic political opponents such as leftists and Islamists.³⁷ Thus, the two policies of the regime were unpopular, and their ramifications led to subsequent political uncertainties. The political gambit that started with the assassination of President Sharmarke on 15th October, 1969 and Prime Minister Igal's overt clannish maneuvering in the parliament to elect a new president were preludes to the military coup of 21st October, 1969.

Against this background, the year 1967 was the culmination of Arabic cultural influence and the maturation of Islamist elites. In the year, the first organization for Arabic educated elites was established under the name *Munadamat al-Nahdah al-Islāmiyah "Nahdah"* and soon other Islamic organizations followed such as *Ahal* and *Wahdah*.³⁸ The climate was ripe for change, and such organizations were responding to various internal and external tensions. The Somali Islamic awakening was not an isolated phenomenon; it was part of a worldwide Muslim upheaval after the defeat of the Arab forces during the war with Israel in 1967. This defeat set off a wave of soul-searching and the demand for a new ideology to replace the defeated secular Arab nationalism. The answer to the national cataclysm was to seek solace in Islamism, which was until then suppressed by the Arabic nationalist/socialist regimes. Therefore, Islamist movements inspired by Hassan al-Banna, al-Maududi, and Sayyid Qutb were gaining ground and amassing support. This awakening had been simmering since the suppression of the Muslim Brotherhood in Egypt in 1954

---

³⁶ See Ibrahim Farah, "Foreign Policy and Conflict in Somalia, 1960-1990" (PhD diss., University of Nairobi, 2009), 107.
³⁷ Ibid., 117.
³⁸ *Nahdah*was established in 1967 in Mogadishu, and had engaged in various Islamic activities, such as the establishment of libraries with contains MB literature and the *Da'wa*programs. The most popular program was the Qur'anic commentary of Sheikh Mohamed Moalim Hassan (1934-2000), which started in 1968 and continued until 1976.

and the execution of the famous Egyptian Islamic scholar Sayyid Qutb along with two other members of the MB in 1966.[39] This event greatly shocked and inspired Muslims all over the world. Many Somali Islamic scholars changed their positive views on the Egyptian regime that they had held because of its earlier provision of educational opportunities for Somalia and its ardent support for the Somali nationalistic cause. As a result of this incident, the MB literature garnered immense interest and attracted huge readership. In particular, two of Sayyid Qutb's works became extremely popular such as *Ma'alim fi al- Ṭariq* (Milestones) and Fi Ḍilal al-Qur'an (In the Shade of the Qur'an), the latter being a 30-volume commentary on the Qur'an with an innovative method of interpretation.

The Islamic awakening in Somalia acquired a new momentum with the military coup in 1969 and the adoption of Socialism as the national ideology. The military regime had adopted modernization policies in line with Socialism which went against the culture of the people and Islamic laws, thereby widening the fissure and ideological polarization in the society. By the end of 1960s, three "Proto-Muslim Brotherhood" organizations were established. These organizations are *Nahdah*,[40] *Ahl al-Islam* (the People of Islam) "Ahal"[41] and *Wahdat al-Shabab al-Islami* (the Union of Islamic

---

[39] Sayyid Qutub (1906-1966) was an Islamist scholar and the leading intellectual of the MB in the 1950s and 1960s. He was imprisoned (1954-64) and then hanged in 1966 by Jamal Abdi-Nasser. The other two members were Muhammad Yusuf Awash and Abd al-Fattah Ismail. See Zafar Bangash, "Remembering Sayyid Qutb, an Islamic intellectual and leader of rare insight and integrity", available from http://web.youngmuslims.ca/online_library/books/milestones/remember.htm (accessed on January 28, 2010).

[40] The influence of the MB was clear in the bye-laws of Nahdah and its top leaders, the president, the vice president, and the secretary general were members of the MB. For more details refer to AbdurahmanAbdullahi, "The Islamic Movement in Somalia", 172- 176

[41] Ahal was established in 1969 and was transformed from Sufism to proto-MB in late 1960s as they are affected by the Qur'an commentary of Sheikh Mohamed Moalim Hassan and the Islamic library of Nahdah. For more details of Ahal, refer to AbdurahmanAbdullahi, "The Islamic Movement in Somalia", 182-190.

Youth) *"Wahdah"*.⁴² Also, Salafia organization *Jamiyat Ihya al-Sunna* (Revivification of the Prophet's Tradition) appeared in the scene.⁴³ The watershed conflict between the Islamic awakening and the military regime was in the secularization of the Family Law in 1975 and the execution of 10 Islamic scholars and subsequent confrontation between Islamists and the military regime.⁴⁴

In conclusion, five factors played a pivotal role in strengthening Islamic awakening in Somalia in the 1970s. The first factor is the role of Islamic scholars in spreading modern Islamic-movement concepts and ideas through public education programs and lectures. The second factor is the activities of student organizations of *Ahal* and *Wahdah*, especially their enthusiasm and outreach programs. The third factor is the influence of the Muslim Brotherhood literature brought to Somalia by *Nahdah*. The fourth factor is the encouragement by conservative Islamic countries such as Saudi Arabia. The fifth factor is the proclamation of the Socialist ideology and adoption of the secular Family law by the military regime, which ignited enormous Islamic sentiment.

Finally, even though the proto-Muslim Brotherhood organizations of the Islamic awakening that include Scholar's organization of *Nahdah* and youth organizations of *Ahal* and *Wahdah* were short-lived, their Islamic call and impact were significant and lasting. They played different roles and complemented each other's efforts; for example *Ahal* and *Waxdah* focused on recruiting high school and university students in their respective geographical locations, in the

---

⁴² Wahdah was formed in Hargeysa in 1969 and transformed from Sufism to proto-MB transpired in 1974. For more details of Wahdah refer to AbdurahmanAbdullahi, "The Islamic Movement in Somalia", 191-203.

⁴³ *JamiyatIhya al-Sunna* was founded in 1967 by Sheikh Nur Ali Olow (1918-1995) and its role was insignificant even though influenced some prominent personalities like General Mohamed Abshir and Yassin Nur Hassan, former Interior Minister.

⁴⁴ AbdurahmanAbdullahi, "Women, Islamists and the Military Regime in Somalia: The New Family Law and its Implications". In *Milk and Peace, Drought and War: Somali Culture, Society and Politics. (Essays in Honour of I. M. Lewis)*, edited by M. V. Hoehne and V. Luling, 137 Å 160. London: Hurst, 2010.

southern and northern Somalia. *Nahdah* assumed the role of providing Islamic education and supplied Islamic literature. *Nahdah* operated for only three years, although its members remained prominent in the Islamic activism for a long period. *Ahal* ceased to exist in 1977 after about eight years of active work, and its members were divided into different new Islamic organizations. *Wahdah* members were divided and some of them joined *Al-Itihad* in 1983 and others joined Islah in 1999.[45] All three organizations of the Islamic awakening were encountering common challenges of westernization, secularization, and Socialism by employing Islamic activism as their resistance ideology. Moreover, these organizations could be characterized as immature with great emotional attachment to the Islamic teachings and its comprehensive way of life, very low organizational capacity and resources, and idealistic approach to social and political realities in the country. The relationship between these organizations and the military regime gradually developed into an open confrontation which had a lasting impact on the political developments in Somalia.

Phase Four: The Emergence of the Islamic movements (1978-1983)

With the crackdown on Islamists after the Family Law proclamation in 1975, most leading scholars were either imprisoned or fled the country. The Islamic awakening, hitherto united in its ideology and leadership, was fragmented and the ideology of extremism emerged strongly. This was provoked by the harshness of the regime in dealing with Islamic scholars, the encouragement and support by the conservative Arab regimes of the Islamists, and their contact with the varieties of Islamic ideologies and activism that changed the Islamic landscape in Somalia. In August 1975,

---

[45] *Wahdah* and *Jama'a Islamiyah* formed *Al-Itihad al-Islami* in 1983 in a precipitate merging that did not last long. At the end, most of the *Wahdah* members joined *Al-Itihad* or Islah in 1990s. For more details refer to AbdurahmanAbdullahi, *"The Islamic Movement in Somalia"*, 202-203.

seven months after the Family Law fiasco, 60 prominent, high-ranking officers were sacked from their positions. Included in these were the leaders of the Islamic awakening: Sheikh Mohamed Garyare, Sheikh Mohamed Moalim, and Sheikh Abdulqani. Both Sheikh Mohamed Moalim and Sheikh Abdulqani were imprisoned, while Sheikh Mohamed Garyare fled the country. In addition to those imprisoned, some of the activists of the Islamic awakening fled to Saudi Arabia and Sudan, and began to regroup there. It is important to note that the flight of Somali Islamists to Saudi Arabia occurred during a time of booming economies and Islamic revivalism throughout the Arab/Muslim world. This economic well-being and education offered the emerging Islamic movement the impetus to reorganize themselves again. Also, students at Saudi universities who joined the Muslim Brotherhood in Sudan and Saudi Arabia were working among Somalis in Saudi Arabia to recruit them into their underground organization (Islah movement). Also, among those who succeeded to flee was the leader of *Ahal*, Abdulqadir Sheikh Mohamud who regrouped members of Ahal in Saudi Arabia.

As a consequence of the migration of the Islamic activists mainly to Saudi Arabia, three Islamic organizations emerged from the ashes of the Islamic awakening organizations. The first organization that announced itself was the Islah Movement established officially on 11th July, 1978. Its establishment was announced after four months of the retreat by the Somali army from the war with Ethiopia.[46] Islah proclaimed representing an ideological continuation of the *Nahdah* and elected Sheikh Mohamed Garyare as its first leader.[47] The second move towards the Islamist fragmentation was undertaken by Abdulqadir Haji Mohamud, the leader of *Ahal* who professed *Takfir* ideology and succeeded to

---

[46] The Somali government ordered its forces to retreat from Ethiopia on March 9, 1978, and the last significant Somali unit left Ethiopia on March 15, 1978, marking a disastrous end of the war.

[47] Many of the former members of *Nahdah* were in prison and others were made aware of the reorganizing of the organization under a new name.

convince prominent leaders of *Ahal* to adopt ideology of *Takfir*.[48] Other members of *Ahal* who were hesitant to join Islah and the Takfir established a new organization called *Jama'a Islamiyah*. This organization combined former Ahal members who considered themselves belonging to the Muslim Brotherhood and many graduates from the Saudi universities who claimed adhering to Salafism. Gradually, Salafia tendency gained the upper hand and the organization took on the character of a Salafia movement. This organization evolved in 1983 to *Al-Itihad* when *Wahdah* and *Jama'a Islamiyah* were unified.[49] Therefore, in the late 1970s and early 1980s, five organizations based on three different Islamic persuasions had appeared in Somalia: Muslim Brotherhood persuasion *(Islah, Wahdah, Ikhwan "Aala-sheikh")*, Salafia *(Al-Itihad)* and *Takfir*. *Takfir* group were not popular and remain small underground organization while other organizations were growing.

By 1990, there were four major Islamic organizations: *Al-Itihad, Islah, Wahdah and Ikhwan (Aala-sheikh)*.[50] Indeed, the Islamic awakening and its institutions were inclined to the Muslim Brotherhood methodology though lacked much of the organizational expertise until 1980. However, in the 1980s, *Al-Itihad* became the strongest Islamic organization in Somalia, and the Salafia ideology took prominence;[51] while other three organizations adhering to the MB methodology were relatively weak and were competing with each other because of many local and external factors. However, by 1990s, Islah emerged strongly with robust socio-political programs and made an

---

[48] Hassan Haji Mohamud interviewed by the author, April 10, 2010, Nairobi, Kenya.

[49] Itihad is the mother organization of Salafia in Somalia; it was renamed as *Al-Ictisambil-Kitabiwa Sunnah* or Itisam in mid 1990s. Hence, Al-Itihad and Al-Itisam became synonym. In the beginning of 1990s Al-Itihad was drifting toward militancy and was entangled in armed conflicts from 1991 to 1997, after that it became fragmented and its activities were downgraded.

[50] Ikhwan, also known as *Aala-Sheikh*, was established after the release of Sheikh Mohamed Moalim from the prison in 1982. Sheikh Mohamed was designated to be their guide and mentor.

[51] Salafism had spread globally in as part of the rising influence of Saudi Arabia in global politics in 1960s. In Somalia, due to its being part of the Saudi geopolitical sphere, the influence of Salafism was noticeably augmented through students educated in the Saudi Islamic universities and through Somali migrant labour during the economic boom of the 1970s. For more details refer to AbdurahmanAbdullahi, *"The Islamic Movement in Somalia, 276-277.*

impact on other Islamist organizations in the socio-political sectors. Moreover, a new organization under the name of *Jamā'at at-Tablīgh* (Society for spreading faith) have been taking strong roots in Somalia since 1991 targeting grass roots level and reaching out across social and economic spectra.[52]

Conclusion

Historical evolution of the Islamic movements went through four major stages: the Islamic revival, the Islamic consciousness, the Islamic awakening and the Islamic movements. In all these stages, the role of Islam in the state and society was growing and both moderation and militancy were evident in every historical juncture. Militancy was always related to the Salafia influence while moderation was linked to Muslim brotherhood persuasion. This paper had demonstrated that Islamic movements share common historical background and advocate for the application of Islamic principles and values in the state and society. Nonetheless, they are not monolithic in their approaches and could be classified generally into Muslim Brotherhood and Salafia persuasions. Besides these two major persuasions, traditional Sufi brotherhoods remain functional even though some of them have been politicized under the name of "*Ahl-al-Sunna wal-Jama'a*".[53]

Islamic movements in Somalia were not immune from the social culture of fragmentation, internal competition, low organizational capacity and leadership crisis. Nevertheless, they were vital socio-political reality and their contribution in the provision of social services in the absence of the functioning state institutions is matchless. Moreover, the role

---

[52] *Jamā'at at-Tablīgh* or TablighiJama'a This movement was started in 1927 by Muhammad al-Kandhlawi in India to spread faith and spiritual reformation by working at the grass roots level. It became very active in Somalia after the civil war in 1991.

[53] *Ahlu Sunna Wa al-Jama'a* is a paramilitary Sufi group who became prominent in 2008, when it took up arms against al-Shabab, the extremist group who began to destroy the tombs of the country's Sufi scholars.

of Islamist entrepreneurs in reviving economic sectors is incomparable. Furthermore, since 2000, Islamists became prominent in politics and Islamic compliant constitution was adopted. Since 2008, both national leaders and armed oppositions have belonged to the Islamic persuasions.[54] Finally, even though, Somalia lacks competing ideologies with Islamic trends, it is also undeniable that Islamists lack necessary experience and expertise in the political sphere. Thus, current trend indicates growing role of inclusive policy based on equal rights of all citizens without discrimination and narrowing gap between Islamists and non-Islamists and their mutual cooperation in recovering the Somali state.

---

[54] After the election of Sheikh Sharif (2008-2012) and Hassan Sheikh (2012-2016) as the Presidents of Somalia and the emergence of Al-Shabab as the armed opposition to the state, Islamists took unchallenged prominent political role in Somalia.

II

Islamic Moderation in War-torn Somalia: The Views of Islah Movement on the Contemporary Issues

I desire naught save reform so far as I am able.
The Holy Qur'an (11:88)

Islah is a peaceful Islamic Movement in Somalia that adheres to the principles and methodology of the Islamic moderation. It is a success story worth telling in the war-torn Somalia.
It demonstrates the alternative way in approaching Somali puzzle beyond clan cleavages and religious intolerance.

Dr. Ali Sheikh Ahmed, former chairman of Islah
Mogadishu, July 11, 2008

Introduction

The growth of Islamic movements has been attracting greater interest over the last three decades, in particular after the 9/11 attack on US targets and the subsequent declaration of the Global War on Terrorism. Many factors have contributed to this growth; one of the major causes has been the failure of the post-colonial states in many Muslim countries and the attractiveness of the oppositional Islamic approach as an alternative. These movements took various courses to realize their agendas and formulated different methodologies and strategies because of the diverse conditions and environment in which they have grown and are operating.[1] For instance, some movements in dictatorial regimes or in Muslim communities under foreign occupation or those living as a

---

[1] Most Muslim countries are ruled by dictatorial regimes that violate human rights, creating conducive environment for the growth of violent organizations in reaction to the repressive state apparatus.

marginalized minority may resort to violence as the only available means of political expression. On the other hand, movements in the democratic environment usually participate in the democratic political process and implement successful social programs[2]. In the Somali context, Somali students in the Arab World universities in 1960s had been interacting with different Islamic groups, embraced similar ideas and gradually formed comparable movements. In particular, two main organizations have become more prominent since the 1980s; namely the Muslim Brotherhood affiliated to Islah (reform) Movement (1978) and the neo-Salafia associated with Al-Ittihad (Islamic Union) Movement (1980) and its successive offshoots[3].

Moderation is a general feature of Islam called *"al-Wasadiyah"* that sets itself up against all kinds of extremism: Ghuluw (excessiveness), Tanattu' (transgressing; meticulous religiosity) and Tashdid (strictness; austerity). The concepts of "moderation" and "extremism" are not newly coined terms used to classify Muslims since the 9/11 event and the Global War on Terrorism. Rather they were evident in early Muslim history since the "Kharijites" rebelled against the legitimate authority of Imam Ali bin Abidalib in the year 658 and initiated a path deviating from the mainstream Islamic moderation. Currently, all armed Islamic groups that subscribe to the ideology of "Takfir and Jihad" (judging an individual to be an infidel on the basis of difference in practice of Islam and then fighting them) could be called a neo-Kharijites and

---

[2] There are examples of armed Islamic movements in Kashmir, Afghanistan, Chechnya, Palestine, Algeria and Somalia. Examples of peaceful organizations are found in Kuwait, Bahrain, Yemen, Jordan, Turkey, Morocco, Algeria, Somalia and Egypt.

[3] At first, the neo-Salafia Movement in Somalia was named *"al-Jama al-Islamiya"* (1980); after uniting with the *Wahdat al-Shabab* Islamic organization, the name was changed to *"al-Ittihad al-Islami"*(1982); this was changed again to *"al-I'tisam bil kitabi wa Sunna"* in 1996 after their conflicts with the armed factions in Kismayo (1991), Puntland (1992) and Gedo (1995-96). The most recent name, *"Jama'at al-wifaaq al-Islaami,"* appeared in 2008 in the aftermath of the Islamic Court defeat with the allied forces of the TFG and Ethiopia. Al-Itihad is the backbone of the Union of the Islamic Courts.

extremists[4]. In this paper, moderation simply means the natural condition of the majority of the Muslims who are tolerant among themselves and with others, and avoid extremism either in belief or in behaviour.[5] Therefore, moderate Islamic movements are collective ventures of those individuals who reject violence as a political means and *"Takfir"* as a religious conviction while vigorously seeking to modernize their societies in the context of Islamic authenticity.

Scholarly studies of the Islamic movements in Somalia remain very superficial, based mostly on sensational media coverage and security related studies in the post-9/11 event and increased curiosity in the political Islam in the Horn of Africa.[6] Moreover, more interest was observed after the emergence of the Union of Islamic Courts (UIC) in 2006 and the subsequent Ethiopian intervention that captured the attention of the world. In the coverage of this, the Union of the Islamic Courts was branded as an alliance including the whole spectrum of Islamic groups. On the other hand, the Islah Movement officially distanced itself from being part of the UIC and demonstrated its distinctive nature and

---

[4] Other names such fundamentalists, radicals and terrorists are recently coined terms, mostly used pejoratively. For instance, Al-Qaida and its offshoots come under this category.

[5] The four main manifestations are: (1) Bigotry, prejudice and intolerance to differing opinions. (2) Perpetual commitment to excessiveness and tireless attempts to force others to emulate them. (3) Continual emphasis on out-of-time and out-of-date religious excessiveness. (4) Harshness, roughness and crudeness in calling people to Islam. See Abdurahman Baadiyow and Ibrahim Farah. "Reconciling the State and Society in Somalia: Reordering Islamic Work and Clan System." A paper presented at the International Somali Studies Association Conference in Ohio, August 2007. see http://www.geeskaafrika.com/academics_21jul08.pdf

[6] This type of literature includes International Crisis Group reports on Somalia. See http://www.crisisgroup.org. Also, Medhane Tadesse. "Islamic Fundamentalism in Somalia: its Nature and Implications," see www.somaliawatch.org. Also, Medhane Tadesse. *Al-Ittihaad*. (Addis Ababa, 2002). See also Shauy Shaul. *Somalia between Jihad and Restoration*. (London: Transaction Press, 2008). The more objective literature through focused on the security concerns includes: Le Sage, Andre. *Somalia and the war on terrorism: Political Islamic movements and US counter terrorism efforts*. (DPhil Thesis, Cambridge University/Jesus College, 2005). Menkhaus, Ken. *Somalia: State Collapse and the Threat of Terrorism*. (Oxford, New York: Oxford University Press for the International Institute for Strategic Studies; London, New York: Routledge, 2004).

programs.⁷ In doing so, it reaffirmed its firm adherence to the peaceful reform program that has persisted since its formation on July 11, 1978. This moderate approach was sustained during the ruthless dictatorial rule (1969-1991) and vicious civil war (1991-2008) that were highly tempting of violent approaches.

On August 12, 2008, Islah publicly announced the result of its five-year term election, in which its fourth chairman was elected by the Consultative *(Shura)* Council,⁸ demonstrating its firm commitment to the tradition of internal democracy, even in these tumultuous times in Somalia.⁹ A medical Doctor and former member of the transitional parliament was re-elected for five years in the his second term in 2013 Following table (6) illustrates the four chairmen of Islah elected in the last 38 years and their qualifications.

---

⁷ See the communiqué of the Islah Movement dated 21/06/2006 on revoking the membership of Dr. Mohamed Ali Ibrahim and denying any Islah's involvement in the Union of the Islamic Court. See http://www.islaax.org/arabic/bayaan

⁸ See http://www.Islah.org/arabic/Dorashada

⁹ According to the Islah by-law, every five years the organization has to elect its Consultative (Shura) Council which elects the Chairman and the two Vice-chairman. During the last 30 years, four chairmen were elected. Each chairman can be elected for only two terms of five years. The membership of Dr. Mohamed Ali Ibrahim was revoked after he joined the Islamic Court Union in 2006 in defiance of the organization's laws and policies.

Name of the Islah leaders (1978-2010)	Term in the office	Qualifications and current status
Sheikh Mohamed Nur Garyare	1978-1989	BA in Islamic Studies in 1965, Islamic University of Medina, Saudi Arabia. He was director of Islamic affairs, Ministry of Islamic affairs (1969-1973). Currently lives in Toronto, Canada.
Dr. Mohamed Ali Ibrahim	1989-1999	PhD in Hadith Science in 1994, Islamic University of Medina, Saudi Arabia, expelled from Islah in 2006 after joining Union of Islamic Courts defying non-violence Islah policy.
Professor Ali Sheikh Ahmed Abubakar	1999-2008	PhD in Islamic Studies in 1984, Islamic University of Medina, Saudi Arabia. Currently, he is former President of Mogadishu University.
Dr. Ali Basha Omar	2008-2018	Medical Doctor in 1976 specialized in ophthalmology and lectured in the Medical Faculty of Somali National University, former member of the Somali Parliament (2000-2008)

Table 4: The chairmen of Islah Movement and their qualifications

Historical Background of the Islamic Revival in Somalia

In the modern history of Somalia, Islam has been used as a strong mobilizing ideology in the early anti-colonial response led by the Islamic scholars and in the subsequent nationalist struggle.[10] However, the Somali Islamic League is considered to be the first effective Islamic organization, established in

---

[10] Differences between the anti-colonial and modern movements is that the former was led by the Sufi brotherhood sheikhs and therefore was traditional in nature, while the modern movement had all the characteristics of modern organizations, such as bylaws, programs and policies.

1952 in Mogadishu in reaction to the increased role of Christian missionary organizations after the return of Italian rule as administrator of the UN trusteeship in 1950.[11] This organization supported by the Somali Youth League (SYL) was mainly promoting education in the Arabic language and lobbied Egypt to open Arabic schools in competition with the Italian education system.[12] These schools were very effective in creating a new Somali elite educated in Arabic culture, with a close affinity to the Arab world. The role played by the Islamic League was to prepare the cultural grounds on which modern Islamic revivalism was to be formed later. After independence in 1960, a few students who had graduated from Arab universities carried modern Islamic ideas and introduced them to Somalia.[13] These Islamic scholars were inspired by the activities of the Muslim Brotherhood in Egypt, the Wahabi School of Saudi Arabia, the appearance of innumerable items of new Islamic literature and the existence of an intolerably corrupt regime in Somalia. All these factors provided ample fuel for the revival of Islamic consciousness and the formation of new social organizations led by modern Islamic scholars. *Al-Nahdah* (the Renaissance), the social club for young returnees from the Arab universities, was formed in Mogadishu in 1967 to promote Islamic values and Arabic

---

[11] The first Somali Islamic organization was founded by Farah Omar in Eden in 1925. The second was founded by Sheikh Sheriff "Mara-adde" and Sheikh Zahid under the name of the Islamic League in 1952. See Abdullahi, Abdurahman. "Non-State Actors in the Failed State of Somalia: Survey of the Civil Society Organizations in Somalia during the Civil War." *Darasaat Ifriqiyayyah*, 31 (2004): 57-87.

[12] Somali Youth League (SYL), the major nationalist movement sent a letter to the Egyptian prime minister Mustafa Nohas, requesting educational assistance for Somalia. See Sayyid Omar (2006). *Somali-Egyptian Relation*. MA Thesis, submitted to the Institute of Islamic and Arabic Studies in Cairo.

[13] Islamic scholars in Somalia had mainly graduated from the learning circles inside Somalia. However, new scholars began to graduate from the renowned Islamic universities such as Al-Azhar in Egypt and Al-MadinaUniversity in Saudi Arabia. Among these are Sh. Abdulqani Sh. Ahmed, Sh. Mohamed Ahmed Nur Garyare, Sh. Mohamed Moalim and others. These scholars had founded *Al-Nahda* society in Mogadishu. For a more detailed account see Abdurahman Abdullahi. "Political Islam in Somalia." *Middle Eastern Affairs Journal*. 1:3 (1993): 46-47.

language and to advocate for other relevant national issues.[14] Moreover, other similar small organizations were also active in Hargeysa and Mogadishu like *Wahdat al-Shabab* and *Jamiyat humat al-Diin,* and *Jamiyat Ihya al-Sunna* respectively. In addition, some other political parties and personalities with Islamic inclinations had come into view.[15]

After the military regime took over power in 1969, all non-state organizations were completely banned, including the burgeoning Islamic organizations. Nevertheless, Islamic activism took greater strides by 1970s in reaction to the military regimes' abolition of the Diya-paying system and espousal of Marxist ideology. The newly found student organization of *Ahl, Wahdah* and scholars of the banned *Nahdah* were coordinating stiff defiance to the regime's ideology. They had confronted socialist ideology with promoting Islamic awareness through establishing many Islamic study circles that were reproduced in every corner of Somalia. This revivalism was part and parcel of the wave of Islamic revivalism gaining impetus in the entire Muslim world after the Arab-Israel war of 1967. It was encouraged by the massive Somali migrant work force in the Gulf during the boom of the oil price in the aftermath of 1973 Arab-Israel war. Moreover, Somalia's membership in the Arab League in 1974 offered more vigour and confidence. Somali Islamic scholars carried the vision and strategy, and gradually propagated the comprehensiveness of Islam. Initially, the majority of Islamic revivalist movements in Somalia claimed affinity with moderate methodologies for propagating Islam, similar to that of Muslim Brotherhood in its matured stage in the

---

[14] Sheikh Mohamed Ahmed Nur Garyare, the vice-president of the *Al-Nahda* organization stated in my interview with him in 1992 in Toronto that this organization was established in Mogadishu in 1967. The founders were: President: Sh. Abdul-Qani Sh. Ahmed; Vice-president: Sh. Mohamed Ahmed Nur Garyare; Secretary: Abdurahman Farah; Vice-secretary: Abdullahi Moallim; Treasurer: Mohamed Osman Jimale; Vice-treasurer: Abdurahman Samatar.

[15] Among these personalities are Sh. Ali Ismael, MP who used to read *Tafsiir* (exegesis of the Holy Qur'an) in Mosques and the founders of *Hizbu Allahi* which had participated in the elections of 1969. See Abdurahman Abdullahi, *"Political Islam"*: 46-7.

seventies.[16] However, that situation changed after the regime's approval of the new Islamic discordant family law in 1975. Peaceful protestation of some Islamic scholars provoked ruthless suppression of the Islamic movement in 1975, when 10 leading scholars were executed and hundreds of Islamic activists were prosecuted.[17]

As a result of oppression and prosecution, many Islamic activists fled to Sudan, Egypt and the Gulf States, getting employment there and education mainly in the Islamic universities in these countries. Conservative Arab countries in the Gulf had been supporting forces opposing socialist ideology in Somalia and thus, facilitated Somali Islamists to join Islamic universities. In these countries, Somalis came into contact with Muslim scholars from all over the world and with all kinds of Islamic revivalist groups having different visions and strategies. In the aftermath, the time from 1975 until 1978 could be characterized as a period of intensive Somali exodus to Saudi Arabia, emergence of internal disputes among Islamic activists and defeat of the Somali army in the war with Ethiopia. Thus, formerly unified Somali Islamists became ideologically divided and brought back home these divisive ways of Islamism, introducing them to the younger generations in Somalia, from 1976 to 1980. In addition to the Muslim brotherhood's peaceful methodology, certain groups, more extreme either in their opinion or in their activities, such as the neo-Salafism and *Takfir (Jama'at al-Muslimuun)* were establishing their footholds in Somalia. Somali Islamic movements could be characterized in the 1970s as having immature and emotional attachment to the Islamic revivalist ideology, very low organizational capacity, meagre economic

---

[16] Abdurahman Abdurahman, 'Political Islam in Somalia," (*Middle Eastern Affairs Journal*, 1, No. 3, 1993).

[17] Somali religious scholars had voiced their concerns with respect to the regime's interference in the family law by introducing articles making the genders equal in terms of inheritance. This legislation directly contravenes Islamic law and indicates the lack of respect that the regime holds to the Islamic laws and values.

resources, and a romantic approach to social and political realities. Moreover, all these organizations were in the early stages of their formative period and were working in secret, since all peaceful avenues of social and political participation were firmly blocked by the military regime.

The Islah Movement: Its Nature and Strategy

After a long pregnancy of the Islamic revival in Somalia, the Islah Movement was finally formed, mainly, by university students who had became active members of the Muslim Brotherhood in Sudan and Saudi Arabia. The popular name of the organization took the catchy word of Islah, derived from the Qur'anic word *Al-Islah*, signifying that all its activities is founded on the profound meaning of that simple word. This word carries various meanings, such as "reforming, betterment, reconciling and correcting." Its logo, consisting of four elements, symbolizes this basic philosophy of the organization. It features the descending light illuminating an open book under which a handshake is depicted; this is surrounded by an oval frame of banana leafs joined at the bottom, with a ribbon on which Qur'anic verse *"inurīdu ila al-Islāh ma astada'atu"* is written. This means, "I decide naught save reform as far as I can able." (11:88).

Fig 4: The logo of Islah Movement

The descending light signifies revelation that, by falling on an open book, transforms into the divine guidance of the Qur'an. This symbolism demonstrates that the ultimate reference of Islah is transcendental and universal. The handshake represents the strategy of Islah, based on peacefulness, dialogue, reconciliation, and cooperation. This notion may reflect Islah's attitude in the war-torn Somalia, which completely contravenes violent and extreme approachesin the name of primordial sentiment or those under the Islamic banner. Finally, the two oval-shaped banana leafs represent the theatre of Islah's operation, Somalia, known for its abundant banana plantations.[18] The cosmology of Islah's logo is "Peace, Qur'an, and Banana." It defied the famous Somali dictum "Nabad iyo Caanno" (Peace and Milk) or "the Gun, the Hand, the Helmet, and the Qur'an," which symbolized the first white paper of the 1969 military coup.[19] Besides the agreed-upon Islamic symbol of the Qur'an, the Islah logo snubbed two elements well attributed in the traditional Somali society: milk and weapons, the symbols of nomadism and war in the Somali context. Instead, Islah chose banana leaves and a handshake, the symbol of settlement and peacefulness.

Islah is a peaceful and moderate Islamic organization, the main goal of which is to advocate and lobby for the harmonisation and calibration of the indigenous culture, state laws and policies with Islamic legal framework and values. It also aims to promote these values in order to stimulate the religious adherence of the individuals and community in accordance with the principles of Islamic moderation. Moreover, Islah strives for the sovereignty and development of the Somali people in order to be able to embrace Islamic values such as Shura (consultation "democracy"), justice and

---

[18] Somalia was the largest exporter of bananas in Africa, with 12,000 hectares under cultivation and employing more than 120,000 people. However, it was affected by the civil war, and bananas ceased to be exported, though the potential remains. See E.Baars and A. Reidiger, "*Building the Banana Chain in Somalia: Support for Agricultural Marketing Service and Access to Markets (SAMSAM) experience*", available from http://www.new-ag.info/pdf/SAMSAM-report.pdf (accessed on May 18, 2010).
[19] See the symbol of revolution issued on 21 October, 1969 in Cabdulaziz Cali Ibrahim"Xildhiban", *Taxanaha Taariikhda Somaaliya* (London: Xildhiban Publications, 2006), 40.

equality. Furthermore, it strives to contribute in the reshaping of the Horn of African region to be a place secure from disastrous conflicts and instabilities through cooperation among its nations. Finally, Islah aims to contribute to world peace, social justice, freedom of nations, tolerance among different religions and races, mutual respect for multiculturalism and development for all nations.[20]

Islah is also a non-exclusionist movement and its inclusive policy and cooperation with other Islamic organizations, Sufi brotherhoods, traditional elders and nationalists has given it a centre stage among the elites. Moreover, the movement's strong commitment to democratic and inclusive programs of restoring the Somali state had succeeded in bridging the gap between worldly and spiritual aspects of the Somalis that hitherto appeared to be irreconcilable. Islah is neither an anti-western movement nor does it imitate western patterns of culture that contravenes Islamic values. Instead, it is a realistic, mature and forward looking pro-Somali movement, struggling to create an enabling environment for the Somali people on the basis of their social and cultural realities. It is also not a fundamentalist movement, a negatively used term, Christian in its original roots,[21] which is alien to the Muslim culture, but an indigenous reformist movement. Its moderate views and peaceful programs are demonstrated by its consistent denunciation of all sorts of extremism and violence. Moreover, Islah considers itself as part of the burgeoning civil society movement in Somalia, having a proven record of promoting civil society values such as protection of human rights, democratic values, women's political rights and so on. All the

---

[20] See the objectives of Islah in Somali and Arabic languages, broadly translated by the author. http://www.islaax.org/about.htm

[21] The origin of the word fundamentalism dates to an early 20th Century American religious movement which took its name from twelve volumes published between 1910 and 1915 by a group of Protestant laymen entitled: *The Fundamentals: A Testimony of the Truth*. It came to embody both principles of absolute religious orthodoxy and evangelical practice which called for believers to extend action beyond religion into political and social life. It has been used by the western scholars and media to explain Islamic movements in the Muslim world.

above stated principles and policies are maintained through an educational curriculum and training programs for its members, and within the framework of moderate interpretation of the Glorious Qur'an and Sunna of the Prophet Mohammad, peace be upon him.

Islah is neither a political party focusing only to gain political power nor merely a social organization focusing on purely social issues. It is, rather, a movement for reawakening Islamic faith and promoting national consciousness in the Somali society. Indeed, Islam provides guidelines for all aspects of life and requires its faithful to abide by certain rules and principles. This means, in contrast to the compartmentalization of spheres of life into social and political, secular and religious, Islah views these spheres as unified aspects of the Islamic doctrine and therefore, extends its operation to all of them[22]. Islah functions as a decentralized grass-roots organization and its members share common vision, mission, values and broad strategy. Its membership is open to all Somalis who meet the requirements in the due process procedure that is centred on the individual's Islamic commitment, adherence to the organization's goals, objectives and policies. The minimum level of the individual's commitment is measured by his/her regular payment of the financial contribution and active participation in its programmes. All members follow the same education and training programmes that unify their understanding of Islam, their country and the world affairs. The organization's activities are coordinated through the office of General Secretariat of the Chairman with the support of the executive Bureau and Consultative Council.

The strategies for attaining the above stated goals are founded on implementing comprehensive programs and

---

[22] In doing so, an organization creates specialized institutions for each aspect; for instance, non-governmental organizations (NGOs) for different social activities and political parties for political activities.

curricula of social reform, aimed at the gradual reform of individuals, families, communities, public and private institutions. These curricula and programs include:

(1) An internal curriculum and program targeting Islah members and conducted as regular education circles, training programs, seminars, symposia and conferences. Different levels of Islah membership qualify for different programs as they ascend the leadership hierarchy; these consist of theoretical and practical sections.

(2) Curricula and programs targeting communities that aims to raise the Islamic awareness of the public and to improve their loyalty and adherence to Islamic principles and values. These programs are generally implemented in the public mosques, Islamic circles, Friday sermons, community activities and conferences, and so on.

Beside all these, Islah related charities are designated to reach out to communities through distribution of charity programs and Zakat funds, opening schools, and building and operating hospitals and health posts. Also, these charities work in sustainable developmental projects in various sectors such as agriculture, health, employment, educational initiatives and so on. They work as well in humanitarian and disaster relief operations, caring for orphans, the widowed and the vulnerable people. Some of these charities are specialized, like women's and youth organizations. Furthermore, Islah members participate actively in public debates and dialogue, political activism, and civil society activities. All these initiatives serve to fulfil Islamic obligations and address the comprehensive social reformation programs.

The formative period of Islah (1978-1992)

The initial program of Islah, from 1978 to 1992, was meant to lay a strong foundation for the modern Islamic organization by attracting and recruiting more educated members through effective education circles and by comprehensively propagating Islam among the Somali people. Politically, Islah had adopted a policy of peaceful struggle against the repressive regime of Siyad Barre and had refrained from indulging in the mushroom armed opposition movements in the 1980s[23]; instead, it had been following peaceful means of political opposition, like raising awareness about the atrocities of the regime and mobilizing public opinion against the regime. By 1980s, while working underground, some leaders of Islah in Mogadishu were discovered, persecuted, and imprisoned as part of the regime's crackdown on Islamic activists in Somalia. Gradually, the regime was loosening its iron hand and its security apparatus was weakening drastically. Specifically, the regime was hard hit after a disastrous confrontation with the armed Somali National Movement (SNM) forces in Hargeysa in 1988 and the ensuing mass exodus of people to the refugee camps. This event had caused the drastic drying up of international assistance to the regime, due to its gross violations of human rights and waging war against its people. During the years 1987 to 1990, Islah focused on providing relief operations in the refugee camps in the Northern Regions affected by the war. On the other hand, it was expanding its Islamic activities on the campuses of the Somali National University in Mogadishu and among students in the Diaspora. The movement was also attracting to its ranks more experienced members that could play more active social and political roles. In the final years of the regime, Islah overtly expressed its socio-political program and played an important role in the bloody demonstrations of "Black Friday" on July 14, 1989. It had been issuing press releases and sending open letters to the leaders of the regime calling for the resignation

---

[23] In 1980s, armed opposition movements like SSDF, SNM, USC and SPM was established to topple the regime in support of Ethiopia. "Islah was invited to join these movements but refused to do so in believing that violent conflict and Ethiopian support will not solve Somali debacle, rather exacerbated it." Interview conducted with Sheikh Mohamed Garyare, first Chairman of Islah, Toronto, October 25, 1999.

of the President and the formation of a transitional national unity government.[24]

On 26th January, 1991, a new chapter of Somali history began, which had a profound and lasting imprint on Somali society in the following years. It was a turning point in the history of the nation characterized by the failure and collapse of the post-colonial state after 30 years of self-government. Initial joy at the disappearance of the repressive regime was, at the same time associated with the unimaginable risks of the civil war. A new dark era had befallen the Somalis and the fate of the Somali State was in the hands of feuding clannish factions. All types of weapons were available for the angry militias who fully exercised their culture of revenge, looting and destruction of the symbols of civilization. The outcome was the outbreak of senseless civil war in every corner of the country. This war caused unprecedented destruction of lives and properties and more than a million Somalis migrated to all continents of the world while other millions perished, some became internally displaced or became refugees in the neighbouring countries.

In Southern Somalia, in the first years of the civil war, the politics of guns and bullets, starvation, agony, and unprecedented human suffering were widespread in most regions. Unfortunately, during those years, the warlords in the South and their savage militia were recognized by the international community as the sole legitimate representatives of the country. On the other hand, the SNM faction in the northern part of Somalia was proclaiming a separate state of "Somaliland". The national vision inherited from the fathers of the nation was entirely lost and a myopic clannish agenda was digging its roots deeply into the Somali society. During

---

[24] On July 14, demonstrations were organized from the mosques in protest against the detention of leading Islamic scholars after the killing of Bishop Salvatore Colombo, the Vatican representative in Somalia. About 200 Somalis had died in "black Friday". Also, the *"Sawt-al-Haq"* (the righteous voice) communiqué was released later on by Islah, calling on the president to resign and safeguard the country from imminent civil war.

this challenging time, although hampered by its limited capacity, Islah did not give up its programs and activities and its involvement in the affairs of the country. The movement had been trying hard to voice its concerns and express its positions on major national issues; Islah considered that what had happened in Somalia was a cataclysmic and senseless clannish conflict and secured its members from being part of such conflicts, maintaining its internal unity in the volatile environment. It issued statements, communiqués and press releases on every important issue. It also courageously and overtly criticized the policy of militarism of the Al-Itihad Islamic movement and its armed confrontation with the faction leaders in Kismayo (1991), Puntland (1992) and Gedo (1996).[25]

While the civil war had devastated the whole nation and caused colossal loss of lives and properties, its damage to Islah was also painful and tremendous. In the first year, the movement had lost many of its active members and field leaders to the civil war, for example its deputy chairman and his chief political officer.[26] Moreover, the war had caused huge displacement among its members and the leadership ranks; and the process of regrouping them was difficult since most of them did not know each other due to the underground nature of the organization at that time. The scope of displacement was vast and covered almost all villages and localities in Somalia and neighbouring countries such as Kenya, Ethiopia, and Djibouti. Migration to Europe, USA, and Canada had started and intensified as well. Furthermore, communications between leaders in the Diaspora and field leaders within

---

[25] Islah issued a communiqué of denunciation with respect to the announcement of Jihad by al-Itihad Movement in 1992 in Puntland and considered all *al-Itihad* wars against armed factions to be part of the civil war conflict.

[26] Sh. Ali Dayar was the Deputy Chairman of Islah in Mogadishu and Inj. Isse Ali was the chief political officer. They actively participated in the efforts to prevent civil war and mobilize Islamic scholars to play role for that endeavour. This information was collected from Dr. Ibrahim al-Dasuqi and Sh. Ahmed Hassan al-Qudubi who were closely working with them. Mogadishu, December 20, 1999.

Somalia was interrupted due to the destruction of communication facilities. Nevertheless, the situation was not absolutely disastrous. On the contrary, this was a great opportunity for Islamic activism to flourish and reach out to the remote areas and to hitherto unthinkable locations. Moreover, in the Diaspora community and among students in universities abroad, migrant members of Islah had been actively reaching out and spreading the message of Islam. During the first years of the civil war, the movement had been working to achieve the following three major objectives:
1. Reconciliation between warring parties *"Islah dat Al-bayn"*.
2. Intensification of Islamic work *"Al-Da'wa Wal Irshad"*.
3. Focusing on relief operations and education *"Al-Igatha wa tacliim"* in support of needy and vulnerable families and to revive education.

Other important policies were also re-affirmed, such as non-violence, political neutrality and establishment of effective community organizations in the Diaspora.[27]

The first inclusive conference of the Islah leadership after the outbreak of the civil war was held in 1992. This conference could be characterized as the second rebirth of the movement, in which the performance of the movement had been re-evaluated, its vision sharpened, new strategy developed and internal restructuring accomplished. In the evaluations, it became clear that the core vision, common values and policies of the movement were being maintained everywhere, although there had been wide displacement and migrations. An overwhelming majority of the members had complied with Islah's policies, such as neutrality and non-alliance, peacefulness and rejection of militarism and clannish wars. The conference had approved main strategic objectives, including, amongst other things, intensification of Islamic works, and publicly and vigorously denouncing the use of

---
[27] See "Brief history of Islah" in http://www.islaax.org/arabic/history.htm.

Islamic legitimization of the internecine wars. It also included in its objectives reaching out to the educated Somali elite, improving relations with the traditional elites, such as Ulama and tribal elders, and keeping a policy of neutrality with respect to the clannish wars. Although social services and reconciliation had always been a consistent field of focus since the beginning of the civil war, at the conference, education and national reconciliation were given critical priority for the years to come.

The Islah Movement during the Civil War (1992-2008)

Participation of Islah in the socio-political affairs of Somalia after 1992 was growing progressively. The movement participated in the international conferences on Somalia, established relevant institutions, and conducted specific public programs. The movement participated in the two reconciliation conferences held in Addis Ababa under the auspices of the United Nation Operation in Somalia (UNOSOM) in January and March in 1993, and issued communiqués and press statements at the conferences that were widely distributed.[28] Also, it had organized conferences on various national and religious occasions, such as Independence Day, the birthday of Prophet Mohammad, peace be upon him, and the Eid Festivities. These conferences were used as a way of reviving national identity and explaining the principles of the movement. In the Diaspora, too, annual conferences, community meetings, and social gathering on different occasions were organized. Moreover, student and community organizations were established, as well as national study groups. During these years, in 1994, Islah had established the Somali Reconciliation Council (SRC) as a specialized NGO for promoting and

---

[28] Radio of Peace in Addis Ababa broadcast in 1993 a serious of lectures and interviews with Dr. Ibrahim Al-Dassuqi about Islah and its position in the Somali reconciliation.

making peace between clans, communities and political factions. Its branches in the major conflict areas in Southern Somalia had played a vital role in mobilizing traditional elites to mediate disputes and resolve conflicts.[29] Moreover, all over Somalia, many NGOs had been formed by members of Islah to provide humanitarian assistance to the needy, orphaned, widowed and vulnerable segments of the society. Most of these NGOs were focused on education, health, accessibility of clean water, and on building mosques and Islamic centres. These NGOs became the backbone of the burgeoning Somali civil society networks.

In the absence of national institutions of the state and peaceful political parties, and with the supremacy of the armed clannish factions, participation in the political affairs is not an easy undertaking for a modern Islamic organization. As stated above, isolation is not an appropriate solution and participation means dealing with clannish realities. The current Somali social and political activism is tribally organized, driven, and supported. In such a radical clannish and hostile environment and a poisonous political culture, how could a trans-clan organization, such as Islah, be involved effectively in the community affairs without compromising its core values and while maintaining its essential internal unity? Theoretically, the issue is more complicated than it seems at first glance. However, referring back to the time of the Prophet Mohammad (PBUH), when there were clans similar to those in present-day Somalia, reviewing the biography of the Prophet and deriving lessons of how clans were dealt with, the issue becomes simple and easy in one respect, turning out even easier since all Somali clans are Muslims. On the other hand, the issue becomes more complex, given the scarcity of modern studies on this topic and a complete absence of theoretical background from the Muslim Brotherhood

---

[29] See the activities of Somali Reconciliation Council (1994-1998) in which 18 reconciliation conferences were held in different regions of Southern Somalia.

literature on how to deal with the stateless situation.[30] Moreover, continuous instruction of Islah members in order to weaken clannish attachment and behaviour, and witnessing the savagery of the clans during the war, had created negative attitudes among Islah members in dealing with the institutions of the clans. To create an atmosphere of common understanding, an exhaustive dialogue and discussions was opened in 1991 on the issue of how to deal with the clannish communities and a gradual development of the policy known as "Dealing with the Reality" was finally adopted in 1995.[31]

Since 1995, new developments that weakened the authority of the armed faction leaders had taken place in Somalia. They include the revival of the local education system up to the tertiary level, epitomized by establishing Mogadishu University in 1996 and the proliferation of networked civil society organizations. Moreover, stronger across-clan business community had emerged vying armed faction leaders in the local politics and community affairs. As a result, Islah adopted an advanced political program in 1998 focusing on working towards national reconciliation. Besides its support for the regional reconciliation efforts in Mogadishu, Islah sent delegates to the various regions to advocate a way out of the political stalemate in Somalia.[32] As a new opportunity emerged

---

[30] Iman Hassan Al-Banna, the founder of Muslim Brotherhood in Egypt in 1928, had theorized how to reform societies ruled by secular nation-states and how to transform them gradually into an Islamic state by reforming individuals, families, communities and state institutions. In the literature of Muslim brotherhood, stateless situations were not envisaged, so Islah had to fill a theoretical gap in studying its social realities, which required a period of reflection, discussion and digestion.

[31] The issue of how the movement should deal with the new realities in Somalia was first discussed in Toronto, Canada, after the fall of the regime in January 1991. The outcome of this discussion was published in an internal pamphlet. The author of this paper had participated in these discussions. However, the official policy of *"Dealing with the Reality"* adopted in 1995 was a turning point and a shift in the policies of Islah to working with the traditional institutions and civil society organizations. Its fruits are that members of Islah were allowed to be part of the transitional parliament selected by their clans. The only limitations imposed on the members were those prohibited and forbidden in Islam.

[32] Islah delegation headed by Sheikh Mohamed Garyare met with Mr. Abdullahi Yusuf, president of Puntland of that time, in Growe and Mr. Mohamed Ibrahim Igal, president of "Somaliland" in Hargeysa in 1999.

with the Djibouti reconciliation initiative on 22 September 1999, the movement not only lent strong support to the initiative but also actively participated in the conference and considered it as "the first genuine political reconciliation in Somalia".[33] During the reconciliation process in 2000, Islah members played a crucial role within different clans and some of its members became members of the Transitional Assembly and held cabinet posts. However, the low capability of the leadership, the weakness of the national institutions, and strong opposition from the armed factions reorganized by Ethiopia under the umbrella of the Somali Reconciliation and Restoration Council (SRRC); encouraged a new call for a reconciliation conference in Kenya in 2002, under the auspices of Inter-Governmental Authority on Development (IGAD).

The prominence of Islah in the Djibouti held Somali peace conference and its international exposure after 9/11 demonstrated its true nature as a moderate movement and its firm commitment to the formation of national state institutions. Moreover, Islah's social programs in education, health, and peace promotion were growing fast across the regions. The Islamic moderation that Islah represents in Somalia took a centre stage in all public forums and among civil society organizations. Consequently, memberships of Islah increased significantly, though its political role was later curtailed in the warlord-dominated Reconciliation Conference in Kenya (2002-2004). However, Islah maintained its strategy of peacefulness and reconciliation in dealing with the new regime created in Kenya. Absolute priority was given by Islah to the maintenance of the national transitional institutions without which Somalia disintegrates into clannish ghettos, and to the curbing of violence and internal strife. To bolster national reconciliation, Islah supported reconciliation between the two factions of the Transitional Federal Institutions that

---

[33] All other conferences were warlord-dominated conferences though their names were given to be national reconciliation conferences.

were divided on the issue of relocation of the state institutions established in Kenya; either to the town of Jawhar or to the capital city of Mogadishu.³⁴ It also proposed a national plan for rebuilding national institutions and offered its support to this venture.

Islah's role of reconciliation, developmental programs and relief assistance was very much in evidence when the conflict erupted between Mogadishu warlords and Union of Islamic Courts (UIC) in 2006. Reconciliation teams of Islah met continually with the two conflicting sides, attempting to broker a peace deal. However, war broke out and the notorious faction leaders were easily crashed. Moreover, the humanitarian assistance of Islah-affiliated NGOs continued to provide assistance to the population displaced by the conflict. Furthermore social services continued to provide education, health services and awareness rising in the mosques, mass media and community centres. These programs intensified when war between Union of the Islamic Courts and Transitional Federal Government allied with Ethiopia was imminent. For that purpose, Islah established a special reconciliation committee to work out reconciliation initiatives between the two sides and to continue promoting peace and dialogue.³⁵

The Islah Movement had distanced itself from being part of the UIC Council and prohibited its members from joining a group using violence against other Somalis. Nonetheless, the whole notion of moderation in politics and religion had been weakened during and after the emergence of the UIC and the

---

[34] An Islah delegation visited Baidoa in February 2006 and met with the President, Abdullahi Yusuf, the Speaker, Sheriff Hassan and the Premier, Ali Mohamed Gedi. The aim of the visit was to bolster reconciliation and contribute in the rebuilding of the national institutions.

[35] See Islah communiqué dated 22/07/2006 in which the formation of the special reconciliation committee was announced. http://www.islaax.org/arabic/bayaan22-7-06.htm. The author was appointed to lead this committee. For the historical record, TFG accepted the reconciliation initiative, but UIC categorically rejected it and sent a letter of admonition to Islah Movement warning it not to get involved in any future reconciliation. A copy of this letter signed by Sheikh Sheriff, the Chairman of UIC, is available at the Islah secretariat.

subsequent Ethiopian Intervention. As a result, civil society organizations were marginalized, their activities curtailed, their leaders targeted and many of them were killed in cold blood.[36] Moreover, all Islamic organizations and many clan-based forces in Mogadishu except Islah and the Sufi orders had joined hands and participated in this venture. It had also been supported by the most Somalis in the Diaspora influenced by the skilful use of the media outlets by the UIC supporters. On the other hand, the UIC clever use of Islamic, nationalistic, and clan mobilization tactics had attracted great popular support, and Islah was temporarily isolated and looked at as unfaithful to its Islamic and nationalistic agenda. Moreover, some members of Islah, departing from the policy and the program of their organization, were fascinated by the impressive success of the UIC and joined it. This situation pressured Islah leadership to take strong public action in distinguishing themselves from the UIC and to expel from Islah's ranks all persons who joined the UIC, including its former chairman Dr. Mohamed Ali Ibrahim.[37] This undertaking caused Islah high security risk to its members and institutions, and as a result, its activities were restricted, festivities banned including the annual commemoration of its 28th anniversary and some of its prominent members were assassinated or displaced.[38] During this difficult period, Islah continued its program of reconciliation and tried to broker peace between the UIC and the government; nevertheless, this

---

[36] Prominent civil society activists eliminated in Mogadishu include the peace activist, Abdulqadir Yahye, the prominent Islamic scholar, Sheikh Mohamed Sheikh Ahmed (Kashk), a well-known military commander, General Mohamed Abdi, The civil society activist, Ali Iman Sharmarke, the business leaders, Abdikarim Sheikh Ibrahim and Abbas Mohamed Du'ale, the women peace activist, Medina Mohamud Ilmi and many others.
[37] See Islah Communiqué on 21/6/2006 of the expulsion of Dr. Mohamed Ali Ibrahim from Islah, available from http://www.islaax.org/arabic/bayaan21-6-06.htm (accessed on August 14, 2010).
[38] See Islah Communiqué on 17/8/2006 on the banning Islaax festivities organized to commemorate its 28th anniversary, available from http://www.islaax.org/arabic/bayaan%2017-8-2006.htm (accessed on August 14, 2010).

effort failed miserably by the rejection of the UIC.[39] Thus, Islah with its insightful understanding of the situation, personalities involved in the UIC, and looming extremist ideologies, adamantly and consistently distanced itself from their venture.

After the defeat of the UIC, oppositions gathered in Asmara, the capital city of Eritrea, and Alliance for the Re-liberation of Somalia (ARS) was formed in September 2007. Islah also refused to be part of ARS and while continuing condemning Ethiopian intervention and Transitional Federal Government policies.[40] It persistently remained firm in its policy of supporting Transitional Federal Institutions (TFIs) considered to be necessary for the existence of the Somali state. In maintaining this delicate balance of refusing to seek foreign power assistance to gain political power and objecting to all forms of violence among Somalis, which both the Transitional Federal government and the oppositions of ARS were exercising, Islah remained true to its principles of moderation. Moreover, it also encouraged reconciliation between the TFG and ARS held in Djibouti in 2009, which finally produced new TFIs that combine former TFG and ARS. However, the precipitate reconciliation process sponsored by the United Nations proved ineffective, and TFIs remain dysfunctional under the protection of African forces (AMISOM). On the other hand, Al-Shabab, an extremist group ideologically affiliated with Al-Qaida, was in control in most regions of southern Somalia and extended its terrorist attacks to Uganda, threatening other African countries that are contributing troops to Somalia security mission. Finally, Islah always believes the only way-out from the Somali peril is through genuine reconciliation, improved security, refraining

---

[39] See Islah Communiqué on 22/7/2006 on the formation of reconciliation committee between the UIC and the TFG, available from http://www.Islah.org/arabic/bayaan22-7-06.htm (accessed on August 14, 2010).

[40] See IslahCommuniqué on 26/7/2006 on the Ethiopian Intervention in Somalia, available from http://www.Islah.org/arabic/bayaan26-7-06.htm (accessed on August 14, 2010).

from arbitrary violence, avoiding monopoly of religious interpretation and conducting popular election to produce legitimate state institutions for Somalia.

Islah's Policies and Views on Contemporary Issues

Almost 40 years of uninterrupted work with its immense challenges and experiences has cultivated Islah movement in ways that have sharpened its common vision, mission and improved its views, strategies and operations. These views are shared among all Muslim Brotherhood affiliated organizations with slight differences regarding their diverse social realities.

1. Opening up to Society

Organizations face difficulties in the transition period from underground movement to open organization. This process requires not only changes of attitudes and norms, but also projection of a clear set of rules and policies. Social and political realities in Somalia changed drastically after the collapse of the state in 1991 and the transition from the rule of the state to clan supremacy. In reality, Islah was not well prepared to deal with new situations during the initial stages. The reason being that its training programs were focused mainly on reforming society ruled by state institutions and not in conflict. Theories of dealing with the clan conflicts were not well developed in the Muslim brotherhood literature, especially when the scope of the conflict was so wide and causes the total collapse of state institutions. Moreover, the general understanding of the members of Islah was that the clans were very much connected with clanism that is abhorred and disavowed in Islam. Furthermore, after the collapse of the state, leadership of communities shifted from the state bureaucracy to the traditional leaders and armed political factions. To interact with such situation, the policy of "Dealing with the Reality" was finally adopted in 1995. The core philosophy of this policy was to break isolation of the movement and to open it up to the society at large. Objectives of this policy included encouraging members of Islah to participate actively in the existing social and political organizations and to engage assertively with all groups. The syndromes of isolation from society and assimilation with the clan culture are not healthy symptoms of modern Islamic activism. Instead, prudent and positive engagement is the only right way for the Islamic reformers. Indeed, it was realized after the implementation of this policy that Islah members could play skilfully the role of "cement or glue" to hold together the segmented blocks of Somali society.

2. Focusing on the Educated Elites

Islam is a religion based on knowledge that shows great respect to scientists and the educated (ulama)[41]. Social change not only requires an enlightened elite but also an understanding of the core philosophy of the movement, undertaking that change, inculcating the masses and taking a leadership role. Bearing these imperatives in mind, Islah generally recruits to its ranks young and educated segments of the society; young because they are energetic and open, educated because they may grasp the message easily and convey it to others.[42] This means that majority of its members are from the young educated generations. Moreover, Islah had discovered that its perception and outreach program to the Somali intellectuals was poor. The new policy adopted had considered these intellectuals as partners for reform and looked for communalities instead of seeking uniformity. The fruits of this policy were tremendous and its application in the

---

[41] In the Holy Qur'an the word *al-Ilm*, knowledge, and its derivatives are used more than 780 times. The first few verses that were revealed to our Holy Prophet (SAW) mention the importance of reading, the pen, and teaching for human beings. In the Qur'an Allah says: *"Say: Are those who know and those who do not know alike?* (39:9)

[42] History of Islam shows that the age of the Prophet Mohammad (PBH) was 40 years when he was sent as a messenger and all his early believers were younger than him except his wife Khadija.

field brought tangible benefits for the Somali community. The space and reservations between modern Islamic activists and Somali intellectuals has been narrowed, whereas both the nationalistic intellectuals and Islamic activists were marginalized during the civil war by the warlords and the bearers of clannish banners. Finally, Islah believes that creating a common front and forging an alliance of nationalists and moderate Islamists is the only way to dislodge clannish and extremist forces and to restore a functioning Somali state.

3. Respecting and Cooperating with Traditional Islamic Scholars

Islah considers itself as the continuation of the endeavours of generations of traditional Islamic scholars and the leaders of the national movements for independence. In fact, traditional Islamic scholars were the sole intellectuals until colonial schools produced new elites. They represent the spirit of Islam, they are leaders and teachers of the communities, protectors of the faith, and saviours of the nation from the attempted Christianization.[43] Also, they remain the founders and core pillars of modern Islamic movements and always play a vital complementary role, particularly in the rural areas and among the mostly uneducated masses.[44] Islah widened its vision and discarded previous imprudent relations with the Sufi orders, by looking upon them as teachers, fathers and leaders of the communities and giving them due respect, encouragement and support. This deep understanding of the social dynamics of Somalia is an antithesis to the prejudiced isolationist views that loomed earlier in the circles of the Islamic movement. These ideas were as a result of late Salafia

---

[43] The French Roman Catholic Mission established in 1891 was located in Daimole near Sheikh and abolished by the Dervish Movement.
[44] The modern Islam movement cannot move forward without having on hand thousands of young educated students graduated from the Qur'anic schools and Islamic education circles in the Mosques.

influence that focused on the traditional scholars of the Sufi orders and considered them as innovators and an obstacle to the revival of Islam. Conversely, while promoting and advancing authentic Islamic teaching and knowledge within the context of Islamic moderation, Islah respects and cooperates with the Sufi brotherhoods.

4. Respecting the Leaders of the Nationalist Movement

Leaders of the national movement for independence and statehood in Somalia have also received great respect and admiration from Islah. Certainly, considering the scarcity of human capital and the limited organizational capacity that was available in the 1940s and after, these leaders had an exalted vision for Somalia. Their vision for Somalia was to establish a strong and all-inclusive Somali state in the Horn of Africa, where all Somalis might live in peace, harmony and dignity. To give them due respect, one has simply to imagine what Somalia would have been without their sacrifice and struggle. Modern activists of Islamic movements are graduates from the schools they established and beneficiaries of the opportunities they provided. Understanding this, Islah is very proud of what earlier fathers of the nation achieved with meagre resources and limited capacities. This perception, based on respect and acceptance of all the good things they did, departs from the previous idea looming among Islamic movement circles of calling these leaders, secular, anti-Islamic and colonial lackeys. Inclusiveness instead of sectarianism, and tolerance, patience and focus on major issues, agreed upon by the majority of the Somalis, is the only way to rebuild Somalia with a new vision rendering due respect for its historical personalities and sacred heritage. Doing so does not mean relinquishing critical review of our past in order to rebuild a new Somalia.

5. Downplaying Disputed Issues of Islam

The basic references of Islam are the Qur'an and the Sunna of the Prophet Muhammad (PBUH). However, these fundamental sources have been variously interpreted by scholars in different Muslim regions and times. Therefore, differences of interpretations in the doctrinal and legal aspects appeared, yielding four famous Sunni legal schools of thought: *Shafi'i, Hanafi, Maliki* and *Hanbali*. Somalis adhere mostly to the Shafi'i school of legal thought, so to protect community cohesion and avoid religious squabbles; Islah chose to adopt Shafi'i school of jurisprudence, while being open to the views of other scholars. Moreover, Islah rejects all divisive discourses and disputations on the detailed legal matters and focuses on major fundamental issues, mostly agreed by all Muslims. It also cooperates with other religious organizations, groups and individuals, to safeguard the religious unity of the Somali people. Furthermore, modern studies of Islam on state building and its institutions, and on what is in accord with Islamic principles and what is not, remain academic discourses. Certainly, politics is a less developed field in the Islamic thought; hence, there is plenty of space for *Ijtihad* offering many options to various organizations.

6. Rejection of Extremism and Violence

Islam is a religion of peace, mercy and humanism, and forbids its believers to commit any acts of violence against innocent human beings. Thus, Islah rejects such violence and all forms of extreme views such as the idea of inevitability of clash of civilizations. Instead, it promotes cooperation, dialogue, understanding and co-existence of all people, races and religions. Islah understands that extremism and violence is a product of frustration, humiliation, feelings of injustice and lack of true understanding of Islamic values. Therefore, it is the conviction of Islah that respect of multiculturalism, democratization, narrowing of economic and political marginalization, and better understanding of cultures and religions will eventually create an environment of peace and cooperation among nations. In accordance with this understanding, Islah has denounced and rejected all forms of violence currently taking place in Somalia.

7. Restoration of National State Institutions

Many post-colonial African states have been pushing themselves to the brink of abysmal failure due to misguided programs of nation-building and economic development. Somalia is a classic example of such a collapsed state that polarized the population into clan lines and led to continuous clan fighting and conflicts. Reviving clan consciousness and weakening national awareness was evident during the civil war. Islah, being a national organization, strongly believes that reviving national consciousness and disowning clanism is the only way to recover the Somali state. Divisive clan interference in the affairs of the state and clan competition for winning political power is the major element threatening the existence of Somalia as a state. Accordingly, Islah contributed to the reconstitution of the national state during the Djibouti reconciliation conference in 2000, and always defends and supports national institutions, even if these institutions are established imperfectly and weakly, like the current Transitional Federal Government. The worst scenario and greatest disaster for Somalia would be the absence of a national state, which would eventually lead to the total disintegration of the nation into clannish cages and ghettos.

8. Promotion of Civil Society Organizations

Islah believes strongly that without vibrant civil society organizations, Somalia will remain at the mercy of segmented clannish groups. In pursuit of that viewpoint, from 1994 to 1999, the movement worked towards promoting more organized civil society organizations in Somalia. Members of Islah were encouraged to establish community-owned organizations and/or to join existing civil society organizations. Particularly in Mogadishu, many networked social and professional organizations emerged during these years, and Islah members were part of them.[45] These organizations had succeeded in unifying the public voice on the issues of peace, human rights and democracy. In the area of reconciliation, Islah established the Somali Reconciliation Council in 1994 to offer logistical support for reconciliation efforts in Somalia. As a result of these policies, hundreds of community initiatives in the fields of education, health, reconciliation, and developmental programs were directed to the communities. Civil society values, such as protection of human rights, promotion of democratic values and good governance, and promotion of peace received wider participation and support from Islah members. The growth of civil society organizations, such as professional bodies, charities, women and youth organizations, those promoting human rights and political parties, is the only way out of messy political clanism.

9. Promotion of Democracy

Democracy is a western terminology; nevertheless, in its essence as a process is no different from the Islamic concept of consultation (*Shura*).[46] Some scholars have said that democracy is similar to *Shura* that have developed modern institutions of political parties; and consultation is like democracy that is bounded by the Islamic ceiling and

---

[45] These are Peace and Human Rights Network (PHRN), Formal Private Education Network (FPEL), Grass Roots Women's Organization (COGWO), Medical Doctors' Association, Lawyers' Association, etc. The author of this paper was the chairman of PHRN in 1999.

[46] Murad Hoffman.*Islam: The alternative*. (Maryland: Amana publications. 1999), 81-82. Also, see Fathi Osman, "Modern Islamist and Democracy" *Arabia*, London (May, 1986): 6. Also, see Gazali, Abdulhamid. *Hawla Asaasiyat al-Mashru'c Al_Islami Li Nahdat Al-Ummah*. (Qahira: Rar Al-Tawzi'c WA Nashr Al-Islamiyah, 2000): 178-80.

conforms to the general Islamic principles.[47] The concept of consultation is characterized in Islam not only as necessary code to healthy faithful communities, families, and individuals but also as a required value for piety.[48] Simplifying this notion, democracy in its ideal form is like pure water that does not have a shape and color; however, takes the shape and color of its container. Likewise, democracy takes the color and the shape of the society in which it is applied. Therefore, democracy exists in different forms corresponding to the will and the choice of the different people. Since nations are different in their culture, religions and system of governance, their application of democracy eventually takes different forms. This means that democracy is applicable to all races, religions and cultures. Western democracy is not unique; it is necessarily secular and takes a color and shape in accordance with the western society's culture, values and belief system. On the other hand, democracy in Muslim societies has to abide with the Islamic values, and culture of the people. In that understanding of democracy, Islah promotes democracy and stands firmly against any form of dictatorial rule in any place in the world and under the pretext of Islam. Finally, Islah firmly exercises democracy within its organization and has been holding internal elections periodically over the last 30 years.

10. Protection of Human Rights

Somalia is one of the many nations suffering from the worst kinds of human rights violations. During 21 years of military rule and 25 years of intensive civil wars, the basics of human rights have been grossly violated. Protection of human rights is a divine obligation and a God-ordained concept. In Islam, the human being is dignified and the whole Islamic legal

---

[47] Sadiq Al-Mahdi. *"Al-Shura ka Asaas li-Nidum Al-Hukm Fi Al-Alam Al Islami."* Unpublished paper submitted to the 15th Conference of the Muslim Affairs held in Cairo (May, 2003): 9-12.
[48] See Qur'anic verse *"Those who hearken to their Lord, and establish regular Prayer; who (conduct) their affairs by mutual consultation (Shura); who spend out of what We bestow on them for Sustenance"* [are praised] (42:38)

system is founded on protecting the rights of that human being[49]. Mostly, the non-binding Universal Declaration of Human Rights of 10 December, 1948, and the other two international pacts of 19 December, 1966 on civil and political, economic, social and cultural rights do not contravene completely the Islamic law. Since these declarations are not binding, different religious groups and civilizations may have specific reservations and Muslims likewise, while abiding by the declarations in general, may disagree with some issues that could contravene Islamic principles. However, in general, Islah promotes the protection of human rights and believes strongly that without it a civilized society cannot be established.

11. Promotion of Women's Rights

Women's rights, particularly their rights to political participation, are widely misunderstood by many Islamists and non-Islamists alike in the Muslim world and beyond. It seems that the ancient culture of societies and religious interpretations on the issues of women have been intermingled in the Muslim world. As a result, those communities where women's rights are undermined by the culture tend to justify those practices from the religious point of view. However,

> any fair investigation of the teaching of Islam or into the history of the Islamic civilization will surely find a clear evidence of women's equality with men in what we call today political rights.[50]

The position of Islah is very clear in this point. Islah openly advocates the advancement of the rights of women and strongly supports their social and political participation in community affairs. Moreover, Islah promotes women's education in all its social development programs. The effect of

---

[49] There are five main rights that Islam always bases its legal judgments upon: these are protection of religion (al-Diin), intellect (al-Aql), property (al-Maal), life (al-Nafs) and family (al-'ird).
[50] Badawi, Jamal. *The Status of Women in Islam.* (Plainfield:American Trust Publications, 1976): 23-24. Also, see Gazali, Abdulhamid. *Hawla asaasiyat.*

these policies was so great that Somali women are now playing important roles in politics and social life that were hitherto believed to be the domain of men.

Conclusions

This paper aims to fill the knowledge gap in the study of Islamic movements in the Horn of Africa. It comprises a brief background of the revival of Islam in Somalia and Islah's historical development since 1978 and its major views on the contemporary issues. The emergence of modern Islamic movement in Somalia is the culmination of a long process of Islamic revival since the anti-colonial resistance and the formation of the Somali Islamic League in 1952 linked with similar world-wide phenomena. From that time until the 1970s, traditional Islamic education, modern Arabic schools and graduates from the Arab universities have been paving the way for the emergence of modern Islamic movement. The military regime (1969-1991) with its rigorous socialist programs provoked Islamic sentiments by executing Islamic scholars in 1975 and blocking the Islamic activism that was growing in the 1970s. Early years of the Islamic movements could be characterized as a period of immature and emotional attachment to the revivalist ideology, very low organizational capacity, and an idealistic approach with respect to social realities. The Islah movement was established on 11th July, 1978 with the goal of reviving Islamic values in the society, promoting harmonization of Somali culture, state laws, and policies with the Islamic legal framework and values. Islah is not merely a political party nor a social organization; rather it is a comprehensive movement for reawakening Islamic faith and promoting national consciousness in the Somali society. It functions as a decentralized grass-roots organization that shares common vision, mission, values, and broad strategy. Also, Islah focuses on education, reconciliation, and peace promotion to realize its objectives. The period 1978 to 1992 is considered the early years of its formative period, facing challenges of establishment, persecution and survival during the civil war.

In the period 1992 to 2008, Islah had applied policies such as opening up to the society, focusing on an educated elite; respecting and cooperating with traditional Islamic scholars; celebrating the fathers of the nationalist movements; downplaying disputed issues of religion; rejection of violence and extremism; restoration of national state institutions; promoting civil society organizations, democracy, women's rights; and protection of human rights. Application of the above stated policies, flexibility of its organizational structures and internal democratic practices puts Islah Movement in the category of moderate Islamic movements.

Finally, Islah's continuous developmental programs, peace promotion policies, support for the national state institutions and rational political participation gives it a unique position in the Somali society. Its future trend shows that it will consolidate above stated policies and programs and at the same time contribute more in restoring Somali state institutions. This will be done through engaging more assertively in the peaceful political process. Besides, the growing role of Islah in Somalia will eventually promote the culture of good governance, social cohesion and Islamic moderation in Somalia and the Horn of Africa at large.

III

Militancy of Sufi Orders in the History of Somalia

> The person guided by Mohamed's law, Will not follow the faction of Satan [Salihiyah]; who deem it lawful to spill the blood of the learned? Who take cash and women too: they are anarchist; publicly, they sell paradise for cash, in our land; they are a sect of dogs.
>
> Synopsis of a poems vilifying Salihiyah Order Compiled by Sheikh Aweys Al-Barawi

> A word to the backsliding apostates, who have gone astray, from the Prophet's way, the straight path? Why is the truth, so plain, hidden from you?
>
> Synopsis of diatribe poem vilifying Qadiriyah Order by Sayyid Mohamed

> Behold, at last, when we slew the old wizard, the rains began to come!
>
> A victory hymn recited by Sayyid Mohamed when he heard the assassination of Sheikh Uweys

Militancy simply means having a combative character; aggressive, especially in the service of a cause. Adding Islamic adjective signifies that certain interpretations of Islam is used as the guiding ideology of that militancy. The first such militancy in the history of Islam was labeled *"al-Khawarij"* ["the Seceders" or "the Rebels"] because of their rebellion [*khuruj*] against fourth Imam of Islam 'Ali ibn Abi Talib. In the opposite stands the terminology of moderation "balanced" *"al-Wasadiyah"* which signifies being within reasonable limits; not excessive or extreme, and not violent or subject to extremes. Islam calls for moderation in everything: in belief, worship, conduct, and legislation; and warns against all forms of extremism: Ghuluw (excessiveness), Tanattu' (meticulous religiosity) and Tashdid (strictness). Moderation, or balance, is not only a general characteristic of Islam, it is a fundamental landmark. In the Qur'anic verse Allah says:

> Thus, have we made of you an Ummah (Nation) justly balanced, that you might be witnesses over the nations and the Messenger a witness over yourselves (2:143).

The phenomenon of extremism in the name of Islam was well articulated by Sheikh Yusuf Al-Qardawi in his booklet "Islamic Awakening between Rejection and Extremism" which is very useful to briefly understand current militancy in a balanced way.

Looking into the history of Somalia in the 18th and 19th centuries, the revival of Islam was carried by the Sufi Brotherhood movements and legendary Sufi scholars belonging to the two main Sufi Orders: Qadiriyah and Ahmadiyah had emerged. Sheikh Madar, Sheikh Abdirahman Al-Zayli, Sheikh Aweys al-Baraawi, Sheikh Mohamed Guleed, Sayyid Mohamed Abdulle Hassan, Sheikh Ali Maye, Sheikh Sufi and many others are well known teachers and respected Islamic Scholars in Somalia. Sufi brotherhoods are generally moderate and use peaceful means of propagating Islam that offer due considerations to the norms and customs of the people. Often, they use innovative means to assimilate and absorb the pastoral and illiterate masses and mobilize them into common action. Bloodlettings being the most heinous crime in Islam, Islamic scholars usually abstain from recurrent clan fighting in the harsh pastoral environment. Their role is limited to conflict resolution, community education and conducting various religious functions. However, there were historical events in the history of Somalia when militancy in the name of Islam emerged and certain Islamic scholars led internal fighting to gain politico-religious hegemony. Such historical events have historical importance and constitute precedents for current militancy and extremism in Somalia. It offers lessons that doctrinal differences and political ambitions may develop into violent wars under the leadership of charismatic and ambitious scholars.

Background Setting

Although Sufism existed and was practiced since the early Islamic history, most of the organized brotherhoods emerged in the eleventh, twelfth and thirteenth centuries AD. For instance, Qadiriyah was founded by Sheikh Abdulqadir al-Jeylani (1077-1166); Ahmadiyah was founded by Ahmad Ibn Idris al-Fasi (1760-1837); and Shadaliyah was founded by Abu-Xasan al-Shadali (1196-1258). In the Somali peninsula, the advent of Sufism has been recorded since early fifteen century with the arrival of 44 Islamic scholars under the leadership of Sheikh Ibrahim Abu-Zarbai in 1430. It was also reported that Sheikh Jamaal al-Addiin bin Yuusuf al-Zaylici (d. 1389), the author of the book *Nasbu al-Rāya li Ahādi li Ah-Ruāyah*, possibly was one of the Sufi Sheikhs in the Horn of African region. However, this remains a mere speculation, since there are no detailed historical accounts of him.[1] Nevertheless, its renewal and reform as an organized movement was noted from the last quarter of the nineteenth century to the middle of the twentieth century. Indeed, Said Samatar wrote, "These years between 1880 and 1920 can be described as the era of the Sheikhs in Somali history."[2] Revival is an important dimension of the historical experience of Muslims; Sufi reformation entailed shifting from individual Islamic activities to institutionalized orders.[3] Traditionally, Sufi order masters belong to all three categories of Islamic scholars in Somalia, the *Culumo* or *Wadaado*. In their communities, they are easily identified by the titles attached to their names: Sheikh (Islamic

---

[1] See Mohamed Ahmed Jum'āle, *Dawr 'ulamā Junub al-Somāl fī al-Da'wa al-Islāmiyah* (1889-1941) (PhD thesis submitted to the University of Omdurman, Khartoum, 2007), 84.
[2] Said Samatar, *Oral Poetry and Somali Nationalism: The Case of Sayyid Mohamed Abdulle Hassan* (Cambridge: Cambridge University Press, 1982), 97.
[3] Scott Steven Rees, *Patricians of the Banadir: Islamic Learning, Commerce and Somali Urban Identity in the Nineteenth Century* (PhD thesis submitted to the University of Pennsylvania, 1996), 306.

jurist and teacher), Macallin (Qur'anic teacher), and Aw (a person with an elementary Islamic education). After joining a Sufi order by taking the oath of allegiance called Bay'a and receiving a banner, a chain, and the litanies (Awrad) of the order, some of them retain their original titles, while others may change to the title Khaliif, the marker of the Sufi masters.[4] The stimulus for their revival, as described by Trimigham, was the emergence of charismatic spiritual preachers with a talent for mass mobilization during this period.[5] However, this raison d'être is not enough to explain the phenomenon. It seems that this revival is not an isolated occurrence in Somalia but could be related to similar revivalist movements in the Muslim world that could be linked with the increased awareness of external threats and the decline of morality in Muslim societies. Traditional Sufi orders have taken mainly peaceful approaches to socio-religious reform through Islamic propagation and spiritual revitalization.[6] As such, they dominated religious life, reaching out to populations in the urban and rural areas alike, most of whom had identified with one of the Sufi orders by the nineteenth century. Sufi sheikhs, besides their complementary role in running community affairs, established Islamic commonwealth centers Jamaacooyin (somalized Arabic word of Jama 'a in plural form) whose dwellers gave their allegiance only to their Sufi masters/sheikhs.[7]Moreover, in contradiction to conventional

---

[4] Since there is no certification system in traditional education, the minimum requirement to bear the name of "Sheikh" is the capacity to contract marriages and administer the law of inheritance. On the other hand, the title of "Macallin" is carried by those who have dedicated their life to the teaching the Qur'an, and "Aw" is a less significant title demonstrating simply that a person went through some kind of elementary Islamic education. See Abdurahman Abdullahi, "Tribalism and Islam: The Basics of Somaliness" in *Variations on the Theme of Somaliness*, edited by Muddle Suzanne Liluis (Turku, Finland: Centre of Continuing Education, Abo University, 2001), 233.
[5] See Trimigham, *Islam in Ethiopia*, 1952. Also, Rees, *Patricians of the Banadir*, 302-303.
[6] The nature of peacefulness of Sufi Orders may be interrupted because of external provocations, such as colonialism in the case of many scholars, exemplified by Sayyid Mohamed Abdulle Hasan, and internal doctrinal conflicts, such as the conflict between Baardheere Jama'a and Geledi Sultanates and current fighting between Al-Shabab and Sufi Order of Ahl al-Sunna wa al-Jama'a.
[7] Certainly, all Jama'a communities in Somalia, estimated by I.M. Lewis in the 1950s to account for more than 80 communities, are under the leadership of a master/sheikh, and the clan factor has no much space. Of these, over half were Ahmadiyah, and the remaining was distributed

historiography that considers Sufi orders to be mainly apolitical, many leaders of the Sufi orders and their disciples became the supreme leaders of their communities. In this way, clan allegiances and loyalties were diluted and at times transformed into ideological loyalties. Occasionally, both religious and secular authorities are combined in one leader creating a strong Sufi master or sheikh. Moreover, most of the Islamic education centers were located in settlements in agricultural areas and around water wells and many of these were later transformed into villages, towns, and cities. In this way, the Sufi orders transformed pastoral society into settled communities engaged in agriculture and/or trade.[8]

These Sufi orders remain active across Somalia with popular support, despite the fact that modern elites who do not belong to any Sufi order have emerged with the development of modern education and modern Islamic movements eschewing Sufism. Briefly, the main characteristics of Sufi orders in Somalia are as follows. They are affiliated with the wider networks of Sufi brotherhoods in the Muslim world. Their leadership is absolute and authoritative, and succession is not necessarily based on heredity; however, the *Khalif* (Sufi master) designates his successor in his lifetime. Often, most of the Sufi masters nominate their sons, believing that their blessing (*Baraka*) is dormant in them, and members of the order will pay great respect to the son derived from respect for his father. Every Sufi master has an official Sufi genealogy connecting him to the founder of his order. Membership is acquired by new aspirants through direct formal initiation (allegiance). Every member has to comply with the policies and procedures of the orders that include

---

almost equally between Qadiriyah and Salihiyah (note here Lewis is not including Salihiyah in Ahmadiyah which is incorrect). See Lewis, *Saints*, 35. Moreover, Professor Mukhtar produces 92 Jama'a in 1920s in the Italian colony, where 50 Jama'a were located in the upper Juba, 30 in Banadir, 4 in Lower Juba, and 8 in Hiiraan. See Mohamed Mukhtar, *Historical Dictionary of Somalia*. African Historical Dictionary Series, 87 (Lanham, MD: Scarecrow Press, 2003), 127.

[8] Laitin, and Samatar, *Somalia: Nation*, 45.

regular recitation of litanies. Finally, members take the common name of *Ikhwaan* (brethren) that connotes their relation to pan-Islamic brotherhood.[9]

There are two main Sufi orders in Somalia: Qadiriyah and Ahmadiyah. Each Sufi order has its local offshoots.[10] Qadiriyah has two main branches, Zayli'iyah and Uweysiyah. Zayli'iyah was founded by Sheikh Abdirahman al-Zaylici (1815-1882), who was based in Qulunqul near Dhagahbur in the Western Somalia (Somali State of Ethiopia). Uweysiyah was founded by the spiritual master Sheikh Uweys ibn Ahmad al-Baraawe (1846-1907), and its seat was located in Balad al-Amiin near Afgoye, about 40 km south-west of Mogadishu. Ahmadiyah has three offshoots in Somalia: Rahmaniyah, Salihiyah, and Dandarawiyah. Rahmaniyah was founded by Maulana Abdurahman ibn Mohamud (d. 1874). Salihiyah, founded by Sheikh Mohamed Salah around 1890s. It has two branches: southern branch introduced by Sheikh Mohamed Guuleed al-Rashiidi (d.1918) and northern branch by Sayyid Mohamed Abdulle Hasan (1856-1920). Dandarawiyah was introduced by SayyidAdan Ahmed and has a limited following in northern Somalia.[11]

In gathering together the pieces of the early history of the Sufi orders, it is important to note that there were two regional centers of Islamic learning in pre-colonial Somali territories. These centers were connected with Yemen, Zanzibar, Oman, Saudi Arabia, and Egypt. One of these centers was in the Banadir region, where the cities of Mogadishu, Barawe, Marka, and Warsheik are located. In these centers, famous Islamic scholars and prominent Sufi sheikhs have been spreading Islam to the clans of the interior. They also established pan-

---

[9] Spencer Trimigham, *Islam in Ethiopia*, 236-237.
[10] Most scholars fail to distinguish between the original Sufi order and their later derivatives. Sometimes these Sufi orders are said to be three, making Salihiyah a separate order from Ahmadiyah and also neglecting the existence of the Rufaiyah order. See Laitin and Samatar, *Somalia: Nation*, 45.
[11] Cabdirisaq Caqli, *Sheikh Madar. Asaasaha Hargeysa* (biographical work on Sheikh Madar written in Somali Language, no date or publishing house).

clan networks through common affiliation to one of the Sufi orders. Students traveled to Banadir via trade routes connecting this area with the southern and middle regions of Somali territories.[12] The other Islamic education centers were located in the historical cities in western Somali territories (currently, Somali state of Ethiopia) such as Harrar, Jigjiga, and surrounding areas. In particular, Qulunqul is renowned as the Qadiriyah Sufi center and had its special importance as the site of the founder of Zayli'iyah branch of Qadiriyah, Sheikh Abdirahman al-Zaylici. Islamic scholars and students of Islamic studies were traveling between Harrar, Jigjiga, and surrounding areas and the northern and northeastern Somali regions that include the current Somaliland and Puntland administrations. Other Sufi orders were marginal late-comers. The two main Sufi orders, Qadiriyah and Ahmadiyah, and their offshoots were spreading their messages along with Islamic education centers.

Names of the Orders	Founders of the Orders in Somalia	Headquarters of the Orders
Qadiriyah Zayli'iyah Uweysiyah	Sheikh Abdirahman al-Zaylici (d.1882) Sheikh Uweys al-Barawi (d.1909)	Qulunqul (Dhagahbur) Beled al-Amin (Afgoye)
Ahmadiyah Rahmaniyah Salihiyah (south) Salihiyah (north) Dandrawiyah	Mawlana Abdirahman Mohamud (d. 1874). Sayyid Mohamed Guled Al-Rashid (d. 1918) Sayyid Mohamed Abdulle Hasan (d.1920) Sayyid Adan Ahmed (the second half of 19th century)	Basra (Afgoye) Misra weyn (Jowhar) Qoryaweyne(Las-Anod) Haahi village and Sheikh town

Table 5: Somali Sufi Orders and their Headquarters

---

[12] See trade routes in early Somalia in Laitin and Samatar, *Somalia: Nation*, 9-10.

Incidents of Militancy among Sufi Orders

In the context, militancy is the use of violent approaches to achieve doctrinal objectives and to impose leadership within Sufi brotherhoods, whereas, moderation simply signifies tolerance and the avoidance of all forms of violent behavior to achieve political and doctrinal objectives. In general, Sufi brotherhoods are moderates and use peaceful means of propagating Islam that offer due considerations to the norms and customs of the people. Sometimes they use innovative means to assimilate and absorb pastoral and illiterate masses and mobilize them into common action. With blood-shedding being in principle the most heinous crime in Islam, Somali scholars usually abstain from clan fighting in the harsh pastoral environment. Their role is limited to conflict resolution, community education, and conduction of religious functions. However, there were four historical events when militancy emerged, and Islamic scholars led internal fighting to gain politico-religious hegemony. These events constitute historical precedents for current militancy and extremism in Somalia and offer lessons that doctrinal differences may develop into violent confrontation between Islamists.

The first incident occurred in the town of Baardheere as a confrontation between the Baardheere Jama'a and the Geledi Sultanate at Afgoye.[13] The Baardheere Jama'a was founded in 1819 by Sheikh Ibrahim Yabarow, introducing some reforms such as outlawing tobacco and popular dancing, and prohibiting ivory trade.[14] The Jama'a began to implement some

---

[13] The narration of this event was misnamed as "*Baardheere Jihad*" by most historians and, in particular, professor Cassanelli. In fact, internal wars between Muslims should not be called *Jihad*. It is a misnomer that militant Baardheere Jama'a used to justify their war with the other Muslims. Note that Sultan of Geledi did not call it *Jihad*. See details of this event in Cassanelli, *Shaping*, 136-139.

[14] Baardheere was founded in 1819 by Sheikh Ibrahim Xasan Yabarow, a native of Dafeed (Wanlaweyn), a town between Afgoye and Buur-Hakaba, who was refused to establish a reformist religious community in his home district. Dafeed sources claim that Sheikh Ibrahim was affiliated with the Ahmadiyah order. See, Cassanelli, *Shaping*,136. However, the nature of Jama'a is highly disputed as a Qadiriyah settlement, as Trimigham argued. See Trimigham, *Islam in Ethiopia*, 240-

elements of Islamic Sharia such as the wearing of decent Islamic dress for women. In the mid-1830s, after receiving strong adherents among new pastoral immigrants, the Jama'a decided to expand its sphere of influence to other regions during the era of Sharif Abdirahman and Sharif Ibrahim, who originated from the Ashraf Sarman residing in Bakool region.[15] By 1840, the Jama'a warriors reached Baidoa area and Luuq and finally sacked Barawe, the historic seat of the Qadiriyah order where both Sultan Yusuf Mohamed of Geledi and Sheikh Maadow of Hintire had studied.[16] Barawe accepted the capitulation conditions that included prohibiting tobacco and popular dancing, and adopting Islamic dress code. They also agreed to pay an annual tax of 500 Pessa.[17] This action provoked a concerted response from the clans of the inter-river areas under the charismatic leadership of the Geledi Sultan Yusuf Maohamed. The Geledi sultanate mobilized an expedition force of 40,000 from all clans in the reverine areas, stormed Baardheere, and burned it to the ground. Cassanelli characterized this conflict as one between the rising power of Islamic reformists and the established traditional power of the Geledi. Moreover, he adds the economic factor of curbing the lucrative ivory trade as well as a clan aspect, which stemmed from the armed immigrant nomads, the followers of the Jama'a, being perceived as a threat to the local population.[18] The external actors' role in this conflict was not well researched; however, it is said that Sayyid Bargash, the Sultan of Zanzibar, was in good terms with the Geledi Sultanate in the confrontation to the threat perceived was a Salafia

---

41. Moreover, it was also labelled as being Wahabiyah by many European explorers. See, Cassanelli, *Shaping*, 136.
[15] Cassanelli, *Shaping*, 137.
[16] Sultan Yusuf Mohamed and Sheikh Maadow were the most powerful leaders who together reacted to the Baardheere militant expansionists.
[17] Aw-Jāma Omar Isse, *Safaḥāt min Tārikh al-'allāma al-Ḥāji 'Ali 'Abdiraḥman Faqigh (1797-1852)*. Sana: Markaz Ibādi li dabat wa nashri, 2009, 124.
[18] Cassanelli, *Shaping*, 140-14. Also see, Virginia Luling, *Somali Sultanate: The Geledi City-State over 150 Years* (London: Haan Publications, 2002), 23.

penetration which was considered antagonistic to the traditional Islam in the southern Somalia.[19]

The second incident is connected with the arrival of Sheikh Ali Abdirahman (Majerteen) (1787-1852) in Marka in 1846 and his confrontation with the dominant Geledi sultanate. Sheikh Ali Majerteen was born in Nugal region between Garowe and Lascanod in the current Puntland State of Somalia. He traveled to Mecca and Baghdad for further studies where he met and studied "with the disciples of Mohammad Abdulwahhab and came back to his home area.[20] He established an Islamic education center at Haalin wells near Taleex in Nugal Valley. However, he emigrated from his home after getting into conflict with his clan and moved to the eastern region under the tutelage of Majerteen Sultan Nur Osman. Here also, Sheikh Ali found it unacceptable to live with the overt violation of Islamic Sharia by the Sultan Nur of Majerteen and formed an alliance with Haji Farah Hirsi, a rebel Sultan of Majerteen. Haji Farah attempted to establish a new sultanate or to overthrow his cousin. Under the arrangement between Sheikh Ali and Haji Farah, Haji Farah would take political responsibility and Sheikh Ali would administer religious affairs.[21] To achieve this goal, Sheikh Ali sent a letter to the ruler of Sharja Sheikh Saqar al-Qasimi offering his allegiance and requesting his support.[22] However, Sheikh Saqar could not respond promptly and, dismayed, Sheikh Ali traveled to India and then Zanzibar and remained there for 15 months under the custody of Sultan Said al-Bu-Saīdi (the father of Sayyid Barkash). Having in mind to establish an Islamic Emirate, Sheikh Ali arrived in Marka in 1847, four years after the defeat of Baardheere Jama'a by the dominance

---

[19] Jum'āle, *Dawr 'ulamā*, 41.
[20] Aw-Jāma, *Safahāt*, 12.
[21] This form of alliance is similar to the alliance of King Saud and Sheikh Mohamed Abdul-Wahhab in creating SaudiKingdom.
[22] See the letter in Aw-Jāma, *Safahāt*, 110-117. The writer of this letter is controversial and other report informs that it was written by one of the Idagale Sultanate of Isaaq sub-clan.

of Geledi Sultanate that ruled over the vast territories of the southern Somali regions. However, the Biyomaal clan, the major clan of Marka, was rebelling against the Geledi Sultanate. Sheikh Ali Majerteen arrived in Marka in alliance with the Biyomaal clan.[23] He settled in the area near Marka with the consent of the Biyamaal clan and began his activities and education programs. According to Virginia Luling (1939-2013), it is believed that "he himself had had plans to form a colony at the port of Mungiya (the point where the Shabelle River was closest to the Indian Ocean coast), and has obtained a permission to do so from Sayyid Sa'id of Zanzibar."[24] However, initially, he attempted to play the role of a peacemaker between Sultan Yusuf of Geledi and the Biyomaal clan and sent a letter to Sultan Yusuf requesting him that he accepts his reconciliation proposal. However, when Sultan Yusuf refused his offer, he arbitrarily declared war against him and seemingly "have raided some of Yusuf's dependent villages near the river" like Golweyn.[25] The reaction of Geledi Sultanate was rapid and Sheikh Ali's followers confronted the Geledi Sultan in 1847 and were easily defeated. Sheikh Ali's expectation of receiving assistance from the Sultan of Zanzibar was dashed; instead, it is thought that the Sultan of Zanzibar helped the Sultan of Geledi to confront what was perceived as the threat of the Wahabiyah. The doctrinal inclination of Sheikh Ali Majerteen is evident in the letter he sent to the clans of Barawe, showing that he considered the Geledi Sultanate to a polity adhering to deviated sect (firqa al-Ḍālah). Commenting on the outcome of the war, Sheikh Ali stated that "in reality ours [deaths] are in the paradise and theirs are in the hell" and "if you are among the deviated sect which Sultan Yusuf leads, there is no relation between us, and

---

[23] Sheikh arrived Marka with five boats, 150 followers, and substantial quantities of firearms and ammunitions estimated to be 40 rifles and 4 cannons. See Luling, *Somali Sultanate*, 24.
[24] Ibid.
[25] Ibid.

your blood will not be saved from us."[26] The intolerance of Sheikh Ali to the propagation of Islam among his people, his mobilization of armed followers, and his siding with the Biyomaal clan against the Geledi Sultanate all indicates that he belonged to a militant ideology akin to that of Baardheere Jama'a, a new militant tendencies that was emerging during this period in many Muslim countries.

The third significant event was the arrival in Berbera in 1895 of Sayyid Mohamed Abdulle Hasan. This was not only the beginning of armed encounters with the colonial powers but also the initiation of an internal conflict among Somali Sufi orders. Upon his arrival in Berbera, Sayyid Mohamed challenged the authority and credentials of the Qadiriyah establishment, setting up the competing Salihiyah order and building his own mosque, the Salihiyah propagation center. Sayyid Mohamed began to publicly criticize some practices of Qadiriyah Sheikhs and introduced fatwa on some controversial issues. These issues included prohibition of chewing Qaad and tobacco, the practice tolerated by Qadiriyah scholars.[27] However, Qadiriyah scholars succeeded in overcoming Sayyid Mohamed's challenges through religious public debate. Scholars such as Aw Gaas and Haji Ibrahim Hirsi invited Sheikh Madar from Hargeysa, head of the Qadiriyah order in the region, and Sheikh Abdullahi Arusi, the teacher of Sayyid Mohamed Abdulle Hasan, to participate in a meeting held in Berbera in 1897 aiming to discuss the issues of what is lawful and what is prohibited in Islam. However, after heated discussions on the issues, followers of Qadiriyah in Berbera repudiated Sayyid Mohamed, and the British authorities intervened to maintain public order and the religious status quo of the city. As a result, Sayyid Mohamed was compelled to emigrate from Berbera, carrying with him doctrinal enmity

---

[26] Aw-Jāma, *Safahāt*, 152.
[27] Khat (Catha edulis Forks.), known in Somalia as Qaad or Jaad, is a plant whose leaves and stem tips are chewed for their stimulating effect. Its lawfulness and prohibition in Islamic the jurisprudence is highly disputed. On June 24, 2014, the sale of khat was also prohibited in Britain.

against Qadiriyah. This deep-rooted conflict between Qadiriyah and northern Salihiyah had two dimensions, one political and one doctrinal. First, Sayyid Mohamed was aiming to establish an Islamic Emirate under his leadership without consulting other prominent scholars. His unilateral, authoritarian, and controversial approach annoyed many scholars and clan leaders. Second, Salihiyah questioned the doctrinal credentials of the rival Qadiriyah order, condemning them as heretical and claiming that only Salihiyah was authentic and original. This theological controversy escalated into a polemic exchange and then developed into bitter propaganda against each other.[28] For instance, Sheikh Uweys wrote poems vilifying the Salihiyah order. Here are some selected excerpts from the poem, translated by B.G. Martin.[29]

> The person guided by Mohamed's law,
> Will not follow the faction of Satan [Salihiyah]
> Who deem it lawful to spill the blood of the learned?
> Who take cash and women too: they are anarchist
> Do not follow those men with big shocks of hair,
> A coiffure like the Wahabiyah!
> Publicly, they sell paradise for cash, in our land; they are a sect of dogs
> They have gone astray and make others deviate on earth,
> By land and sea among the Somalis
> Have they no reason or understanding? Be not deceived by them
> But flee as from a disaster, from their infamy and unbelief.

This verbal polemic was countered by a similar diatribe of poems by Sayyid Mohamed, which concluded: "A word to the backsliding apostates, who have gone astray, from the Prophet's way, the straight path? Why is the truth, so plain,

---

[28] See Sheikh Uweys's poems in Samatar, Said S., 1992. *Sheikh Uways Muhammad of Baraawe, 1847-1909. Mystic and Reformer in East Africa*, in: Said S. Samatar (ed.), *In the Shadows of Conquest. Islam in Colonial Northeast Africa*. Trenton, NJ: The Red Sea Press, 48-74.
[29] See complete translation in Ibid, 55-56.

hidden from you?"[30] This verbal polemic developed into physical attacks on the leaders of Qadiriyah, and on April 14, 1909, followers of Salihiyah attacked and murdered Sheikh Uweys al-Barawi at Biyoley village in southern Somalia. When Sayyid Mohamed heard of the death of Sheikh Uweys he recited a victory hymn saying, "Behold, at last, when we slew the old wizard, the rains began to come!"[31] The implications of this conflict in Somalia were tremendous, affecting anti-colonial resistance and tarnishing the image of the Salihiyah order among the southern Somali population.

The fourth incident occurred among Salihiyah and Dandarawiyah in northern Somali territory. Before the arrival of Sayyid Mohamed in northern Somali territory, there was the Dandarawiyah order, an offshoot of Ahmadiyah, in the towns of Sheikh and Haahi. Sayyid Mohamed demanded from the Dandarawiyah order to follow him claiming absolute authority over the order. After refusing the Sayyid's initiative, the conflict between the Dandarawiyah and Sayyid Mohamed escalated. Sayyid Mohamed dispatched to the town of Sheikh, the seat of the Dandarawiyah, about 80 cavalry troops with the message that they should participate in the Jihad against the British infidels. Sending an armed mission without consultation was perceived as a threat by the Dandarawiyah. They captured most of the soldiers and surrendered them to the British forces stationed in Laylis between Sheikh and Berbera.[32] In reaction, Sayyid Mohamed dispatched a strong military expedition and razed Sheikh to the ground.[33] Later,

---

[30] Martin, Bradford G., 1993. *Shaykh Uways bin Muhammad al-Barawi, a Traditional Somali Sufi*, in: G. M. Smith and Carl Ernst (eds.), *Manifestations of Sainthood in Islam*. Istanbul: ISIS, 225-37. Also, Samatar, *Shadows of Conquest*, 59.
[31] The Somali version is "Candhagodoble goortaan dilaa roobki noo da'aye." See Samatar, *Shadows of Conquest*, 61.
[32] Sultan Maxamuud Axmad Sheikh Ciise interviewed by the author on December 16, 2009, Hargeysa.
[33] The leadership genealogy of the Dandarawiyah in Somalia is as follows from top-down; (1) Sheikh Aadan, (2) Sheikh Nuur, (3) Sheikh Mohamed Xuseen (d. 1964), (4) Engineer Cali Sheikh Mohamed Xuseen (d. 2009), (5) Suldaan Maxamuud Axmad (collective leadership). This information was reported by Suldaan Maxamuud Axmad Ciise on December, 16, 2009, Hargeysa.

the Sayyid Mohamed's bright points were romanticized by Somali nationalists in their efforts to nurture national consciousness by narrating a glorious past and reconstructing symbols, heroes, and myths. In this approach, self-inflicted wounds, civil wars, massacres, and human atrocities are downplayed and belittled.[34] However, in tracing the background of the current extremism in the name of Islam, it is necessary to bring up other episodes of Sayyid Mohamed that suggest the historical roots of the current extremism in Somalia.[35] The roots that are similar to the early militancy between the Sufi orders and modern Islamists – points to the influence of the Salafia ideology based on "exclusivity and absolutism", and the use of violent means to impose their Islamic interpretation on other Muslims.[36]

Conclusion

The controversies and polemics that occurred between Sufi Orders in Somalia in the 19th and early years of the 20th centuries could be characterized mainly as between the rising power of Islamic reformists and established traditional Sufi Order. The three incidents that took place in the Southern Somalia were between followers of Qadiriyah Order on one side and reformists on the other. Reformists such as Sharif Ibrahim "Baardheere", Sheikh Ali Majerteen (Marka) and Sayyid Mohamed were attempting to expend their area of influence in the traditionally Qadiriyah regions. Other factors may have motivated controversies such as cultural treats of the leaders, Islamic orientation, economic and clan factors.

---

[34] Adeed Dawisha, *Arab Nationalism in the Twentieth Century: From Triumph to Despair* (Princeton Press, 2003), 63.

[35] There are resemblances between Sayyid Mohamed's activities and slogans and current extremist organizations like Al-Shabab and Hizbul-Islaam. These are (1) personal rule; (2) exclusion of other Islamic organizations and monopoly of religious legitimacy; (3) excessive use of violence against other Muslims; and (4) selective and haphazard application of Sharia. All these actions are disguised under the slogan of *Jihad* against the enemies of the Islam and infidels.

[36] Abdurahman Abdullahi, "Recovering the SomaliState: the Islamic Factor." In *Somalia: Diaspora and State Reconstitution in the Horn of Africa*, edited by A. Osman Farah, Mammo Mushie, and Joakim Gundel (London: Adonis & Abby Publishers Ltd, 2007), 196-221, 211.

Moreover, reformist leaders had the objective and ambition of establishing polity (sultanate) while southern Qadiriyah's objective was limited to keeping the status quo and building harmonious and pious communities. Furthermore, the influence of Salafia doctrine were evident from all reformist leaders and their ardent opposition to the some practices of traditional Sufi Orders and to discredit their doctrinal credentials . Conversely, the fight between Dandrawiyah and Salihiyah who are two branches of Ahmadiyah in the town of Sheikh could be described simply as internal legitimacy tussle motivated by their different policies in encountering colonial power.

Finally, current militancy in the name of Islam forcefully emerged after the event of 9/11 attack on US targets and intensified during the short rule of the Union of the Islamic Courts in 2006. Linking to Al-Qaida and adopting extremist ideology, Al-shabab began to desecrate venerated Sufi scholars' shrines. As a reaction, peaceful Sufi Orders in some regions were compelled to take up armies and to defend themselves. As a result, they also became militants with political ambition under the name of "*Ahlu Sunna waa Al-Jamaa'a*". Though, current militancy, its scope, objectives and impact is incomparable to the historical random incidents among Sufi Orders, nevertheless, it is important to portray historical lessons in connecting past to the present and to explore communalities and shared features.

References

Abdi Gadiid, "Yaan laga Tegin Cadaaladda Danbiilayaasha ma yaro". Availablefrom http://www.qubanaha.com/2012/08/16/yaan-laga-tagin-cadaaladda-dambiilayaasha-ma-yaro-faalo-xiiso/.

Abdi, Sheik Abdi, Divine Madness: Mohammed Abdulle Hassan (1856-1920). Zed Books Ltd., London, 1993.

Abdulkadir, Fowsia&Abdulkadir, Rahma, "Transitional Justice& Limited or Failed Statehood: A Case Study of Somalia."www.wiscnetwork.org/porto2011/papers/WISC_2011-769.pdf.

Abdulkadir, Rahma."Gender, Transitional Justice and failed statehood: can Somali Traditional Customary Law be the basis for Viable and inclusive Mechanism (s) of Transitional Justice in Somalia?"PhD *Diss., The University of Texas at Dallas, 2011.*

Abdullahi, Abdurahman Baadiyow and Ibrahim Farah. "Reconciling the State and Society in Somalia: Reordering Islamic Work and Clan System." A paper presented at the International Somali Studies Association Conference in Ohio, August 2007.

Abdullahi, Abdurahman, "Non-state Actors in the Failed State of Somalia: Survey of the Civil Society Organizations during the Civil War (1990-2002)." DarasatIfriqiyah, 31 (2004): 57-87.

Abdullahi, Abdurahman, "The Islamic Movement in Somalia: A Historical Evolution with the Case Study of Islah Movement (1950-2000)". A PhD thesis, Institute of Islamic Studies, McGill University, 2011.

Abdullahi, Abdurahman, "Tribalism, Nationalism and Islam: The crisis of the political Loyalties in Somalia (MA thesis, Islamic Institute, McGill University, 1992).

Abdullahi, Abdurahman. "Conceptions of Transitional Justice in Somalia: findings of Field research in

Mogadishu."*Northeast African Studies,*Vol. 14, No. 2 (Fall 2014).

Abdullahi, Abdurahman. "Islam and Transitional Justice: principles, mechanisms, and historic role in Somalia". A paper produced as part of research project on Transitional Justice in Somalia commissioned by Max Planck, Institute for Social Anthropology, Halle/Saale, Germany,2013.

Abdullahi, Abdurahman. "Somalia: phases of modern Islamic development."www.academia.edu/13227041/Phases_of_the_Islamic_Movement_in_Somalia.

Abdullahi, Abdurahman. "The roots of the Islamic conflict in Somalia." In *Somalia: Exploring aWay Out*. National Civic Forum, Somalia, 2011.

Abdullahi, Abdurahman. "Islah movement in Somalia: Islamic moderation in war-torn Somalia."Presented at the Second Nordic Horn of Africa Conference, Oslo University, 2008. www.hiiraan.com/oct2008/ISLAH.pdf.

Abdullahi, Abdurahman. "Penetrating Cultural Frontiers in Somalia: History of women's Political Participation during four Decades (1959-2000)."African Renaissance. 4:1 (2007): 34-54.

Abdullahi, Abdurahman. "Perspectives on the State Collapse in Somalia." In Somalia at the Crossroads: Challenges and Perspectives in Reconstituting a Failed State, edited by Abdullahi A. Osman and Issaka K. Soure. London: Adonis & Abby Publishers Ltd, 2007.

Abdullahi, Abdurahman. "Recovering the Somali state: the Islamic factor." In *Somalia: Diaspora and State Reconstitution in the Horn of Africa*, edited by A. Osman Farah, Mamo Mushie, and Joakim Gundel. London: Adonis & Abby Publishers Ltd, 2007: 196-221.

Abdullahi, Abdurahman. "Women, Islamists, and the military regime in Somalia: The new family law and its implications." In Markus Hoehne and Virginia Luling (ed.)

Milk and Peace, Drought and War: Somali Culture, Society and Politics. London: Hurst&Company, 2010, 137-160.

Abdullahi, Abdurahman. "Tribalism, Nationalism and Islam: Crisis of the Political Loyalties in Somalia". MA Thesis, McGill University, 1992.

Abdullahi, Abdurahman the Application of Shari' a Law in Somalia, available at http://www.hiiraan.com/comments2-op-2009-mar-the_application_of_shari_a_laws_in_somalia.aspx.

Abdullahi, Abdurahman. "Political Islam in Somalia." Middle Eastern Affairs Journal. 1:3 (1993): 46-47.

Abu Sulayman, Abdul Hamid A., The Islamic Theory of International Relations: New Directions for Islamic Methodology and Thought. Herndon, VA: The International Institute of Islamic Thought, 1987.

Abubakar, Ali Sheikh. Al-Somal: Judur al-Ma'sat al_Rahina. Beirut: Dar-Ibn Hazm, 1992.

Adam, Hussein M., "Political Islam in Somali History," in Milk and Peace, Drought and War: Somali Culture, Society and Politics, ed. Markus Hoehne and Virginia Luling (London: Hurst & Company, 2010).

Adam, Hussein. "Historical Notes on Somali Islamism." A paper presented at the Conference of the Somali Studies Association, Djibouti: December 12-15, 2007.

Agence France Press, Somali warlords hold 'secret anti-terrorism' talks with US agents: witnesses", February 28, 2006.

Al-Asqalani, Ibn Hajar, al-Nukat Ala Kitab ibn al-Salah. Maktabah al-Furqan, Ajman, U.A.E., 2 edition, vol. 1, 2003.

Al-Banna, Hassan, The Message of Teachings. http://web.youngmuslims.ca/online_library/books/tmott/index.htm#understanding (accessed on Jan. 20, 2012).

Al-Barakaat Case Study: The Somali Community and al-Barakaat, available from http://www.9-

11commission.gov/staff_statements/911_TerrFin_Ch5.pdf (accessed on August 25, 2010).

Al-Gazali, Abdulhamid. Hawla Asaasiyat al-Mashru'c Al_Islami Li Nahdat Al-Ummah. Qahira: Rar Al-Tawzi'c WA Nashr Al-Islamiyah, 2000

Ali, Jan A., Tabligh Jama'at: A trans-national movement of Islamic faith regeneration. European Journal of Economic and Political Studies. IJIPS-3, (SI), 2010, (103–131).

Ali, Salah Mohamed, Hudur and the History of Southern Somalia. Cairo: Mahda Bookshop Publisher, 2005.

Al-Mahdi, Sadiq, "Al-Shura ka Asaas li-Nidum Al-Hukm Fi Al-Alam Al Islami." Unpublished paper submitted to the 15th Conference of the Muslim Affairs held in Cairo: May, 2003.

Al-Maududi, Abul Ala. The Islamic Law and Constitution. Islamic books, 1980.

Al-Mawardi, Abu l-Hasan Ali b. Muhammad, al-Ahkam al-Sultaniyya wa al-wilayat al-Diniyya. Cairo: Maktaba wa Matba'a Mustafa al-Babi al-Halabi, 1966.

Al-Naqira, Mohamed Abdallah, Intishar al-Islam fi SharqIfriqiyahwaMunahadat al-GarbiLahu. Riyadh: Dar al-Marikh, 1982.

Al-Qaradawi, Yusuf. Islamic Awakening between Rejection and Extremism. International Institute of Islamic Thought, (IIIT), 2006.

Al-Qaradawi, Yusuf. Priorities of the Islamic Movement in The Coming Phase. Al-Dar; 1st edition, 1992.

Al-Raysouni, Ahmed,http://www.suhaibwebb.com/islam-studies/islam-101/misconceptions/freedom-of-religion-and-apostasy-in-islam-by-dr-ahmed-raysuni; accessed on Jan. 31, 2012.

Alsaid, Muhammad Ata, The Hudud: The Hudud are the Seven Specific Crimes in Islamic Criminal Law and their mandatory Punishments. Kuala Lumpur: Muhammad Ata al Sid Sid Ahmad, 1995.

Al-Shafi'i, Muhammad ibn Idris. n.d. Islamic Jurisprudence: Shafi'i's Risala, trans. by Majid Khadduri, Baltimore: The Johns Hopkins Press, 1961.

Al-Tibrizi, Mishkat al-Masabih, Vol.2, al-Maktab al-Islami, Dimashq, 1961.

Anderson, Benedict, Imagined Communities: Reflections of the Origin and Spread of Nationalism. Verso, 1991.

Annan, K., UN Secretary-General, The Rule of Law in Conflict and Post-Conflict Societies. NY: United Nations, 2004.

Aqil, Abdallah, Min I'lam al-Da'wa wa al-Harakah al-Islamiyah al-Muasirah. Dar al-Tawzi wa al-Nashr al-Islāmyah. Qāhira: 2000.

Aqli, Abdirisaq, Sheikh Madar: AsaasahaHargeysa. biographical work on Sheikh Madar written in Somali Language, no date or publishing house.

Badawi, Jamal. The Status of Women in Islam. Plainfield: American Trust Publications, 1976: 23-24.

Bangash, Zafar, "Remembering SayyidQutb, an Islamic intellectual and leader of rare insight and integrity", available from http://web.youngmuslims.ca/online_library/books/milestones/remember.htm.

Barnes, Sedric, SOAS and Harun Hassan, The Rise and Fall of Mogadishu's Islamic Courts, Chatham House, 2007.

Barons, Maria, Society, Security Sovereignty and the State in Somalia: From Statelessness to Statelessness. Netherlands: Utrecht: International Books, 2001.

Barre, Mohamed Siyaad, My Country and my people: Selected Speeches of Jaalle Siyaad. Ministry of Information and National Guidance, 1979.

Bauman, Michael, Law and Morality, http://www.equip.org/article/law-and-morality/.

Bouhdiba, Abdelwahab and Dawalibi, Muhammad Ma'ruf, The Different Aspects of Islamic Culture: The Individual and Society in Islam. UNESCO, 1998.

Bradbury, Mark, Becoming Somaliland. London: Progresso, 2008.
Brief history of Islah" in http://www.islaax.org/arabic/history.htm.
Caqli, Cabdirisaq, Sheikh Madar: Asaasaha Hargeysa. biographical work on Sheikh Madar written in Somali Language, no date or publishing house.
Carosseli, Francesco, Ferro e Fuoco in Somalia: VentiAnni di Lotte Contro Mullah e Dervisc. Roma: SindicatoItaliano ArtiGrafiche, 1931.
Cassanelli, Lee, The Benaadir past: essays in southern Somali history. Philadelphia: University of Pennsylvania Press, 1973.
Chapra, M. Umer, The Future of Economics: An Islamic Perspective. Leicester: The Islamic Foundation, 2000.
Contini, Poalo, The Somali Republic: an Experiment in Legal Integration. London: Frank Cass & Company LTD., 1969.
Dawisha, Adeed, Arab Nationalism in the Twentieth Century: From Triumph to Despair.Princeton Press, 2003.
Dobbins, James, Seth G. Jones, Keith Crane, and Beth Cole DeGrasse. The Beginner's Guide to Nation-Building. Santa Monica, Calif.: RAND Corporation, 2007.
Drysdale, John, Whatever Happened to Somalia? London: HAAN Publishing, 1994.
Dusuk, Asyraf Wajdi and Abdullah, Nurdianawati Irwani, Maqasid al-Shari`ah, Maslahah, and Corporate Social Responsibility. The American Journal of Islamic Social Sciences 24:1. http://kantakji.com/media/2699/0308914.pdf.
El-Azhary, Amira Sobol (ed.) Women, the Family and Divorce laws in Islamic History. New York: Syracuse University Press, 1996.
Elmi, Afyare Abdi, Understanding the Somalia Conflagration: Identity, Political Islam and Peace building. London: Pluto Press, 2010.

Farah, Ibrahim, "Foreign Policy and Conflict in Somalia, 1960-1990". PhD diss., University of Nairobi, 2009.

Gilbert, William &Condon Gilbert, Edwyna. The Renaissance and the Reformation, ed. by Judith C. Galas, electronic edition, 1998.

Haji, Abdirizak."Somali vs. Rwanda –Transitional Justice". www.linkedin.com/pulse/somali-vs-rwanda-transitional-justice-abdirizak-hagi.

Haji, Awes Osman and Haji, Abdiwahid Osman, Clan, Sub-clan and Regional Representation in the Somali Government Organization 1960-1990: Statistical Data and Findings. Washington DC, 1998.

Hallaq, Wael, "On the Authoritativeness of Sunni Consensus". International Journal of Middle Eastern Studies 18 (1986), 427–454.

Hansen, Stig Jarle and Mesoy, Atle, "The Muslim Brotherhood in the Wider Horn of Africa." Norwegian Institute for Urban and Regional Research (NIBR) Report 2009.

Hansen, Stig, Al-Shabaab in Somalia: The History and Ideology of a Militant Islamist Group, 2005-2012. London: Hurst and Co., 2013.

Hirschkind, C. "What is political Islam?" Middle East Report Oct/Dec (1997).

Hoffman, Bruce."Inside Terrorism." *Columbia University Press, 1998.*

Hoffmann, Murad. Islam: The alternative. Maryland: Amana publications. 1999.

http://siteresources.worldbank.org/INTSOMALIA/Resources/conflictinsomalia.pdf.

Huntington, Samuel, "The Clash of Civilizations?" Foreign Affairs 72 (Summer 1993): 22-49.

Hussin, Nasimah and Muhammad, Ramizah Wan, Sulh in the Islamic Criminal Law: Its Applications in Muslim Countries. Available from http://webcache.googleusercontent.com/search?q=cache: http://documents.mx/documents/33-nasimah-hussin-ramizah-wan-muhammad.html.

Ibn Farhun, Ibrahim ibn Ali , Ibn Salmun, Abdallah Ali , Kitab Tabṣirat al-Hukkam fi Uṣul al-Aqḍiyah wa-manahij al-Ahkam. Dar al-Kutub al-Ilmiyah, 1983.

Ibn-Khaldun, Muqaddimah: An Introduction to History. Transl. by Franz Rosenthal, (2nd ed.). London: Routledge & Kegan Paul, 1967.

International Crisis Group, "Somalia's Islamist". African Report No. 100, December 12, 2005. Available from http://www.crisisgroup.org/en/regions/africa/horn-of-africa/somalia/100-somalias-islamists.aspx.

Isse, Aw-Jāma Omar, Safaḥāt min Tārikh al-ʿallāma al-Ḥāji ʿAli ʿAbdiraḥman Faqigh (1797-1852). Sana: Markaz Ibādi li dabāt wa nashri, 2009.

Jardine, Douglass, The Mad Mullah of Somaliland. London: Herbert Jinkines, 1923.

Jeng, Abou. "Transitional Justice and Post-Conflict Reconstruction in Somalia: The Role of the African Union and Pointers Provided by It."North Eastern African Studies, Vol.14, No.2, 2014, 45-76.

Jumʿāle, Mohamed Aḥmed, Dawr ʿulamā Junub al-Somāl fi al-Daʿwa al-Islāmiyah (1889-1941). A PhD thesis submitted to the University of Omdurman, Khartoum, 2007.

Kapteijns, Lidwien, Clan Cleansing in Somalia. Philadelphia: University of Pennsylvania Press, 2013.

Kapteijns, Lidwien. "Women and Crisis of Communal Identity: The Cultural Construction of Gender in Somali History." In The Somali Challenge: From Catastrophe to Renewal?, edited by Ahmed Samatar. Boulder: Lynne Reinner Publishers, 1994.

Karamé, K. Social and economic reasons for the recruiting to political Islam (in Norwegian). Internasjonal Politikk, 1996.

Kassam, Karim-Aly, "The clash of Civilization: The selling of Fear", 2011. Available from https://dspace.ucalgary.ca/bit stream/1880/44170/1/Islam.pdf.

Khan, Qamaruddin. Political Concepts in the Quran. Lahore: Islamic Book Foundation, 1982.

Knudsen, Are. "Political Islam in the Middle East". Chr. Michelsen Institute Development Studies and Human Rights, Bergen,2003.

Kritz, Neil J. (ed.), Transitional Justice: How Emerging Democracies Reckon with Former Regimes. US Institute of Peace Press, 1995.

Laitin, David and Said Samatar,Said, Somalia: Nation in Search of a State. Boulder: Westview Press, 1987.

Le Sage, Andre. Somalia and the war on terrorism: Political Islamic movements and US counter terrorism efforts. A DPhil Thesis, Cambridge University/Jesus College, 2005.

Lewis, Bernard, The Political Language of Islam. Chicago: University of Chicago Press, 1991.

Lewis, I. M., A Modern History of Somalia: Nation and State in the Horn of Africa. London: Longmans, 1980.

Lewis, I. M., Pastoral Democracy. Oxford: Oxford University Press, 1961.

Lewis, I. M., Saints and Somalis: Popular Islam in a Clan-based Society. Lawrenceville, N.J.: Red Sea Press, 1998.

Lewis, I.M., A Modern History the Somali: Nation and State in the Horn of Africa, Revised/Fourth Edition. Columbus: Ohio University Press, 2003.

Luling, Virginia, Somali Sultanate: The Geledi City-State over 150 Years. London: Haan Publications, 2002.

Lyons, Terrence and Samatar, Ahmed, Somalia: State Collapse, Multilateral Intervention, and Strategies for Political Reconstruction. Washington DC: Brooking Occasional Papers, 1995.

Mansur, Abdalla, "Contrary to a Nation: The Cancer of Somali State'" in Ahmed, Ali Jimale (ed), The Invention of Somalia. Lawrenceville, NJ, Red Sea Press, 1995.

Marchal, Roland, "Islamic Political Dynamics in the Somali Civil War," in Islamism and its Enemies in the Horn of Africa, ed. Alex De Waal. Indiana University Press, 2006: 114-146.

Marchal, Roland, The Rise of a Jihadi Movement in a Country at War: Harakat Al-Shabaab al-Mujaheddin, 2011.

Martin, Bradford G., Shaykh Uways bin Muhammad al-Barawi, a Traditional Somali Sufi, in: G. M. Smith and Carl Ernst (eds.), Manifestations of Sainthood in Islam. Istanbul: ISIS, 1993: 225-37.

Menkhaus, Ken.,Somalia: State Collapse and the Threat of Terrorism. Oxford, New York: Oxford University Press, 2004.

Migdal, J.S., Strong Societies and Weak States: State-Society Relations and State Capabilities in the Third World. Princeton, NJ: Princeton University Press, 1988.

Mire, Hassan Ali, "On providing for the future," in Ahmed Samatar, ed., The Somali Challenge: From Catastrophe to Renewal? London: Lynne Rienner, 1994.

Mobekk, Erin, Justice in Post-Conflict Society – Approaches to Reconciliation, 2005. Available from http://www.gsdrc.org/go/display&type=Document&id=1685.

Mohamed, Hamdi, Multiple Challenges, Multiple Struggles: A History of Women's Activism in Canada. A PhD Thesis submitted to the University of Ottawa, 2003.

Mohamud, Mohamed Sharif, "Faslun fi al-Alaqat al-Somaliayah al-Saudiyah", 2010 (Somali-Saudi relations), available from http://arabic.alshahid.net/columnists/8598.

Mukhtar, Mohamed, Historical Dictionary of Somalia. African Historical Dictionary Series, 87. Lanham, MD: Scarecrow Press, 2003.

Nasr, Sayyid Vali Reza, Mawdudi and the Making of Islamic Revivalism. Oxford University Press,1996.

Northampton-Shire Somali Community Association, Dhaawac ama Waxyeelo Maskaxeed, a Report on Post-Traumatic Stress in the Somali Community in Northampton and their experiences of Health Service, 2008. Available from http://www.nmhdu.org.uk/silo/files/post-traumatic-stress-disorder-in-the-somali-community-northampton.pdf.

Omar, Sayyid. Somali-Egyptian Relation. MA Thesis, submitted to the Institute of Islamic and Arabic Studies in Cairo, 2006.

Osman, Fathi, "Modern Islamist and Democracy" Arabia. London, May, 1986.

Osman, Hussein Abdi, "Malaf al-Sarā' beyna 'Ali Mahdi wa 'Aidīd." unpublished paper submitted to the Horn of African Center for Studies, Mogadishu, 1993.

Osseina Alidou and Meredith Turshen, "Africa: Women in the Aftermath of Civil War", Race &Class, 2000:41(4): 81-92.

Paolo Tripodi, The Colonial Legacy in Somalia: Rome and Mogadishu: From Colonial Administration to Operation Restore Hope. London: McMillan Press, 1999.

Pastaloza, Luigi, The Somali Révolution. Bari: Édition Afrique Asie Amérique Latine, 1973.

Peace and Human Right Rights Network (PHRN), Annual Report from July 2010- June 2011submitted on September, 2011.

Peters, Rudolph, Crime and Punishment in Islamic Law: Theory and Practice from the Sixteenth to Twenty-First Century. Cambridge University Press, 2005.

Qutb, Muhammad, Islam the Misunderstood Religion. www.Islambasics.com(accessed on May 24, 2016)

Rees, Scott Steven, Patricians of the Banadir: Islamic Learning, Commerce and Somali Urban Identity in the Nineteenth Century, A PhD thesis submitted to the University of Pennsylvania, 1996.

Reese, Scott S., Urban Woes and Pious Remedies: Sufism in Nineteenth-Century Banadir (Somalia). Indiana: Indiana University Press, 1999.

Refugee Survey Quarterly, Vol. 13, Nos. 2 and 3, 1994.

Roht-Arriaza, Noami ,'The new landscape of Transitional Justice,' in," in Naomi Roht-Arriaza and Javier Mariezcurrena, eds., Transitional Justice in the Twenty-First Century. Cambridge University Press, 2006.

Roht-Arriaza, Roht-Arriaza, N. and Mariezcurrna, J. (eds.), Transitional Justice in the Twenty-First Century: Beyond Truth Versus Justice. Cambridge: Cambridge University Press, 2006.

Rutherford, Kenneth, Humanitarianism under fire: The US Intervention in Somalia. Kumerian Press, 2008.

Sahih al-Bukhari, Volume 9, Book 89, Number 281.

Sahnoun, Mohamed, "Somalia: the Missed Opportunities." A paper delivered to the United State Institute of Peace, 1994.

Samatar, Ahmed, Socialist Somalia: Rhetoric and Reality. London: Zed Press, 1988.

Samatar, Said, 1992. Sheikh Uways Muhammad of Baraawe, 1847-1909. Mystic and Reformer in East Africa, in: Said S. Samatar (ed.), In the Shadows of Conquest. Islam in Colonial Northeast Africa. Trenton, NJ: The Red Sea Press, 48-74.

Samatar, Said, Oral Poetry and Somali Nationalism: The Case of Sayyid Mohamed Abdulle Hassan. Cambridge: Cambridge University Press, 1982.

Sayed Sabiq, Fiqh-us-Sunnah (10 Edition). Mecca: Bab al- log, 1993.

Shaw, Rosalind, & Waldorf, Lars (eds.), Localizing Transitional Justice: Interventions and Priorities after Mass Violence. Stanford University Press, 2010.

Shay, Shaul, Somalia between Jihad and Restoration. New Brunswick: Transaction Publishers, 2008.

Sii'arag, Duale, "The Birth and Rise of Al-Ittihad Al-Islami in the Somali Inhabited Regions in the Horn of Africa", 2005. Available from http://wardheernews.com/articles/November/13__Alittihad_Sii'arag.html.

Simpson, J.A. and Weiner E.S.C, The Compact Oxford English Dictionary, 2nd ed. Oxford, GB: Clarendon Press, 1991.

Smith, Anthony, "State-Making and Nation-Building" in John Hall (ed.), States in History. Oxford: Basil Blackwell, 1986.

Somali Provisional Constitution Available from http://unpos.unmissions.org/LinkClick.aspx?fileticket=RkJTOSpoMME=.

Stan, Lavina and Nedelsky, Nadya, Encyclopedia of Transitional Justice.

Stephenson, Carolyn, Nation-building, January, 2005. Available from http://www.beyondintractability.org/essay/nation building.

Tadesse, Medhane, "Islamic Fundamentalism in Somalia: its Nature and Implications." Available from www.somaliawatch.org.

Tadesse, Medhane, Al-Ittihad: Political Islam and Black economy in Somalia: Religion, Clan, Money, Clan and the Struggle for Supremacy over Somalia. Addis Ababa: Meag Printing Enterprise, 2002.

Tahir, Mahmood, Personal Law in Islamic Countries. New Delhi: Academy of Law and Religion, 1987.

The International Crisis Group Report. "Understanding Islamism." Middle East/North Africa Report no. 37-2 (March, 2005).

The Royal Aal al-Bayt Institute for Islamic Thought. The Amman Message. Jordan, 2009.

The World Bank, "Conflict in Somalia, drivers and dynamics, 2005", available from

Thompson and Della ed., "State", Concise Oxford English Dictionary (9th ed.). Oxford University Press, 1995.

Touval, Saadia, Somali Nationalism: International Politics and the Drive for Unity in the Horn of Africa. Cambridge: Cambridge University Press, 1963.

Trimigham, J.S, Islam in Ethiopia.Frank Cass, 1952.

Tripodi, Paolo, The Colonial Legacy in Somalia: Rome and Mogadishu: from Colonial Administration to Operation Restore Hope. London: Macmillan Press, 1999.

Villalba, Clara Sandoval, Briefing paper: Transitional Justice, key concepts, Processes and Challenges, 3. http://www.idcr.org.uk/wp-content/uploads/2010/09/07_11.pdf.

Voerman, Jan, The Reign of Terror. Andrews University Seminary Studies, Vol. 47, No. 1, 117-134.

Wagemakers, Joas, 'Seceders' and 'Postponers'? An Analysis of the "Khawarij" and "Murji'a" Labels in Polemical Debates Between Quietist and Jihadi-Salafi.

Wallis, R. & Bruce, S. "Secularization: The orthodox model."In S. Bruce, ed., *Religion and Modernization*. Oxford University Press, Oxford, UK, 2001.

Wiktorowicz, Quintan (ed), Islamic Activism: A Social Movement Theory Approach. Indiana University Press, 2003.

Xarakow, Moxamed Cali, "Cadaaladda Xilliga kala-Guurka". Available from http://www.hiiraan.com/op4/2012/july/25249/cadaaladda_xilliga_kala_guurka.aspx.

Zuin, Margherita, "A Model of Transitional Justice for Somalia". *PRAXIS The Fletcher Journal of Human Security*, Vol. XXIII,2008, 89-108.

Index

A

Abdulqadir Mosque, 53
Abidalib, Imam Ali bin, 23, 208
Abu-Zarbai, Ibrahim, xi, 186, 245
Adam, Hussein, 46, 61, 121, 124, 185, 261
Afghanistan, 17, 208
African Union Mission in Somalia, 30, 140, 148
Ahmadiyah, 63, 132, 133, 136, 188, 189, 244, 245, 246, 248, 249, 250, 256, 258
Ahmed, Christine, xii, 21, 45, 46, 47, 53, 63, 73, 134, 142, 143, 145, 181, 188, 192, 198, 207, 211, 212, 213, 222, 229, 248, 249, 262, 266, 267, 268, 270
Aidid, Mohamed Farah, 143, 144, 145, 146, 169
al- Ghazali, Abu Hamed, 133
A'la Maududi, Abdul, 17
Al-Itihad,, 136, 139, 164, 184, 204
Al-Qaradawi, Yusuf, 20, 21, 89, 262
Al-Shabab, 115, 129, 133, 139, 149, 164, 169, 175, 182, 184, 187, 206, 230, 246, 257
Alternative Dispute Resolution, 152
Arab League, 48, 213
Arabian peninsula, 34
Arab-Israeli, 49
Authoritarianism, 16

B

Barons, Maria, 45, 73, 263
Barre, Siyaad, 39, 45, 47, 51, 52, 55, 142, 144, 183, 220, 263
Besteman, Catherine, 46
Blessed Revolution, 55
British Somaliland, 49, 77, 193

C

Caliph, xi
Caliphate, 16
Christian colonizers, 192
Christian Missionaries, 64
Christianity, 27, 28, 76
Civil society activism, v
Cold War, 99, 191, 193, 194
Constitution of Medina, 78
Consultative Governance, 85
Cultural Revolution, 48

D

Darawish Movement, 180, 189
Dheel, Abdulkadir, 48
Diaspora communities, 66, 77, 93
Djibouti conference of 2000, 128
Djibouti Peace Process, 62, 68, 183

E

Elmi, Afyare, 186, 264
Ethiopia, 49, 55, 66, 76, 77, 93, 128, 140, 147, 148, 163, 183, 184, 188, 192, 198, 203, 208, 214, 220, 222, 227, 228, 246, 248, 249, 250, 272
European ascendance, 18
European powers, 76
European Renaissance, 18

F

Family Law, vii, 37, 39, 40, 42, 44, 45, 46, 48, 49, 50, 51, 52, 53, 54, 55, 56, 57, 58, 59, 65, 127, 181, 201, 202
French Revolution, 25

G

Global War on Terrorism, 146, 175, 182, 207, 208
Godless' socialist ideology, 57
Greater Somalia, 49, 76, 194, 198
Guled, Mohamed Ainanshe, 48
Gulf States, 49, 133, 214

H

Hadith, 64, 80, 104, 108, 109, 113, 121, 211
Halal, 83
Halane Training Camp, 51
Haram, 83
Hassan, Nurta Haji, 50, 51, 129, 187, 192, 201, 244, 261, 263
Hawo, Hawo, 51, 52
Helander, Berhard, 73
Hijab, 127, 157
Hoffman, Bruce, 25, 26, 237, 265
Horn of Africa, xi, 32, 34, 44, 76, 92, 134, 145, 147, 164, 181, 183, 184, 185, 190, 191, 198, 209, 234, 240, 241, 257, 260, 265, 267, 268, 271, 272
Hudud crimes, 110

I

Ikhwan, xiii, 134, 136, 204
Industrial society, 19
International Criminal Court for Rwanda, 173
International Crisis Group, ix, 19, 147, 185, 209, 266, 271
Iranian Islamic Revolution of 1979, 24
Islah, viii, xiii, 33, 34, 66, 88, 127, 136, 173, 177, 179, 184, 185, 202, 203, 204, 207, 208, 209, 210, 211, 215, 216, 217, 218, 219, 220, 221, 222, 223, 224, 225, 226, 227, 228, 229, 230, 231, 232, 233, 234, 235, 236, 238, 239, 240, 241, 259, 260, 263
Islah Society, xiii
Islami, xiii, 86, 113, 164, 200, 202, 208, 237, 238, 261, 262, 271
Islamic civilization, 18, 80, 239
Islamic fundamentalism, 21, 180
Italian Communist Party, 51
Italian Fascism, 190
Italian Somalia, 77

J

Jama'a communities, 85, 246
Judaism, 27, 101

K

Kapteijns, Lidwien, 45, 142, 266
Khalifah, 16
Khomeini, Grand Ayatollah Rohollah., 25
Kismayo, 165, 167, 193, 208, 222

L

Laitin, David, 45, 75, 134, 187, 188, 247, 248, 249, 267
Lewis, I.M., 16, 43, 44, 48, 73, 87, 145, 180, 188, 190, 201, 246, 247, 267
Lower Shabelle region, 54, 164
Lulling, Virginia, 43, 73

M

Mahmood, Tahir, 52, 271
Marxist ideology, 213
Marxist revolution, 49
Masculinity, 43
Mauritania, 17
McGill University, Canada, v, 42, 70, 127, 173, 179, 196, 259, 260
Middle Eastern Muslim societies, 100

Militancy, vii, 24, 34, 177, 205, 243, 250
Moderate Islamic movements, 88, 92, 94, 96
Mogadishu, vii, xi, xii, xiii, 33, 39, 47, 48, 51, 52, 54, 63, 129, 134, 139, 140, 141, 142, 143, 144, 145, 148, 149, 158, 162, 163, 164, 167, 168, 169, 170, 171, 172, 174, 181, 184, 190, 191, 193, 197, 199, 207, 211, 212, 213, 220, 222, 226, 228, 229, 237, 248, 259, 263, 269, 272
Moral, ii
Mujadiddin, 20
Muslim political elites, 26

N

National Reconciliation Conference, 128, 131, 146
Nation-building, 73, 74, 75, 271
Nuremburg Tribunals, 99

O

Organization of Islamic Cooperation, 17
Organization of the African Union, 48

P

Pakistan, 17, 78
Paradigm shift, v, vi
Pastoralism, 43
Police Academy, 54, 55
Political Islam and Black Economy in Somalia, 93, 183
Predatory elite culture, v
Prophetic traditions, 16, 100, 110, 111, 112
Puntland, 115, 136, 155, 208, 222, 226, 249, 252

Q

Qadiriyah, 63, 133, 136, 186, 188, 243, 244, 245, 247, 248, 249, 250, 251, 254, 256, 257
Qisas punishments, 114
Qur'an and Hadith. Memorization, 64
Qutb, Muhammad, 15, 21, 53, 199, 200, 269

R

Restorative justice, 116, 153
Retribution, 107, 109, 110, 114, 115, 117, 171
Revolutionary Islam, 21, 24, 25
Roht-Arriaza, Naomi, 100, 150, 270
Roman Catholic Church, ix, 193

S

Salihiyah order, 188, 254, 256
Samatar, Said, 45, 46, 75, 134, 142, 143, 144, 145, 180, 181, 186, 187, 188, 192, 213, 245, 247, 248, 249, 255, 256, 266, 267, 268, 270
Saudi Arabia, 55, 58, 65, 88, 133, 134, 157, 173, 193, 197, 201, 203, 204, 211, 212, 214, 215, 248
Saudi Islamic universities, 134, 204
Secularism, 26, 40, 43, 46, 131, 181
Shafi'i Jurisprudence, 42, 49, 52, 136
Shah, Mohammad Reza, 24
Sharia, viii, 19, 22, 31, 32, 50, 53, 101, 103, 105, 110, 117, 126, 128, 129, 130, 131, 136, 137, 141, 151, 152, 155, 156, 157, 159, 160, 172, 176, 251, 252, 257
Sheikh, Ali, xii, xiii, 47, 50, 51, 52, 53, 54, 55, 57, 85, 89, 112, 133, 134, 136, 180, 181, 186, 188, 189, 192, 199, 200, 201, 203, 204, 206, 207, 211, 212, 213, 220, 226, 228, 229,

233, 243, 244, 245, 246, 248, 249, 250, 251, 252, 253, 254, 255, 256, 257, 258, 261, 263, 264, 270
Somali customary law, 33, 152, 159, 171, 173, 176
Somali National Movement, ix, 139, 144, 220
Somali politics, v
Somaliness, 35, 47, 68, 75, 191, 246
South African Truth and Reconciliation Commission, 173
Sufi brotherhoods, 34, 63, 85, 186, 205, 217, 234, 244, 247, 250
Sufism, 15, 64, 126, 132, 133, 152, 181, 186, 200, 201, 245, 247, 270
Sunna, ix, xiii, 80, 104, 107, 115, 133, 187, 201, 205, 208, 213, 218, 235, 246, 258

T

Tokyo, 150
Touval, Saadia, 75, 76, 272
Transitional Federal Government, x, 62, 115, 147, 183, 228, 230, 236
Transitional Justice, i, iii, iv, v, vii, x, 29, 30, 32, 33, 97, 99, 100, 101, 103, 107, 109, 110, 114, 116, 117, 118, 123, 125, 126, 132, 136, 137, 139, 140, 149, 150, 151, 153, 155, 156, 157, 158, 160, 172, 173, 174, 176, 259, 265, 266, 267, 270, 271, 272

Traore, Karim, ii
Turkey, 53, 56, 208

U

Umayyad Dynasty, 63
Unifiers, 94
Union of Islamic Courts, x, 129, 139, 148, 149, 175, 209, 211, 228
Union of the Islamic Courts, 184, 208, 209, 258
United Nations, x, 50, 100, 140, 145, 148, 149, 150, 175, 230, 263
Utvik, Bjørn Olav, 19

W

Wahabi School, 88, 212
Wahdah, xiii, 136, 199, 201, 202, 204, 213
Western Criminal Laws, 114
World War II, 150

X

Xeer, 42, 64, 115, 126, 128, 139, 151, 152, 159, 160, 165, 176

Z

Zakat, 83, 106, 219
Zanzibar, 248, 251, 252

www.ingramcontent.com/pod-product-compliance
Lightning Source LLC
Chambersburg PA
CBHW051632230426
43669CB00013B/2268